Disaster and Crisis Management

T0300157

A wide range of natural hazards pose major risks to the lives and livelihoods of large populations around the world. Man-made disasters caused by technological failures, industrial accidents, spillages, explosions, and fires, compound this threat. Since 9/11, security threats based on violence (terrorism, insurgency, and civil strife) have attracted much governmental attention and a great deal of public resources. As the scale, frequency, and intensity of disasters and crises have dramatically increased over the last decade, the failures in responding to these crises have prompted a critical need to evaluate the way in which the public sector responds to disaster.

What have we learned? What has changed in the management of disasters and crises? What do we know about the causes, patterns, and consequences of these events? This book looks at some of the approaches that can be taken to empirically examine disaster and crisis management practices. It contributes to the literature on crisis and disaster management, as well as social policy and planning. Introducing approaches that are applicable to a variety of circumstances in the US and other countries, it offers ways to think through policy interventions and governance mechanisms that may enhance societal resilience.

This book was originally published as a special issue of *Public Management Review*.

Naim Kapucu is Professor of Public Policy and Administration in the School of Public Administration at the University of Central Florida, Orlando, USA. He has published widely in areas of public administration and emergency management, and has developed and taught emergency management and homeland security programmes at UCF.

Arjen Boin is Professor of Public Institutions and Governance at the Institute of Political Science, Leiden University, The Netherlands. He has published widely on topics of crisis and disaster management. He is co-editor of *Public Administration* and managing partner of Crisisplan BV.

Disaster and Crisis Management

Public management perspectives

Edited by
Naim Kapucu and Arjen Boin

Routledge
Taylor & Francis Group

)NDON AND NEW YORK

First published 2016
by Routledge

2 Park Square, Milton Park, Abingdon, Oxon OX14 4RN
711 Third Avenue, New York, NY 10017, USA

Routledge is an imprint of the Taylor & Francis Group, an informa business

First issued in paperback 2017

British Library Cataloguing in Publication Data
A catalogue record for this book is available from the British Library

ISBN 13: 978-1-138-93516-7 (hbk)
ISBN 13: 978-1-138-09890-9 (pbk)

Typeset in Perpetua
by RefineCatch Limited, Bungay, Suffolk

Publisher's Note
The publisher accepts responsibility for any inconsistencies that may have
arisen during the conversion of this book from journal articles to book chapters,
namely the possible inclusion of journal terminology.

Disclaimer
Every effort has been made to contact copyright holders for their permission to
reprint material in this book. The publishers would be grateful to hear from any
copyright holder who is not here acknowledged and will undertake to rectify
any errors or omissions in future editions of this book.

Contents

CONTENTS

Citation Information

The following chapters were originally published in *Public Management Review*, volume 15, issue 3 (March 2013). When citing this material, please use the original page numbering for each article, as follows:

Chapter 1

Time and Crisis
Julia Fleischer
Public Management Review, volume 15, issue 3 (March 2013) pp. 313–329

Chapter 2

The Vulnerability of Public Spaces: Challenges for UK hospitals under the 'new' terrorist threat
Denis Fischbacher-Smith and Moira Fischbacher-Smith
Public Management Review, volume 15, issue 3 (March 2013) pp. 330–343

Chapter 3

The Core and Periphery of Emergency Management Networks: A multi-modal assessment of two evacuation-hosting networks from 2000 to 2009
Scott E. Robinson, Warren S. Eller, Melanie Gall and Brian J. Gerber
Public Management Review, volume 15, issue 3 (March 2013) pp. 344–362

Chapter 4

Managing Disaster Networks in India: A study of structure and effectiveness
Triparna Vasavada
Public Management Review, volume 15, issue 3 (March 2013) pp. 363–382

For any permission-related enquiries please visit:
http://www.tandfonline.com/page/help/permissions

Notes on Contributors

Simon A. Andrew is Associate Professor in the Department of Public Administration at the University of North Texas, Denton, TX, USA. His research focuses on the problems of developing and maintaining cooperative solutions to institutional collective action problems, emphasizing the role of inter-organizational relations, and social network structures.

Sudha Arlikatti is Associate Professor and the Emergency Administration and Planning program coordinator in the Department of Public Administration at the University of North Texas, Denton, TX, USA. Her research focuses on risk communication, protective action decision-making, sheltering, long-term housing recovery and community resiliency, and capacity building.

Arjen Boin is Professor of Public Institutions and Governance at the Institute of Political Science, Leiden University, The Netherlands. He is an Adjunct Professor at the Public Administration Institute, Louisiana State University, Baton Rouge, LA, USA.

Richard A. Couto is Distinguished Senior Scholar at Union Institute & University, Brattleboro, VT, USA. He recently edited the two-volume reference handbook, *Political and Civic Leadership*.

Michel J. G. van Eeten is Professor of Public Administration in the Faculty of Technology, Policy and Management, Delft University of Technology, The Netherlands.

Warren S. Eller is Associate Professor in the Department of Health Policy, Management and Leadership in the School of Public Health at West Virginia University, Morgantown, WV, USA.

Denis Fischbacher-Smith is Professor of Risk and Resilience at the University of Glasgow, UK. He holds a PhD in Science and Technology Policy from the University of Manchester, UK, and a DLitt in Management from the University of Glasgow.

Moira Fischbacher-Smith is a Senior Lecturer in Strategy at the Adam Smith Business School, University of Glasgow, UK. She worked in the UK NHS before becoming a full-time academic.

Julia Fleischer is a Research Fellow at the German Research Institute for Public Administration, Speyer, Germany. Her research focuses on crisis management and governance, especially in the fields of homeland security and climate change, as well as on the comparative analysis of administrative elites and central government organizations.

Melanie Gall is a visiting Assistant Professor in the Department of History and Sociology at Claflin University, Orangeburg, SC, USA.

Brian J. Gerber is Associate Professor and Executive Director of the Buechner Institute for Governance in the School of Public Affairs at the University of Colorado, Denver, CO, USA.

Naim Kapucu is Professor of Public Policy and Administration in the School of Public Administration at the University of Central Florida, Orlando, USA. He has published widely in areas of public administration and emergency management, and has developed and taught emergency management and homeland security programmes at UCF.

Tyler Kustra is a Henry M. MacCracken Fellow and a doctoral student in the Wilf Family Department of Politics at New York University, NY, USA.

Claire Menck is the Academic Director for the Culinary Department at the Art Institute of Wisconsin, Milwaukee, WI, USA. Her most recent work is *Recipes of Resolve: Food and Meaning in Post-Diluvian New Orleans*.

Scott E. Robinson is Associate Professor of Public Service and Administration in the George Bush School of Government and Public Service, Texas A&M University, College Station, TX, USA.

Adam Rose is Coordinator for Economics at the Center for Risk and Economic Analysis of Terrorism Events, and Research Professor in the Sol Price School of Public Policy, at the University of Southern California, Los Angeles, CA, USA. His recent research has expanded the economic consequence analysis framework by incorporating resilience and behavioral considerations.

Marina Saitgalina is a doctoral student in the Department of Public Administration at the University of North Texas, Denton, TX, USA. She specializes in non-profit management, and her research interests also include non-profit and voluntary sector involvement in emergency response management.

Paul Stephenson is Assistant Professor in the Department of Political Science at Maastricht University, The Netherlands. His research interests lie in European public policy and the policy process, and include the European Commission and Court of Auditors, cohesion policy and trans-European transport networks, and the politics and society of France and Spain.

Triparna Vasavada is Assistant Professor of Public Administration at Pennsylvania State University, State College, PA, USA. Her research interests are in social networks, non-profit management and leadership, and disaster management. She has published in *American Review of Public Administration*, *Public Administration Quarterly*, and in other international journals.

INTRODUCTION: STUDYING DISASTER AND CRISIS MANAGEMENT[1]

Naim Kapucu and Arjen Boin

Naim Kapucu
School of Public Administration, University of Central Florida, USA

Arjen Boin
Institute of Political Science, Leiden University, The Netherlands

Public Management research tends to focus on patterns and regularities, explaining everyday problems, offering prescriptions to make government more effective and efficient. This type of research is not always well positioned to explain non-regular problems such as crises and disasters. To understand the causes, characteristics, and consequences of crises and disasters, and to prescribe structures and processes that can help control crises and disasters, we need a more specialized approach.

The research field dealing with crises and disasters has grown strongly over the years, especially in the decade after 9/11. The field is increasingly coming into its own, with journals, conferences, professional associations, academic programs, etc. But as crises and disasters are becoming a part of everyday public governance, the time has come for the Public Management field to familiarize itself with some of the key developments and approaches of that field. This is all the more necessary, because the world of crises is changing. New developments (new threat agents) and increasing vulnerabilities have created urgent challenges to public governance.

Three challenges stand out: understanding the causes of crisis (which allows for early recognition and early warning); determining the processes and conditions that give rise effective crisis and disaster management; and developing societal resilience.

This book focuses on the topic of disaster and crisis management in the public sector. wide range of natural hazards – ranging from earthquakes, tornados, tsunamis and floods, to global climate change, environmental degradation, and deforestation – pose major risks to the lives and livelihoods of large populations around the world. Man-made disasters that are caused by technological failures (industrial accidents, spillages, explosions, and fires) compound the threat. In the post-9/11 context, security threats based violence (terrorism, insurgency, and civil strife) have attracted much of government's attention and public resources. The scale, frequency, and intensity of disasters and crises have dramatically increased over the last decade.

After the failures of disasters and crises responses, there is a critical need for careful stocktaking. What have we learned? What has changed in the management of crises and disasters? What do we know about the causes, patterns, and consequences of these events? We need public management research to help address these challenges. This book, based on the special issue of *Public Management Review*, offers a 'sampler' of issues and approaches that can be used for empirical examination of disaster and crisis management.

QUESTIONS

The contributing authors address a variety of relevant questions in this volume. Intriguing questions include the following:

- How can the concept of disaster resilience be operationalized in a way that is useful as a framework to investigate the conditions that lead to stronger, safer, and more sustainable communities?
- What factors account for the variation across geographic jurisdictions in the ability to respond and recover from a disaster?
- Which policy interventions and governance mechanisms can be developed to improve the practice of disaster and crisis management and reduce vulnerability to natural disasters?
- How are disaster and crisis management strategies conceptualized, operationalized and implemented in different parts of the world?
- How have various disasters, as focusing events, impacted policies and practice disaster and crisis management?
- What are some of the key differences between developing and developed countries in respect to disaster and crisis management?
- How did disaster-impacted communities collaborate with multiple stakeholders (local, state, international) during the transition from disaster response to recovery?
- Can the collaborative nature of disaster recovery help build resilient communities?

PERSPECTIVES

This book makes us of various perspectives:

International and comparative

Rather than focusing primarily on one specific country, the book expands the scope empirical analysis to international contexts. This brings additional contextual factors that improve the general understanding of disaster and crisis management and how communities plan for and manage disasters and crisis.

Multi-level

The volume presents chapters that analyze vulnerability and resilience at individual, organizational, and societal levels.

Interdisciplinary

It is important to understand the role of culture, social capital, socio-economic vulnerabilities, and interpersonal social networks and international collaboration. This requires analytical perspectives from different disciplines.

Solution-oriented

Chapters in this volume explore how various conditions and factors may have implications for planning decisions, policy-making, and governance. The volume shifts attention away from a 'silo' approach to a 'collaboration' perspective in creating disaster resilient and sustainable communities. It aims to support the development of effective collaborative governance strategies for improved management in the mitigation, preparation, response to, and recovery from natural and man-made hazards.

OVERVIEW

This book contributes to the literature on crisis management, emergency management, social sciences, policy, and planning. The volume introduces approaches that are applicable to a variety of circumstances in the US, Europe and other countries; it offers ways to think through policy interventions and governance mechanisms that may enhance societal resilience.

Chapter 1, authored by Julia Fleischer, presents a theoretical argument that the study of time provides crucial explanatory factors to the analysis of public sector crisis responses. The chapter asserts that time is an external condition *and* an internalized feature of organizational behaviour in response to crisis and disasters. The author claims that time influences governmental crisis responses but can also be exploited by actors during such critical episodes.

Chapter 2, co-authored by Denis Fischbacher-Smith and Moira Fischbacher-Smith, considers the challenges for hospitals in the UK that arise from the threats of mass casualty terrorism events. The chapter argues that the academic focus is often on the role of healthcare as a major resource and rescuer in terrorist attacks and other mass casualty crises; it often lacks attention for healthcare organizations as a *victim* of disaster. The chapter highlights the nature of the challenges facing the UK healthcare system, with a special focus on hospitals both as essential first responders under the UK's civil contingencies legislation and as potential victims of terrorism and other man-made disasters.

Chapter 3, co-authored by Scott Robinson, Warren Eller, Melanie Gall and Brian Gerber addresses a topic which has recently gained significant attention among scholars in the disaster management community. Disaster preparedness, response, and recovery involve different actors from different sectors (public, private, and non-profit). The chapter assesses the temporal dynamics of disaster networks in two moderately sized communities that have served as large-scale disaster evacuation hosting sites in the past decade in the US. It discusses the potential advantage presented by having a two-tier network for evacuation hosting that mixes core and periphery across multiple sectors in dealing with disasters.

Chapter 4, authored by Triparna Vasavada, studies disaster management networks in the state of Gujarat, India, using social network analysis. It examines the governance structure of a disaster management network and factors affecting its effectiveness. Trust, the number of participants in the network, goal consensus, and the need for network-level competencies based on the nature of the task were analyzed as key factors in network effectiveness in response to disasters.

Chapter 5, co-authored by Simon Andrew, Sudha Arlikatti and Marina Saitgalina focuses on the challenges faced by disaster survivors in developing countries where there is a lack of pre-identified shelters and staging capacities, as well as an inability of public sector entities to manage catastrophic events independent of local and international non-profit organizations. The chapter investigates evacuation decision-making and shelter choice in the wake of the 2004 Indian Ocean Tsunami.

Chapter 6, authored by Paul Stephenson, examines the impact of a public health crisis on French public management. The chapter specifically considers how government agencies across various state institutions have engaged in post-crisis reform. The chapter highlights how state actors drew policy and practical lessons from previous experiences. The chapter demonstrates the discursive use of solidarity in a game of political blame shifting and experimentation in the context of crisis enquiries.

Chapter 7, co-authored by Claire Menck and Richard Couto examines the leadership of one organization, Market Umbrella, which used farmer's markets as spaces of community building to help facilitate the recovery in the wake of Hurricane Katrina. It focuses on the social and cultural role of food in New Orleans. The chapter suggests that informal leadership can use 'free spaces' of community gathering to recreate fractured relationships between people and places affected by disaster.

Chapter 8, co-authored by Arjen Boin and Michel van Eeten discusses a topic that recently gained much attention from practitioners and scholars of disaster studies. The chapter focuses on resilience at the organizational level: it examines relationships between organizational characteristics, processes, and resilience, building on the insights of high reliability organizations theory and crisis management research.

Chapter 9, co-authored by Adam Rose and Tyler Kustra, provides a framework for designing transboundary disaster management institutions and policies based on economic perspectives. The chapter highlights the importance of economic considerations as disaggregating economic losses into direct and indirect components, which vary in terms of their transboundary potential. It applies economic principles, such as scale economies, externalities, and public goods analysis, studying European cooperation in emergency management. The chapter concludes by identifying the type of consequences that might best be addressed by a wider geographic and political authority in dealing with transboundary crises.

NOTES

1 Chapters in the book were published in a special issue of *Public Management Review* (*PMR*). We gratefully acknowledge the guidance of editor Stephen Osborne. The chapters have been peer-reviewed by experts in the field. We acknowledge their contributions to the book as well.

Abstract

This article presents a theoretical argument that the study of time provides crucial explanatory perspectives to the analysis of governmental crisis responses. The article claims that time is an external condition and an internalized feature of organizational behaviour. It follows that time influences governmental crisis responses but can also be exploited by actors during such critical episodes. The article discusses the properties of time and its consequences during crises along these two notions, reviewing existing scholarly work on time and crises. It concludes with a plea for a more explicit and systematic time-centred study of governmental crisis responses.

TIME AND CRISIS

Julia Fleischer

Julia Fleischer
German Research Institute for Public Administration
Speyer
Germany

I think that the people are rightly impatient, similar to all of us involved in the crisis management. (...) However, we have to fight an epidemic and this is no time for abstract discussions of responsibility. (Ilse Aigner, German Minister for Food, Agriculture and Consumer Protection, *Frankfurter Rundschau*, 17 June 2011)

INTRODUCTION[1]

The statement of the German Minister for Agriculture, Food, and Consumer Protection during the recent 'enterohemorrhagic E. coli (EHEC) crisis' refers to at least two crucial characteristics of critical events: they require timely decisions, often based on incomplete information, and they threaten the organizations and politicians responsible for (handling) it.[2] In addition, the statement points to a typical problem that policy-makers face during a crisis: the accelerating conflict between the time *rationally* necessary to cope with the crisis and the *appropriate* time to do so, which is also defined by stakeholders and citizens endangered by the critical episode.

The notion of crisis is fundamentally related to the idea of time. First, crisis limit reaction time. Hermann (1963: 64) defined a crisis as an event that '(1) threatens high priority values of the organization, (2) presents a *restricted amount of time* in which response can be made, and (3) is unexpected or unanticipated by the organization' (emphasis added).

Second, there appears to be a sense of order. Most authors may agree that crises are exceptional situations that arise from multiple causes accumulating into a critical event (Fink, 1986; Turner, 1976; Van Eeten *et al.*, 2011); they also assume that a crisis unfolds in distinguishable sequences between the onset of a critical event and its aftermath (Boin *et al.*, 2005; Boin and 't Hart, 2006). Yet, we lack explicit conceptualizations of time during crisis and its consequences – although such a time-centred perspective adds explanatory value to the comparative study of governmental crisis responses.

Crises have arguably been a battlefield for different theoretical approaches (Boin and 't Hart, 2006: 44–6). This article adds a complementary perspective by theorizing the explanatory relevance of time during crisis and its effects on governmental crisis responses. The article is not confined to governmental crisis management as the reactive activities of executive actors facing a threatening event (Van Wart and Kapucu, 2011: 491–2). It also considers activities by these actors in exploiting a crisis in order to achieve other objectives than dealing with the critical episode.

The article starts by outlining the key assumptions in organizational research about time and organizational behaviour. To advance its theoretical argument, the article illustrates the explanatory relevance of time during the crises along two conceptualizations, perceiving time primarily as a constraint and a resource. The article concludes discussing the added value of a more explicit and systematic time-centred study governmental responses to crises and disasters.

TIME AND ORGANIZATIONAL BEHAVIOUR

Broadly speaking, organizational research assumes that organizations are designed to persist over time.[3] As a consequence, most scholars think about time in their theoretical thinking in a rather implicit way (Roe et al., 2009). The dominant notions of time in organizational research can be differentiated along the two Greek terms for time (Hall, 1983; Jaques 1982; Orlikowski and Yates, 2002: 686): many authors refer to chronos, i.e. to the objective time as a linear condition of organizational behaviour that is divisible and measurable by the clock, and others refer to kairos, i.e. to the subjective time that is socially constructed and expressed in perceptions and expectations.

Both the notions address different analytical foci in organizational research: whereas the objective notion of time is often applied in studies at the macro-level of organizational behaviour, the subjective notion of time is mostly examined for the micro-level of organizational behaviour (Bluedorn and Denhardt, 1988). More importantly, they formulate different assumptions about the influence of time on organizational behaviour.

Contingency theorists advance their key argument as 'time-free', i.e. they claim that organizations adjust their structure and behaviour corresponding to their environment regardless of the time in which these contingent requirements occur (e.g. Pugh and Hickson 1976). They also stress the relevance of different 'ways in which effects emerge at some time after the initial intervention' (Bowers and Taylor 1972; Clark, 1985: 39). Thus, they refer implicitly to objective time by studying the 'time lag' between an environmental stimulus and organizational responses (Likert, 1961). In a similar vein, the configurational approach emphasizes that organizational configurations may change over time in order to secure an organization's competitiveness under changing environmental conditions (Miller, 1987).

The debate about 'organizational life cycles' also applies a chronological notion of time, albeit more explicitly, and argues that organizations are dynamic systems developing through various evolutionary stages (Child and Kieser, 1981; Kimberly and Miles 1980; Whetten, 1980). In contrast to contingency theorists, these authors stress that organizational structures reflect the times in which they were created (Stinchcombe, 1965: 148–50). More importantly, they assume that each evolutionary stage of an organization ends in a predictable crisis requiring adjustments if the organization is to survive and proceed to the next stage (Greiner, 1972; Mintzberg, 1979; see also Selznick, 1957). Path dependency theorists argue that 'critical junctures' occur as periods of significant change, forcing organizations to move onto a particular path, which they follow due to the increasing returns to change direction (Arthur, 1994; Collier and Collier, 1991; Pierson, 2000; Schreyögg and Sydow, 2011; Thelen, 1999). Various studies on governmental responses in crisis management apply a similar albeit less cyclical approach, arguing that the growing complexity and coupling of organizations over time increases their vulnerability to disruptions and crises (Perrow, 1984; Turner, 1976).

9

In contrast, other organization scholars stress explicitly the importance of *subjective* time for organizational behaviour. Following seminal writings about time as a social construct (Durkheim 1915/1965; Gurvitch, 1964; see also Adam, 1990, 1998; Nowotny 1994; Rosa, 2005), they analyse the explanatory relevance of temporal orientations among organizational participants for organizational behaviour, i.e. their time horizons and time senses (Albert, 1995; Berger and Luckmann 1966; Lawrence and Lorsch, 1967: 34; Lewis and Weigert 1981; McGrath and Rotchford, 1983).

Despite Clark's plea for more theoretical attention to such 'organizational times' (1985: 37–8), most organization theorists have widely neglected subjective time (see, for an exception, Butler, 1995). The most comprehensive conceptualization of subjective time and organizational behaviour is provided by sociologist writings on 'timescapes', acknowledging the spatiality, materiality and contextuality of time and analysing different elements such as time frames, temporality, timing, tempo, duration, sequence and temporal modalities (Adam, 2008). Although this timescape approach has been applied in studies of environmental hazards (Adam, 1998), it has been mostly neglected in the crisis management literature.

Political scientists studying organizational behaviour stress that both objective and subjective time matter. Various studies on legislative actors discuss the constraints of chronological time in legislative periods and the importance of individually constructed time horizons of legislative actors (e.g. Döring, 1995, 2004; Riescher, 1994; Schedler and Santiso, 1998). Similar studies have been conducted on the executive branch: research on the US presidency shows that presidential behaviour is related to temporal dynamics caused not only by the electoral cycle but also by subjective time senses (Lewis and Strine, 1996; Skowronek, 1993, 2008). Recently, scholars have begun to analyse the emerging temporal order of objective and subjective time at the EU level (Goetz, 2009; Meyer-Sahling, 2007; Meyer-Sahling and Goetz, 2009). Although these authors ignore explicitly 'how unforeseen and unforeseeable events, crises and "bolt from the blue" may play havoc with well-laid plans and timetables' (Goetz and Meyer-Sahling, 2009: 181), their discussion of time properties can contribute to a theoretical conceptualization of time during crisis.

A TWO-FOLD PERSPECTIVE ON TIME DURING CRISIS

Building on the insights outlined above, this article conceptualizes time for organizational behaviour during crisis along the notions of objective and subjective time. Whereas the former refers primarily to time as a constraint, the latter recognizes the malleability of time during critical events. Such a dual understanding of time may result in circularity problems: the analytical status of time as an independent variable and dependent variable is not confined to either of the two notions (Butler, 1995: 926). This pitfall is to be avoided through asking proper research questions and selecting appropriate methods (Abbott, 1990; Meyer-Sahling and Goetz, 2009: 327; Pollitt

2008). To advance its theoretical claim, the article discusses the distinct properties of objective and subjective time during crisis and explores its consequences for governmental crisis responses.[4]

The relevance of objective time during crisis

This article distinguishes three concepts of objective time that likely matter during crisis. Each time concept imposes different consequences on governmental crisis responses, but they also interact.

First, the most prominent conceptualization of objective time is *political time*, understood as an external condition that unfolds in linear fashion or in cycles: actors 'may not always know the precise duration of any particular sequence, but [they] know for sure that once it passes it will come again when the cycle repeats itself' ('t Hart, 2011: 4). Many authors take the electoral cycle as key example of how political time influences decision-making (Martin, 2004; Pollitt, 2008: 53–4). In what has been termed the 'political business cycle', incumbent governments use expansionary policy to improve their economic performance before general elections (Nordhaus, 1975; Schultz, 1995) Other public administration scholars recognize the effects of political time by stressing the conflicts arising from politicians' short time horizons oriented towards re-election and bureaucrats' comparatively longer time horizons (Jacobsen, 2011; March and Olsen, 1989). Multiple political times exist, as illustrated in studies on policy-making in multi-level systems with more or less synchronized electoral cycles at different levels (Andrews *et al.*, 2012; Goetz, 2009). The key argument in these debates is that political time influences actors' behaviour because it sets irreversible temporal conditions for action.

This article argues that political time exists also in times of crisis, although these critical events have often a 'time compressing' effect – especially for political actors facing the threat of dismissal (Browne *et al.*, 1984; Dewan and Myatt, 2007; Diermeier and Stevenson, 2000). In contrast, bureaucrats are more likely to maintain their long time horizons, expressed in their attempts to apply standard operation procedures – also revealing the difficulties to synchronize different time horizons within and across bureaucratic organizations (McGrath and Rotchford 1983: 71–3). However, crisis responses often require coordinated efforts by various organizations and thus bureaucrats may also defend their areas of responsibility, which increases their perceptions of critical events as threats to their organization's survival (Peters *et al.*, 2011: 20). Consequently, a critical episode may also result in 'time integration' of previous rather divergent time horizons inside the bureaucracy (Schneider, 1995: 38–9).

Empirical studies on crisis management provide evidence for the impact of political time, mostly for critical events occurring at the end of an electoral cycle: think of governmental responses to the 100-year flood in Germany, which occurred a few weeks before the general election in 2002, or the 2004 terrorist attacks in Madrid 3 days before the election day. Incumbent governments aim to respond quickly – but consider also the effects of crisis management on the electoral turnout (Bytzek, 2008; Olmeda, 2008). Other effects have been observed for new governments in office facing a crisis, e.g. for the Obama administration coping with the emergence of the global financial and economic crisis (Masters and 't Hart, 2012; 't Hart and Tindall, 2009: 337). In addition, the lacking synchronization between national and transnational political times may pose problems as evidenced by the formulation of governmental responses to the global financial and economic crisis at the domestic level while crisis decisions were taken at the EU level (Hope, 2011).

Second, *quantic time* refers to the occurrence of irreversible breaks in the linear timeline. Such breaks have been analysed for the United States, distinguishing an 'early' and a 'modern' presidential time marked by the Roosevelt presidency (Lewis and Strine, 1996: 689–90). In a similar vein, the transition of Central and Eastern European countries after the breakdown of the socialist system signifies a break between two eras before and after this quantic event (Beyer *et al.*, 2001; Nunberg, 1999). Similarly, public administration scholars argue that New Public Management (NPM)-driven reforms can cause irreversible breaks of the machinery of government, heralding a new 'era' in public bureaucracies (Hood 1991). A key argument in these debates holds that quantic time often has long-term effects on the basic premises of organizational behaviour by ushering in a new era.

This article applies the same reasoning to crises. It suggests that extraordinary critical events such as '9/11' can impose consequences on immediate and future governmental responses because they configure distinguishable 'eras' of crisis management shaping the general principles of organizational behaviour in crisis responses (Boin *et al.*, 2005; Lagadec, 2006; Lalonde, 2004; Miller and Friesen, 1982). These studies reveal how an irrevocable punctuation such as an extraordinary crisis influences subsequent crisis responses, particularly in similar or adjacent policy areas. This effect has also been noted for the governmental crisis responses to Hurricane Katrina, which relied on a distinct crisis response machinery in the realm of homeland security that had been overhauled after 9/11 (Boin *et al.*, 2010; Kapucu, 2009; Kapucu and Van Wart, 2006; 't Hart *et al.*, 2009).

Lastly, *episodic time* refers explicitly to crisis episodes and describes the temporal realization of governmental crisis responses between the initial recognition of a critical event and its termination (Boin *et al.*, 2005; Stark, 2011). As such, episodic time influences the selection and application of crisis response measures; also affecting other time properties such as timing, sequences and tempo (see below). In addition, these objective elements of episodic time are inherently confronted with individual perceptions about the appropriate time available for crisis responses, which are very likely to differ across actors.

More generally, these expectations reveal different views among actors with regard to the cause of a critical episode, reflecting codifications of the *past* that offer knowledge on how to deal with the crisis (Brändström *et al.*, 2004; Neustadt and May, 1986), as well as different views of desired ends, expressing visions of the *future*. This article argues that such expectations interplay with objective time properties and thus contribute to episodic time as a constraint for governmental crisis responses (Butler, 1995). Another aspect of episodic time that differs from political and quantic time is its likelihood of interruption, e.g. when one crisis overlaps with another, also across territorial boundaries (Ansell *et al.*, 2010) or when crisis effects are temporally linked to another critical event, revealing organizational incapacities to deal with the causes or unintended side effects of the crisis response.

The research on governmental responses to crises and disasters recognizes the importance of episodic time as an external condition, emphasizing time pressure and its effects on routine processing of information, compliant behaviour and functionally divided responsibilities (Hamblin, 1958; Hermann, 1963; Rosenthal *et al.*, 1991). Comparative crisis studies show that the episodic time available to actors influences governmental responses, which, in turn, may also change over time if crises occur repeatedly in a particular policy area (e.g. Hazelwood *et al.*, 1977). Other scholars discuss the challenges of overlapping episodic times of crises for policy-makers (Ansell *et al.*, 2010). Yet, we lack further studies on the crucial interaction between decision-making patterns and the varying episodic time properties, most notably the time horizons of crisis causes and outcomes.

The juxtapositions of these three types of objective time impose constraints on governmental crisis responses. From a time-centred perspective, each crisis emerges at a particular point in the electoral cycle, before or after a potential quantic break, and unfolds in a particular episodic time. The crisis management literature provides empirical evidence for the consequences of temporal interruptions especially for transboundary crises, such as the BSE crisis or the recent global financial and economic crisis (Sato, 2010; 't Hart and Tindall, 2009). These crises are particularly suitable to study the importance of interrupted objective times because they cut across different domestic electoral cycles, unfold in different episodic times at national and transnational levels and can be associated with a distinct era in crisis management. In turn, such transboundary crises are very likely to be perceived as extraordinary, because of their territorial outreach, and thus may even constitute the irreversible break that introduces a new era of crisis management.

Doubled times? The relevance of subjective time during crisis

Various scholars of organizational behaviour perceive time as a social construct that actors can exploit in 'time tactics' (Butler, 1995; Lawrence and Lorsch, 1967; Meyer-Sassling and Goetz, 2009; Pollitt, 2008). They assume that time is experienced as longer or shorter according to the rate at which events occur or how quickly actions are taken by others and responses are needed (Butler, 1995; Waller and Uitdewilligen, 2009). Similar time tactics are used in times of crisis, thus linking the different 'experiences of time' during critical episodes with deliberate actions of governmental actors, most notably organizational leadership ('t Hart, 2011). Crises break the routine, but governmental actors may contribute to the 'how' and with what consequences.[5] Various time properties are discussed in the literature for time tactics during ordinary times (Adam, 2008; Pollitt, 2008); here, we focus on timing, sequences and tempo.

First, *timing* emphasizes the temporal synchronization of activities or rather distinguishes 'good and bad times for action'. It matters 'whether or not the times [of activities] to be synchronized are compatible to achieve good timing' (Adam, 2008: 3). Timing is most prominently discussed in the scholarly debate over policy agenda-setting. Here, timing is the bringing together of policy solutions with policy problems at a point in time when it is politically feasible to implement policy change (Baumgartner and Jones, 1993; Kingdon, 1984). Accordingly, timing has crucial implications for the dynamics of policy processes. In a similar vein, public administration scholars discuss the timing of administrative reforms and the relevance of attention cycles (Van de Walle *et al.*, 2005).

Timing is also a crucial tactic during crisis. Broadly speaking, crises occur 'in the eyes of the beholder' (Albæk, 2001: 454) and the announcement of a crisis can be regarded as a first attempt of timing (Pollitt, 2008: 177), although actors may not necessarily recognize the power that the initiation of a critical episode holds for influencing subsequent organizational processes. In fact, studies on governmental responses to crises argue that such announcements are often issued 'too late', because the critical threat to high-priority values of an organization cannot always be recognized before it happens, the notion of a crisis is often contested and the beginnings of critical episode are often characterized by uncertainty over their intensity and progress (Boin and Hart, 2006: 48). More importantly, timing as a time tactic emphasizes that most governmental crisis responses require a complex temporal synchronization of very different activities and decisions – and actors may differ with regard to their preference for good or bad timing – the latter being especially favourable for those organization actors unaffected by the critical event.

Studies of inter-organizational coordination processes in governments responding to critical events refer to timing rather implicitly and mostly as a constraint. Contingency planning, which seeks explicitly to enable a good timing of different response measures may exist, but opposing interests and additional decision features result regularly in bad timing and poorly synchronized action (Kapucu, 2006, 2009). We lack more systematic knowledge about deliberate activities of certain actors to ensure or sabotage a good timing in governmental crisis responses.

Second, the *sequences* of activities are closely linked to good or bad timing. Basically the literature on sequences in ordinary policy-making suggests that policy processes incorporate different activities that are temporally linked. Their order is assumed to have considerable implications for the dynamics of the policy process (Abbott, 1990).

Sequences matter also in governmental crisis responses, not only as a chronological constraint, as expressed in writings about crisis management (Boin *et al.*, 2005), but also as a key object of 'temporal skirmishing' by actors – exploiting that 'during very

14

bad times (…) no routine will lead to success' (Levitt and March, 1988: 326). In other words, the sequences of action may be pre-formulated in contingency planning, but they are very likely to fall into disorder during crisis. Actors can exploit this situational context for their purposes. Moreover, sequencing signals priorities and posteriorities of action during crisis. But this 'temporal hierarchy' of action depends always upon the definition of the situation – which changes permanently during a crisis (Boin et al., 2005: 57). In turn, the sequences of activities are a very suitable object for time tactics.

Empirical studies provide evidence for tactics in the conduction of these sequences, including their selection and order (Boin et al., 2005; 't Hart et al., 2009). Yet, these sequences are still often perceived as a challenge rather than as a distinct resource that can be exploited. Here, the scholarly debate on crisis management would benefit from more systematic research into the moves and countermoves of actors involving the selection and order of sequences of action during crises. Moreover, 'blame games' during governmental crisis responses could be regarded as a specific sequential tactic because actors involved in these activities expedite deliberately the sequence on accountability and responsibility attribution at the expense of other sequences (Boin et al., 2010; Hood, 2010; Stark, 2011).

Lastly, tempo refers to the pace and intensity at which activities are conducted and have to be completed. A time tactics perspective asks 'whether or not the speed is the same across various [activities] and (…) who establishes the pace for whom and on what basis' (Adam, 2008: 3). Broadly speaking, the literature discusses two time tactics involving tempo during ordinary times: delay and advance.

Delaying seeks to avoid the completion of certain activities in order to influence other activities depending on their completion. It is generally exploitable by more and less powerful actors, especially if actors' competencies cannot be substituted (Pollitt, 2008: 177). The public administration literature perceives delayering as the 'oldest and most lethal weapon in the arsenal of public bureaucracy' (Pollitt, 2008: 62, citing Warwick, 1975: 68), although bureaucratic actors do not always delay in order to influence other activities in government policy-making. Instead, delaying is often caused by the 'time-consuming modus operandi' (Rosenthal and Kouzmin, 1997: 293) of bureaucracies, caused by legal frameworks or consultation mechanisms that have to be followed (Hood, 1974: 447). Moreover, the slow speed of bureaucratic actors regularly conflicts with other social subsystems operating on a higher speed such as industry or science (Laux, 2011).

In contrast, speeding aims to quicken the completion of certain activities in order to enable the beginning of another activity. Scholars studying organizational behaviour suggest that speeding has particularly strong effects on decision-making when the different accelerated activities move in the same direction (Lindblom, 1959; Lindblom, 1979: 517). Speeding up can also result in the deliberate neglect to conduct certain activities within a particular sequence that would be necessary to finished in regular decision-making.

Tempo tactics are also applied in times of crises. The general time-compressing nature of critical events is often argued to reduce the time available for certain activities (Hermann, 1963; Rosenthal *et al.*, 1989: 10). As a response, it is very likely that actors advance processes with the explicit reference to the general speed necessary to terminate the critical episode. Delaying also occurs, either as an explicit strategy to avoid the completion of certain activities or because actors orient their behaviour towards temporal cognitions of ordinary policy-making and are not willing (or able) to advance the pace of their activities (cf. Moynihan, 2012).

Much of the literature on governmental responses to crises discusses tempo as a constraint, reasoning that the notion of a crisis inhibits a sense of urgency that can only be controlled with prompt action (Van Wart and Kapucu, 2011). But multi-actor response constellations are often informed by 'diverging perceptions of the necessity for prompt action' (Rosenthal *et al.*, 1991: 212). The existing scholarly debate refers to delaying tactics mostly with regard to communication strategies during crises, i.e. organizations confronted with a threatening event favour the disclosure of embarrassing information about their performance (Boin *et al.*, 2010; 't Hart *et al.*, 2009). In addition, governmental responses in the aftermath of a critical episode are described in terms of delaying when policy-makers 'set up a committee or an inquiry in order to "kick the ball into the long grass" and defuse current criticism' (Pollitt, 2008: 177; see also Boin *et al.*, 2008; Parker and Dekker, 2008). A more systematic analysis of delaying would offer important insights into the comparative study of governmental crisis responses – especially if it includes not only those governmental actors directly engaged in crisis management but also other actors who may not be involved directly but can influence the tempo of crisis response measures.

In contrast, speeding is particularly advantageous for policy-makers to formulate quick policy responses, even if perhaps not the best solutions, to improve the situation for stakeholders and citizens suffering from a crisis (Peters *et al.*, 2011: 20). The speeding tactic can include the temporal suspension of pre-existing rules, as observed in governmental responses to the global financial crisis in 2008 when rescue packages were adopted in parliaments unusually quickly (Fleischer and Parrado, 2010; Laux, 2011). Again, the literature on governmental crisis management lacks more systematic studies on speeding up; we do not know which activities are particularly suitable for such time tactics during critical episodes.

More generally, the mismatching tempi of actors impose consequences on decision making processes, especially if one actor depends on another in gaining knowledge and information (Rosa, 2005). In times of crisis, the effects of this incongruent speed between actors depending on each other in terms of knowledge and communication about causes and consequences have been illustrated for the Challenger and the Columbia disaster (Garrett, 2004), for 9/11 (Kapucu, 2006) and for the recent accelerating ecological crises, revealing how the decisions of governmental actors respond not quickly enough to decisions made by faster actors in industry or science (Galaz *et al.*, 2011).

CONCLUSION

This article makes a case for a more explicit and systematic study of time during crisis in order to sensitize the study of governmental crisis responses to the varying properties and consequences of time. It not only shows how the current literature treats time as a linear constraint for decision-making under extraordinary circumstances but also highlights studies examining time as an employable resource for governmental actors during crises.

Admittedly, temporal features can be more difficult to observe than institutional or sectoral features. And this article's plea for a more explicit and systematic time-centred research on governmental crisis responses is not to say that a time-reckoning explanatory perspective trumps other explanations. Instead, it acknowledges that time always coexists 'within a wider organizational and institutional setting' (Butler, 1995: 936; cf. Ekengren, 2002). Moreover, it argues that none of the temporal elements discussed above operate in isolation; instead, they 'mutually implicate each other' (Adam, 2008: 4). If time-centred analyses focus on one particular temporal element, the other elements have to be taken into account. As a consequence, a more explicit and systematic time-centred research perspective on governmental crisis responses also seeks to illuminate the dynamics of temporal relationships, interdependencies and embeddedness.

This article calls for comparative studies of governmental crisis responses from a time-oriented perspective, analysing how objective time properties at the level of political, quantic and episodic time influence governmental crisis responses. One could also study this temporal contextualization of crises as a dependent variable, e. g. examining whether policy-makers with the formal authority to determine electoral cycles use their prerogative in critical episodes, whether they are involved in attributing a crisis as quantic in order to shape radical changes in the foundations of the crisis management or whether and how they engage in defining the episodic time of a crisis. This research perspective may also inform studies on incipient crises (Lalonde, 2007), examining how governmental preparations for critical episodes emerging over longer time periods are influenced by the properties of their distinct objective time.

Similarly, the perspective on time as a resource advocates more comparative empirical research into time tactics during crisis, including the selection of tactics by distinct actors, their moves and countermoves, as well as the conditions under which certain time tactics are more likely to be deployed. Although one of the key research interests of current studies in governmental crisis management is to examine the consequences of time tactics on such responses, more research could be done on time tactics as an independent variable, especially with regard to the consequences of timing, sequencing and tempo on other actors rather than on organizational leaders.

The time-centred research perspective highlights the relevance of time in research methods and emphasizes the implications of our 'temporal framework of observation' (Adam, 2008: 2) on the research results. The time span of empirical research is crucial

17

for the detection of temporal dynamics. In turn, a time-centred perspective may not only favour retrospective analyses of past critical events but also offers new research avenues into real-time observations of emerging crises and governmental preparations to respond to such potential critical events of the future.

NOTES

1 I am grateful to Thurid Hustedt and the anonymous reviewers for their valuable comments on earlier versions of the article.

2 In May 2011, an Escherichia coli bacterial outbreak occurred in Germany, causing in many cases the life-threatening haemolytic-uremic syndrome. Only in late June, several weeks later, the government had formally identified its cause, fenugreek seeds imported from Egypt. During the outbreak, a total of 4,321 EHEC infection cases were officially reported, fifty people in Germany died (RKI, 2011).

3 An exception is the Scandinavian school of project studies in 'temporary organizations' (see Lundin and Söderholm, 1995; Sahlin-Andersson and Söderholm, 2002; see also Bennis, 1965; Goodman, 1967; Goodman and Goodman, 1976).

4 This article's argument is confined to governmental organizations.

5 The article neglects the temporal characteristics of policy measures adopted in governmental crisis responses (Goetz and Meyer-Sahling, 2009: 189–90).

REFERENCES

Abbott, A. (1990) Conceptions of Time and Events in Social Science Methods: Causal and Narrative Approaches. *Historical Methods*, 23:4 pp140–50.

Adam, B. (1990) *Time and Social Theory*, Cambridge: Polity Press.

—— (1998) *Timescapes of Modernity: The Environment and Invisible Hazards*, London: Routledge.

—— (2008) *Of Timescapes, Futurescapes and Timeprints*. Paper presented at Lüneburg University, 17 June 2008, Lüneburg.

Albæk, E. (2001) 'Managing Crisis: HIV and the Blood Supply' in M. Bovens, P. 't Hart and B. G. Peters (eds) *Success and Failure in Public Governance: A Comparative Analysis*. Cheltenham: Edward Elgar, pp453–70.

Albert, S. (1995) Towards a Theory of Timing: An Archival Study of Timing Decisions in the Persian Gulf War. *Research in Organizational Behavior*, 17 pp1–70.

Andrews, R., Boyne, G. A., Meier, K. J., O'Toole, L. J. and Walker, R. M. (2012) Vertical Alignment and Public Service Performance. *Public Administration*, 90:1 pp77–98.

Ansell, C., Boin, R. A. and Keller, A. (2010) Managing Transboundary Crises: Identifying Building Blocks for an Effective Response System. *Journal of Contingencies and Crisis Management*, 18:4 pp205–17.

Arthur, W. B. (1994) *Increasing Returns and Path Dependency in the Economy*, Ann Arbor, MI: University of Michigan Press.

Baumgartner, F. R. and Jones, B. D. (1993) *Agendas and Instability in American Politics*, Chicago, IL: The University of Chicago Press.

Bennis, W. G. (1965) Beyond Bureaucracy. *Trans-Action*, 2:5 pp31–5.

Berger, P. and Luckmann, T. (1966) *The Social Construction of Reality: A Treatise in the Sociology of Knowledge* Harmondsworth: Penguin.

Beyer, J. Wielgohs, J. and Wiesenthal, H. eds. (2001) *Successful Transitions: Political Factors of Socio-Econom Progress in Postsocialist Countries*, Baden-Baden: Nomos Verlagsgesellschaft.

Bluedorn, A. C. and Denhardt, R. B. (1988) Time and Organizations. *Journal of Management*, 14:2 pp299–320

Boin, A., McConnell, A. and 't Hart, P. eds. (2008) *Governing After Crisis: The Politics of Investigation, Accountability and Learning*. Cambridge: Cambridge University Press.

Boin, R. A. and 't Hart, P. (2006) 'The Crisis Approach' in H. Rodríguez, E. L. Quarantelli and R. Dynes (eds) *Handbook of Disaster Management*. New York: Springer, pp42–54.

Boin, R. A., 't Hart, P., McConnell, A. and Preston, T. (2010) Leadership Style, Crisis Response and Blame Management: The Case of Hurricane Katrina. *Public Administration*, 88:3 pp706–23.

Boin, R. A., 't Hart, P., Stern, E. and Sundelius, B. (2005) *The Politics of Crisis Management: Public Leadership Under Pressure*, Cambridge: Cambridge University Press.

Bowers, D. and Taylor, J. (1972) *Survey of Organizations: A Machine-Scored Standardized Questionnaire Instrument*. Ann Arbor, MI: The University of Michigan.

Browne, E. C., Fendreis, J. P. and Gleiber, D. W. (1984) An 'Events' Approach to the Problem of Cabinet Stability. *Comparative Political Studies*, 17:1 pp167–97.

Brändström, A., Bynander, F. and 't Hart, P. (2004) Governing by Looking Back: Historical Analogies and Contemporary Crisis Management. *Public Administration*, 82:1 pp191–210.

Butler, R. (1995) Time in Organizations: Its Experience, Explanations and Effects. *Organization Studies*, 16:6 pp925–50.

Bytzek, E. (2008) 'Flood Response and Political Survival: Gerhard Schröder and the 2002 Elbe Flood in Germany' in A. Boin, A. McConnell and P. 't Hart (eds) *Governing After Crisis: The Politics of Investigation, Accountability and Learning*. Cambridge: Cambridge University Press, pp85–113.

Child, J. and Kieser, A. (1981) 'Development of Organizations over Time' in P. C. Nystrom and W. H. Starbuck (eds) *Handbook of Organizational Design*. New York: Oxford University Press, pp28–64.

Clark, P. (1985) 'A Review of Theories of Time and Structure for Organizational Sociology' in S. B. Bacharach and S. M. Mitchel (eds) *Research in the Sociology of Organizations*, vol. 4. Greenwich, CT: JAI Press, pp125–75.

Collier, D. and Collier, R. (1991) *Shaping the Political Arena*, Princeton, NJ: Princeton University Press.

Dewan, T. and Myatt, D. (2007) Scandal, Protection, and Recovery in the Cabinet. *American Political Science Review*, 101:1 pp63–77.

Diermeier, D. and Stevenson, R. T. (2000) Cabinet Terminations and Critical Events. *American Political Science Review*, 94:3 pp627–40.

Döring, H. (1995) 'Time as a Scarce Resource: Government Control of the Agenda' in H. Döring (ed.) *Parliaments and Majority Rule in Western Europe*, Frankfurt/Main: Campus Verlag, pp223–46.

—— (2004) 'Controversy, Time Constraint, and Restrictive Rules' in H. Döring and M. Hallerberg (eds) *Patterns of Parliamentary Behaviour: Passage of Legislation Across Western Europe*. Aldershot: Ashgate Publishing Ltd., pp141–68.

Durkheim, E. (1915/1965) *The Elementary Forms of the Religious Life (Translated by J. W. Swain)*, London: Allen & Unwin.

Ekengren, M. (2002) *The Time of European Governance*, Manchester: Manchester University Press.

Fink, S. L. (1986) *Crisis Management: Planning for the Inevitable*, New York: Amacom.

Fischer, J. and Parrado, S. (2010) Power Distribution in Ambiguous Times: The Effects of the Financial Crisis on Executive Decision-Making in Germany and Spain. *Der Moderne Staat*, 3:2 pp361–76.

Galaz, V., Moberg, F., Olsson, E.-K., Paglia, E. and Parker, C. (2011) Institutional and Political Leadership Dimensions of Cascading Ecological Crises. *Public Administration*, 89:2 pp361–80.

Garrett, T. M. (2004) Whither Challenger, Wither Columbia: Management Decision Making and the Knowledge Analytic. *American Review of Public Administration*, 34:4 pp389–401.

Goetz, K. H. (2009) How Does the EU Tick? Five Propositions on Political Time. *Journal of European Public Policy*, 16:2 pp202–20.

Goetz, K. H. and Meyer-Sahling, J.-H. (2009) Political Time in the EU: Dimensions, Perspectives, Theories. *Journal of European Public Policy*, 16:2 pp180–201.

Goodman, R. A. (1967) Ambiguous Authority Definition in Project Management. *Academy of Management Journal*, 10:4 pp395–407.

Goodman, R. A. and Goodman, L. P. (1976) Some Management Issues in Temporary Systems: A Study of Professional Development and Manpower – The Theater Case. *Administrative Science Quarterly*, 21:3 pp494–501.

Greiner, L. E. (1972) Evolution and Revolution as Organizations Grow. *Harvard Business Review*, 50:4 pp37–46.

Gurvitch, G. (1964) *The Spectrum of Social Time*, Dordrecht: Reidel.

Hall, E. T. (1983) *The Dance of Life: The Other Dimension of Time*, Garden City, NY: Anchor Press.

Hamblin, R. L. (1958) Group Integration During a Crisis. *Human Relations*, 11:1 pp67–76.

Hazelwood, L., Hayes, J. J. and Brownell Jr, J. R. (1977) Planning for Problems in Crisis Management: An Analysis of Post-1945 Behavior in the U.S. Department of Defense. *International Studies Quarterly*, 21:1 pp75–106.

Hermann, C. F. (1963) Some Consequences of Crisis Which Limit the Viability of Organizations. *Administrative Science Quarterly*, 8:1 pp61–82.

Hood, C. (1974) Administrative Diseases: Some Types of Dysfunctionality in Administration. *Public Administration*, 52:4 pp439–54.

—— (1991) A Public Management for All Seasons? *Public Administration*, 69:1 pp3–19.

—— (2010) *Spin, Bureaucracy, and Self-Preservation in Government*, Princeton, NJ: Princeton University Press.

Hope, W. (2011) Crisis of Temporalities: Global Capitalism After the 2007–08 Financial Collapse. *Time Society* 20:1 pp94–118.

Jacobsen, D. I. (2011) Convergence, Divergence or Stability – How Do Politicians' and Bureaucrats' Attitude Change During an Election Period? *Public Management Review*, 13:5 pp621–40.

Jaques, E. (1982) *The Form of Time*, New York: Crane, Russak.

Kapucu, N. (2006) Interagency Communication Networks During Emergencies: Boundary Spanners in Mult Agency Coordination. *American Review of Public Administration*, 36:2 pp207–25.

—— (2009) Interorganizational Coordination in Complex Environments of Disasters: The Evolution of Intergovernmental Disaster Response Systems. *Journal of Homeland Security and Emergency Management*, 6:1, Article 47.

Kapucu, N. and Van Wart, M. (2006) The Evolving Role of the Public Sector in Managing Catastrophe. *Administration & Society*, 38:3 pp279–308.

Kimberly, J. R. and Miles, R. H. (1980) *The Organizational Life Cycle*, San Francisco, CA: Jossey-Bass.

Kingdon, J. W. (1984) *Agendas, Alternatives, and Public Policies*, New York: HarperCollins.

Lagadec, P. (2006) 'Crisis Management in the Twenty-First Century: "Unthinkable" Events in "Inconceivable" Contexts' in H. Rodríguez, E. L. Quarantelli and R. Dynes (eds) *Handbook of Disaster Management*. New York: Springer, pp489–507.

Lalonde, C. (2004) In Search of Archetypes in Crisis Management. *Journal of Contingencies and Crisis Management* 12:2 pp76–88.

Lalonde, C. (2007) The Potential Contribution of the Field of Organizational Development to Crisis Management. *Journal of Contingencies and Crisis Management*, 15:2 pp95–104.

Laux, H. (2011) The Time of Politics: Pathological Effects of Social Differentiation. *Time & Society*, 20:2 pp224–

Lawrence, P. R. and Lorsch, J. W. (1967) *Organization and Environment: Managing Differentiation and Integration* Boston, MA: Graduate School of Business Administration, Harvard University.

Levitt, B. and March, J. G. (1988) Organizational Learning. *American Review of Sociology*, 14 pp319–40.

Lewis, D. E. and Strine, J. M. (1996) What Time Is It? The Use of Power in Four Different Types of Presiden Time. *The Journal of Politics*, 58:3 pp682–706.

Lewis, J. D. and Weigert, A. J. (1981) The Structures and Meanings of Time. *Social Forces*, 60:2 pp432–6

Likert, R. (1961) *New Patterns of Management*, New York: McGraw-Hill.

Lindblom, C. E. (1959) The Science of 'Muddling Through'. *Public Administration Review*, 19:2 pp79–88.

—— (1979) Still Muddling, Not Yet Through. *Public Administration Review*, 39:6 pp517–26.

Lundin, A. and Söderholm, R. A. (1995) A Theory of the Temporary Organization. *Scandinavian Journal of Management*, 11:4 pp437–55.

March, J. and Olsen, J. P. (1989) *Rediscovering Institutions*, New York: The Free Press.

Martin, L. W. (2004) The Government Agenda in Parliamentary Democracies. *American Journal of Political Science*, 48:3 pp445–61.

Masters, A. and 't Hart, P. (2012) Prime Ministerial Rhetoric and Recession Politics: Meaning Making in Economic Crisis Management. *Public Administration*, 90:3 pp759–80.

McGrath, J. E. and Rotchford, N. L. (1983) Time and Behavior in Organizations. *Research in Organizational Behavior*, 5 pp57–101.

Meyer-Sahling, J.-H. (2007) *Time and European Governance: An Inventory*. Paper presented at the Biennial Conference of the European Union Studies Association, 17–19 May 2007, Montreal.

Meyer-Sahling, J.-H. and Goetz, K. H. (2009) The EU Timescape: From Notion to Research Agenda. *Journal of European Public Policy*, 16:2 pp325–36.

Miller, D. (1987) The Genesis of Configuration. *The Academy of Management Review*, 12:4 pp686–701.

Miller, D. and Friesen, P. H. (1982) Structural Change and Performance: Quantum Versus Piecemeal-Incremental Approaches. *The Academy of Management Journal*, 25:4 pp867–92.

Mintzberg, H. (1979) *The Structuring of Organizations*, Englewood Cliffs, NJ: Prentice Hall.

Moynihan, D. P. (2012). A Theory of Culture-Switching: Leadership and Red-Tape during Hurricane Katrina. *Public Administration*, 90 pp4.

Neustadt, R, E, and May, E. R. (1986) *Thinking in Time: The Uses of History in Policy Making*, New York: Free Press.

Nordhaus, W. D. (1975) The Political Business Cycle. *The Review of Economic Studies*, 42:2 pp169–90.

Nowotny, H. (1994) *Time: The Modern and Postmodern Experience*, Cambridge, MA: Polity Press.

Nunberg, B. (1999) *The State After Communism: Administrative Transitions in Central and Eastern Europe*, Washington, DC: The World Bank.

Olmeda, J. A. (2008) 'A Reversal of Fortune: Blame Games and Framing Contests After the 3/11 Terrorist Attacks in Madrid' in A. Boin, A. McConnell and P. 't Hart (eds) *Governing After Crisis: The Politics of Investigation, Accountability and Learning*. Cambridge: Cambridge University Press, pp62–84.

Orlikowski, W. J. and Yates, J. (2002) It's About Time: Temporal Structuring in Organizations. *Organization Science*, 13:6 pp684–700.

Parker, C. F. and Dekker, S. (2008) 'September 11 and Post-Crisis Investigation: Exploring the Role and Impact of the 9/11 Commission' in A. Boin, A. McConnell and P. 't Hart (eds) *Governing After Crisis: The Politics of Investigation, Accountability and Learning*. Cambridge: Cambridge University Press, pp255–82.

Perrow, C. (1984) *Normal Accidents: Living with High-Risk Technologies*, New York: Basic Books.

Peters, B. G., Pierre, J. and Randma-Liiv, T. (2011) Global Financial Crisis, Public Administration and Governance: Do New Problems Require New Solutions? *Public Organization Review*, 11:1 pp13–27.

Pierson, P. (2000) Increasing Returns, Path Dependence and the Study of Politics. *American Political Science Review*, 94:2 pp251–67.

Pollitt, C. (2008) *Time, Policy, Management: Governing with the Past*, Oxford: Oxford University Press.

Pugh, D. S. and Hickson, D. J. eds. (1976) *Organizational Structure in its Context. The Aston Programme I*, Aldershot: Gower.

Riescher, G. (1994) *Zeit Und Politik. Zur Institutionellen Bedeutung Von Zeitstrukturen in Parlamentarischen Und Präsidentiellen Regierungssystemen*, Baden-Baden: Nomos Verlagsgesellschaft.

Robert-Koch-Institut (RKI). (2011) *Informationen zum EHEC/HUS-Ausbruchsgeschehen – Ende des Ausbruchs*, Berlin, 27 July 2011.

Roe, R. A., Waller, M. J. and Clegg S. R. eds. (2009) *Time in Organizational Research*, London: Routledge.

Rosa, H. (2005) *Beschleunigung: Die Veränderung Von Zeitstrukturen in Der Moderne*, Frankfurt/Main: Suhrkamp.

Rosenthal, U., Charles, M. T. and 't Hart, P. eds. (1989) *Coping with Crises: The Management of Disasters, Riots and Terrorism*, Springfield, IL: Charles Thomas.

Rosenthal, U. and Kouzmin, A. (1997) Crises and Crisis Management: Toward Comprehensive Government Decision Making. *Journal of Public Administration Research and Theory*, 7:2 pp277–304.

Rosenthal, U., 't Hart, P. and Kouzmin, A. (1991) The Bureau-Politics of Crisis Management. *Public Administration*, 69:2 pp211–33.

Sahlin-Andersson, K. and Söderholm, A. eds. (2002) *Beyond Project Management: New Perspectives on the Temporary-Permanent Dilemma*, Malmo: Liber Ekonomi.

Sato, H. ed. (2010) *Management of Health Risks From Environment and Food Policy and Politics of Health Risk Management in Five Countries—Asbestos and BSE*, Dordrecht: Springer.

Schedler, A. and Santiso, J. (1998) Democracy and Time: An Invitation. *International Political Science Review*, 19:5 pp5–18.

Schneider, S. K. (1995) *Flirting with Disaster: Public Management in Crisis Situations*, Armonk, NY: Sharpe.

Schreyögg, G. and Sydow, J. (2011) Organizational Path Dependence: A Process View. *Organization Studies*, 32:3 pp321–35.

Schultz, K. (1995) The Politics of the Business Cycle. *British Journal of Political Science*, 25:1 pp79–99.

Selznick, P. (1957) *Leadership in Administration*, New York: Harper and Row.

Skowronek, S. (1993) *The Politics Presidents Make: Leadership from John Adams to George Bush*, Cambridge, MA: Belknap/Harvard University Press.

—— (2008) *Presidential Leadership in Political Time: Reprise and Reappraisal*, Lawrence, KS: University Press of Kansas.

Stark, A. (2011) The Tradition of Ministerial Responsibility and Its Role in the Bureaucratic Management of Crises. *Public Administration*, 89:3 pp1148–63.

Stinchcombe, A. (1965) 'Social Structure and Organizations' in J. G. March (ed.) *Handbook of Organizations* Chicago, IL: Rand McNally, pp142–93.

't Hart, P. (2011) Reading the Signs of the Times: Regime Dynamics and Leadership Possibilities. *The Journal of Political Philosophy*, 19:4 pp419–39.

't Hart, P. and Tindall, K. (2009) 'Public Leadership and the Social Construction of Economic Catastrophe' in P. 't Hart and K. Tindall (eds) *Framing the Global Economic Downturn: Crisis Rhetoric and the Politics of Recessions*. Canberra: ANU Press, pp331–51.

't Hart, P., Tindall, K. and Brown, B. (2009) Crisis Leadership of the Bush Presidency: Advisory Capacity and Presidential Performance in the Acute Stages of the 9/11 and Katrina Crises. *Presidential Studies Quarterly* 39:3 pp473–93.

Thelen, K. (1999). Historical Institutionalism in Comparative Politics. *Annual Review of Political Science*, pp369–404.

Turner, B. A. (1976) The Organizational and Interorganizational Development of Disasters. *Administrative Science Quarterly*, 21:3 pp378–97.

Van de Walle, S., Thijs, N. and Bouckaert, G. (2005) A Tale of Two Charters. *Public Management Review*, 7 pp367–90.

Van Eeten, M., Nieuwenhuijs, A., Luijf, E., Klaver, M. and And Cruz, E. (2011) The State and the Threat Cascading Failure Across Critical Infrastructures: The Implications of Empirical Evidence From Media Incident Reports. *Public Administration*, 89:2 pp381–400.

Van Wart, M. and Kapucu, N. (2011) Crisis Management Competencies. *Public Management Review*, 13 pp489–511.

Waller, M. J. and Uitdewilligen, S. (2009) 'Talking to the Room: Collective Sensemaking during Crisis Situations' in R. A. Roe, M. J. Waller and S. R. Clegg (eds) *Time in Organizational Research*. London: Routledge, pp186–203.

Warwick, P. (1975) A Re-Evaluation of Alternate Methodologies in Legislative Voting Analysis. *Social Science Research*, 4:3 pp241–67.

Whetten, D. A. (1980) Organizational Decline: A Neglected Topic in Organizational Science. *Academy of Management Review*, 5:4 pp577–88.

Abstract

This article considers the challenges for hospitals in the United Kingdom that arise from the threats of mass-casualty terrorism. Whilst much has been written about the role of health care as a rescuer in terrorist attacks and other mass-casualty crises, little has been written about health care as a victim within a mass-emergency setting. Yet, health care is a key component of any nation's contingency planning and an erosion of its capabilities would have a significant impact on the generation of a wider crisis following a mass-casualty event. This article seeks to highlight the nature of the challenges facing elements of UK health care, with a focus on hospitals both as essential contingency responders under the United Kingdom's civil contingencies legislation and as potential victims of terrorism. It seeks to explore the potential gaps that exist between the task demands facing hospitals and the vulnerabilities that exist within them.

THE VULNERABILITY OF PUBLIC SPACES

Challenges for UK hospitals under the 'new' terrorist threat

Denis Fischbacher-Smith
and Moira Fischbacher-Smith

Denis Fischbacher-Smith
Adam Smith Business School
University of Glasgow
Glasgow
UK

Moira Fischbacher-Smith
Adam Smith Business School
University of Glasgow
Glasgow
UK

INTRODUCTION

A patient walks into a hospital dragging a wheeled suitcase. To all intents and purposes, the individual is coming into the hospital for a procedure and seems to be expecting an overnight stay at the very least. No one checks the suitcase. This patient, however, seeks out the nuclear medicine department intending to detonate 20 kg of home-made explosive, called 'Mother of Satan', which is in the suitcase. He hopes not to die in the initial blast so he can roam the hospital attacking people with the 9-mm firearm that he has hidden on his person. The aim of this attack is to cause mass panic and casualties and to render the hospital impotent in dealing with the aftermath of simultaneous attacks planned across the city. As the hospital is designated as a major trauma centre within the city's civil emergencies plan, this attack will prevent it from receiving the casualties from the other attacks. As such, the hospital attack is part of a wider strategy to destabilize the city and its infrastructure.

The opening scenario to this article is based on observations made by the authors within UK hospitals. Whilst such a scenario may seem fanciful, it is far from impossible. The hospital system (like many public services) is permeable and open. Its security-based defences would appear to be underpinned by a key assumption, which is that no one would actively seek to cause harm within a hospital. This view, however, is based on framing the problem through a Western-centric moral lens that would condemn indiscriminate killing of innocents, especially of those who are already ill.

A similar view prevailed within education prior to the fatal attacks at Dunblane (UK), Columbine (USA) and Beslan (Russian Federation), but those attacks changed the dominant mindset around the vulnerabilities of schools to external mass-casualty threats involving firearms. The Oklahoma City bombing, the Oslo shootings and even the Tokyo subway gas attacks all illustrated the vulnerability of public services to terrorism. These cases also illustrate the risks from domestic, often described as home-grown terrorists (Durham, 1996; Mulinari and Neergaard, 2012; Olson, 1999). The shocks caused by such extreme events have been seen to generate shifts in the views held by policy-makers regarding potential risks of this nature (Field, 2009; Savitch, 2003; Vidino, 2007), even in the most consensus-seeking societies (Leader, 2001). The challenge for public management is how to change that dominant paradigm before a terrorist attack so that effective defences can be put in place to prevent it.

A related challenge stems from a growing recognition that cities are the focal point of terrorist attacks in what has been likened to an 'urban battlespace' (Graham, 2009; Sorkin, 2008). Following on from the attacks on Mumbai in 2008 (Tankel, 2011), there has been considerable attention paid to the vulnerability of cities, especially to roving attacks by terrorists (Bishop and Roy, 2009; Fischbacher-Smith et al., 2010; Sassen, 2010). Much of the response to the range of terrorist threats has been the increase of surveillance within cities, although concerns have been raised as to whether such an approach will prove successful in preventing attacks (Haggerty and Gazso, 2005).

What is also clear from Mumbai attack is that the very technologies that underpin both the state and commercial organizations were used against them in the planning and implementation of the attacks (Bratton, 2009; LaRaia and Walker, 2009; Oh et al., 2011). A considerable amount of the hostile surveillance that is necessary to mount an attack against an urban target can now be carried out using online imaging tools, albeit at a rudimentary level. Information technologies have also provided terrorists with increased communication, as well as surveillance capabilities. Terrorists are able to conceal their planning footprints and train and empower new recruits at a considerable distance. Ultimately, this means that the opportunities for early warnings of impending attacks are partially constrained at the local level, with the security services relying heavily on signals intelligence as a means of identifying potential threats.

The urban context in which these activities occur is itself characterized by points of vulnerability that can be attacked by terrorists. The open and transient nature of cities, the presence of key critical infrastructures and the proximity of large numbers of people in crowded spaces, all combine to present a set of attractive targets for terrorists (Bishop and Clancey, 2008; Boin and Smith, 2006; Fischbacher-Smith et al., 2010; Gilbert et al., 2003; Graham, 2008).

Our aim in this article is to consider the vulnerabilities that exist within hospitals in the United Kingdom. The article frames acute health care within a wider urban context and, in particular, considers its importance as part of the wider contingency response within urban areas, whereby hospitals can be seen as part of the infrastructure that underpins the successful functioning of city life. We also discuss how and why the hospital itself might be vulnerable. A conceptual framework is developed that consider how public organizations, and hospitals in particular, can be vulnerable to attack at multiple levels. These vulnerabilities become represented through gaps in the system that create the potential for failure across layers of the organization. It is in these spaces that hostile actors may seek to expose vulnerabilities in order to cause harm. The article is based on a series of observations made by the authors at several hospitals in the United Kingdom as well as through time spent working within the National Health Service (in one case, as a non-executive director of two NHS Trusts).

IT WOULD NOT HAPPEN HERE, WOULD IT? DETERMINING THE POTENTIAL FOR EXTREME EVENTS

Within many Western societies, there is an assumed level of trust in the generally safe environment that prevails, for the most part, within our communities and cities. So much so that some readers may be confident that the regulatory and policy requirements in place will ensure regular testing of security procedures and that violations or gaps within the system, will be addressed by staff at the operating core of the security function. Others will have a belief that no one would ever consider attacking their hospital.

History tells us that our assumptions about likely events are often flawed. For example, the military wing of the Musgrave Park hospital in Northern Ireland was attacked during the 'Troubles' (Hodgetts, 1993); schools have been attacked and children killed by terrorists, fellow pupils and deranged individuals from within the community (Coupland and Meddings, 1999; Cullen, 1996; DeFoster, 2010; Moscardino *et al.*, 2007; Muschert, 2007; Neuner *et al.*, 2009) and the recent attacks in Oslo were initially targeted against government buildings before attention was directed at young people.

The relative ease by which the attackers could access buildings and public areas was a key factor in shaping the fatalities associated with these events. The essentially open nature of public buildings renders them particularly vulnerable to such attacks. Despite a range of mitigation measures (especially relating to vehicles) that have been put in place during the last 20 years, such vulnerabilities remain. To illustrate the ongoing presence of such vulnerabilities, we offer two short vignettes based on our own observations in city-centre hospitals:

1. Several patients with small, wheeled bags were observed walking through the foyer of the hospital. At no point were these patients challenged by security staff regarding the content of their luggage.

2. In a children's hospital, one of the authors was admitted into several locked and restricted areas, having being swiped in by hospital staff past locked security doors and allowed through restricted areas. The basis of this violation of protocol was that the author was en route to a meeting with a senior administrator. The meeting was genuine, but no one asked for identification from the author or sought corroboration from the manager hosting the meeting.

These vignettes illustrate how day-to-day vulnerabilities may give rise to the potential for harm. Essentially, it is often the normality of the process that creates problems for management: such events can pass unnoticed, allowing organizational defences to be bypassed, ultimately resulting in failures that escalate to a point at which managers can no longer control the system (Perrow, 1984; Reason, 1990a, 2008; Turner, 1978).

The focus within the terrorist-related literature is on how health care responds in the aftermath of an attack (Matusitz, 2007; May and Aulisio, 2006). Health care itself tends not to be seen as the target. Hospitals can be seen as potential targets for two main reasons. Firstly, they form part of our critical infrastructure and are invariably a core element in any civil contingency planning process for mitigating the effects of any mass-casualty crisis. Any disruption of the service that they generate will act as a force multiplier for the damage caused elsewhere, i.e. the impact of the attack will be greater than the energy used in that attack.

The role of the doctor in carrying out the attacks on Glasgow airport highlights the role that medical staff can play in such crises (Wessely, 2007). Local hospitals simultaneously became the focus of an active investigation (given that a terrorist had been a member of NHS staff) as well as a treatment centre for one of those attackers who was injured. This necessitated a heightened level of security within the hospital as a member of staff was placed under armed guard. The potential for confusion within this situation was high as staff sought to comprehend the nature of the event, whilst caring for the attackers and simultaneously recognizing that these perpetrators/patients might leave the hospital open to attack by way of attempted rescue or even retribution. Given the fact that one of the attackers had been a medic, it left open the question of whether they had any collaborators who were also in the health care sector. One immediate result was that health professionals dealing with the injured terrorist were required to work with armed guards present close by. Parts of the hospital were then closed, generating further problems for staff security and safety.

Hospitals are soft targets that are often not adequately target hardened, but are essentially open and porous. Any attacks on their urban catchment areas will see the hospital utilized as a casualty centre and, depending on the nature of that attack, may see people self-presenting, thereby causing congestion and an erosion of the service. A Mumbai-style attack on hospitals could generate mass casualties within a confined space. Hospitals also have within them the means for causing further damage through the presence of low-level nuclear materials. By attacking a hospital directly, it would be possible to have long-term impacts that could make considerable portions of the site unusable for many years and cost large sums to decontaminate.

Our aim in the remainder of this article is to provide a broad framework within which vulnerabilities can be contextualized. In order to explore the implications of such attack strategies for a city – and for hospitals in particular – we will now develop the discussion in the context of an urban environment. Given the obvious sensitivities around the use of a particular town or city as a focus for such discussion, we have a hypothetical but nonetheless realistic urban setting in mind. We frame the specific challenges that may confront a hospital if it were to be directly attacked as part of a wider, and expanding, attack scenario.

CONCENTRATED SPACES: CITIES AS TARGETS

Cities provide a range of targeting choices for terrorists given the concentration of people and buildings, permeable boundaries and transient populations (Amin and Thrift, 2002; Fischbacher-Smith et al., 2010; Libicki et al., 2007). The underpinning transport infrastructures allow large numbers of people to be herded together in ways that not only maximize mobility but also maximize vulnerabilities (Boin and Smith, 2006; Fischbacher-Smith et al., 2010; La Porte, 2007).

We can, therefore, conceive of a city as a set of interconnected nodes and pathways in which people are concentrated, with channels through which they pass, and underlying fabrics that allow a range of transformations to take place (communication, transport systems, infrastructures, etc). The interconnections between these various elements and layers of a city generate a myriad of opportunities for harm to be created by using the very fabric of the city to cause that harm. Spaces that connect elements of urban life generate 'spaces of destruction' (Fischbacher-Smith, 2011) in which mass-casualty attacks are mounted. These spaces are permeable and vulnerable as they are, by definition, open to public involvement and it is therefore difficult to put robust defence mechanisms in place without changing the nature of the service.

Invariably, military theorists have spent considerable time and effort exploring this vulnerability. We conceptualize the city as a potential series of interconnected zones in which smart target selection can cause a breakdown of the city as a system with a minimum of force (Warden, 2011). Hospitals are part of the very fabric of the supporting infrastructure that exists within cities and provide a range of core under-pinning processes by which cities function. A range of public health, primary care, acute and emergency services also keep urban areas (relatively) healthy and disease free. Any erosion of the capabilities to provide health care, would therefore impact on the performance of a range of other services and activities. A city that loses its abilities to contain disease will very quickly start to see a denudation of its core functions as those who provide such service become too ill to work.

Many of the debates around urban terrorism have seen health care's role as dealing with major catastrophic events along with the public health implications of damage to the city's underpinning infrastructure (water, sewage, food provision and power). This traditional emergency-response perspective of health care is one of a contingency bureaucracy (Smith, 1992). Whilst acute care and paramedic services are obvious elements of this process, it is also likely that primary care, the blood transfusion service, coroners departments and mortuary provision, as well as public health, would also play a major role in dealing with the demands of any attack. Hospitals are also functionally dependent on other elements of infrastructure for its routine activities, including power, water, sanitation, IT infrastructure/communications and transport, and any attacks on this supporting infrastructure could severely inhibit hospitals' abilities to function effectively.

Whilst the conventional view sees elements of health care acting as rescuers within an extreme event, they may become victims as the nature of the crisis event escalates. When the World Trade Centre towers collapsed, they claimed the lives of many of those trying to rescue civilians trapped in the burning buildings. The capabilities of New York City to deal with further attacks were, at that point in time, severely degraded through the loss of so many key personnel and the additional task demands generated by the collapse. It raises questions about how a city would cope if those personnel were directly targeted as part of the terrorists' attack strategy.

The fear generated by direct attacks on vulnerable populations would be an important consideration in raising the impact of the event. If hospital sites were attacked as casualties from prior attacks were attending for treatment, then the potential for mass panic would be clearly heightened. Hospitals would, at this point, provide terrorists with a vulnerable and highly concentrated population to attack. In order to explore these issues in more detail, we need to consider hospitals as potential 'nodes of destruction' (Fischbacher-Smith, 2012) and to frame these nodes as systems in their own right so as to identify failure modes and vulnerable pathways.

HOSPITALS AS NODES OF DESTRUCTION

Health care can be broken down into a set of interactive components. Each component (and their interactions) can generate vulnerabilities, which, if exposed, may cause an organization to fail catastrophically. In keeping with the broad contextual framework of urban areas outlined earlier, we need to consider the interactions between elements of the organization and their associated networks. Our framework draws on five propositions, which are based upon established research in crisis management.

The first proposition is that *organizations incubate the potential for failure based on their routine decision-making processes*. This proposition is based on the work of Turner who argued that the assumptions and core beliefs of managers would shape their perceptions of risk and help to formulate the associated limits of control (Turner, 1976, 1978, 1994). These perceptions then serve to shape the precautionary approaches taken to risk by the organization (Calman and Smith, 2001; Fischbacher-Smith and Calman, 2010; Mitroff *et al.*, 1989; Pauchant and Mitroff, 1992). Any gap between the potential hazards facing the organization and its associated precautionary norms (Turner, 1976) would allow for a crisis to be incubated – that is, the potential hazards will exceed the controls that are in place.

This incubation potential provides the basis for the second proposition that *the potential for failure can be exposed by the actions of individuals at both an operational and a strategic levels*. This proposition is based on the work of Reason (Reason, 1987, 1990b) and others (Collingridge, 1984, 1992; Perrow, 1984; Sagan, 1993; Shrivastava, 1987; Tenner, 1996) concerning the process of human error within systems failure. Errors can be both latent (i.e. they embed failure potential within the system over a long timeframe) and active (where the errors can have a more immediate effect upon performance). The interplay between latent and active errors generates a complex lattice within organizations in which the interactions between different types of errors, operating in different temporal and spatial settings and at different levels of the organization, will generate vulnerable pathways within the system (Smith, 2000).

The third proposition concerns the difficulties involved in managing information flows and making sense of the codified information and early warnings generated around failure (Boisot, 1995; Brookfield and Smith, 2007; Fortune and Peters 1995). We can frame this proposition in a way that suggests that *organizations experience difficulties in decoding information that is highly codified and which provides early warnings of potential failures*. As a consequence, organizations will often miss the cues that warn them of the potential for failure. Under the conditions of crisis, these issues around information processing become even more acute.

Our fourth proposition is that *the design of organizations and their associated networks ensures that failures will be exposed quickly and possibly over considerable distances from the initiating trigger*. Due to the interconnected nature of modern organizations, a failure in one part of the organization may cascade through the organization bypassing and eroding organizational defences (Van Eeten *et al.*, 2011). The recent financial crisis illustrated the interconnected nature of the system (what Perrow (1984) terms its 'interactive complexity') and how the consequences of the initial erroneous decisions can have consequences for the precautionary norms that are in use within the organization. The speed of that failure cascade can create problems for managers in terms of sensemaking (Weick, 1995, 2001). The closer to the core of an organization where such vulnerabilities are exposed, the greater the potential will be for causing damage across the various interlinked elements.

The final proposition concerns the role of insider threats to service organizations. Having an insider within the organization allows attackers to map the security measures in place, test their robustness and assess how to bypass defences. As a consequence, by being able to deal with the central management or operator elements of the hospital, attackers can create the opportunity to map and expose vulnerabilities. The threat from insiders can be expressed as follows: *service organizations are more vulnerable to the threats from insiders due to their greater reliance on human capital and the need to source the workforce from across society and internationally*. It is this proposition that informs the remainder of this article as a means of highlighting the core vulnerability that exists across health care, namely those who work within it and their potential to cause harm.

THE ENEMY WITHIN: INSIDER THREATS IN A SERVICE ENVIRONMENT

Insider threats are a significant issue for hospitals. The role of doctors in the attacks on the Tiger Tiger nightclub in London and Glasgow Airport leaves little room for doubt that staff working within hospitals have the *potential* to be involved in terrorism (Al-awi and Schwartz, 2008; Day, 2007; Wessely, 2007) or other malicious acts (Clarkson, 2001; Donaldson, 1994; Misen, 2000; Rosenthal, 1987, 1995; Smith, 2002). How managers choose to deal with the task demands associated with screening employees has been the subject of considerable attention within government and there have been a range of cases where individuals affiliated with terrorist groups have sought to gain positions within organizations where they could help to plan and carry out terrorist attacks. There are several issues here although perhaps the most obvious relates to the recruitment and selection of staff into the organization.

There have been cases in health care where individuals have claimed bogus qualifications and experience in order to gain employment. This raises the importance of robust screening and background checking processes at the point of recruitment. A second issue concerns those staff who become malicious in their intent after they have satisfied pre-employment checks around qualifications and expertise. The issue of radicalized[1] or otherwise malevolent staff is a problem that faces many organizations and has recently been the subject of debate, for example, between the government and university administrators in the United Kingdom. It is our contention here that this human component generates a significant vulnerability for hospitals, due to the central role played by people in a service organization, as it allows potential access to a range of critical sources of information within the organization.

Information technology can be a valuable source of intelligence for any attacking group. The ability to access a hospital system (through hacking or employment) provides those who want to attack a system with information on the levels of security, potential access to security codes and access measures, as well as data on the potential storage of hazardous materials on site (bio-waste, nuclear medicine, medical gases and pathogens). Information processing elements of the system could give attackers insights into the likely key nodes (points of attack) and pathways (consequence dynamics of any failure) within the system. Similarly, information about core processes and products supporting infrastructures and supply chains would allow anyone wishing to attack the hospital system to highlight vulnerabilities, especially through the identification of potential interactions between these various, interconnected, elements of the system.

The customers of the system – in this case, patients and hospital visitors – constitute both a potential target group and a means of testing the permeability of the site. Hospitals are designed to allow people to access many of the core functional areas necessary to provide care. This permeability within the system therefore provides both the opportunity for a mass-casualty event and a means of testing many of the under pinning planning assumptions for such an attack without attracting undue levels of attention.

PHYSICIAN, HEAL THYSELF: DEFENDING PERMEABLE ORGANIZATIONAL SPACE

This article has sought to highlight the threats to hospitals from malicious attacks and the issues that arise from the specific threats associated with mass-casualty terrorism. Whilst it may seem obvious to some readers that hospitals are potential targets, our work with UK hospitals suggests that the threat potential is not something that is high on the managerial agenda. In many cases, the potential for such attacks is often passed on to the contingency planning managers for hospitals rather than featuring as an issue for the senior management board and policy-makers.

There are a number of challenges for policy-makers and for hospital managers that arise from our discussion. Hospital managers must raise awareness amongst staff, patients and the local population, of proportionate risks and of risks that exist but that cannot be accurately predicted. They must nurture the vigilance that provide necessary intelligence to pursue potential terrorists (in advance of an attack) a simultaneously ensure that patients and staff feel safe. This is especially difficult in the UK setting where medical staff in particular are frequently rotated from one hospital to another, and where the sheer size of a hospital complex means that it is difficult to know who should – and should not – be in the building at any point in time. Moreover, hospitals are caring environments for vulnerable individuals and families and that ethos must be balanced with the need to reduce the vulnerabilities arising from the openness of the hospital system.

Also difficult is the planning of evacuations that would be required following an attack. They are difficult to model given the transient nature of cities and, in holiday periods, the increased tourist population (Fischbacher-Smith *et al.*, 2010). They are equally difficult to rehearse. Communicating risk and communicating emergency plans is exceptionally challenging and yet, the responsibility of hospital managers, and Government is to do just that.

A major challenge at the national and regional levels relates to how government can capitalize appropriately on the lessons to be learned from an event anywhere in the world, and particularly within the United Kingdom. It is often only in the aftermath of events that core assumptions, beliefs and values become challenged such that we begin to see the potential for other extreme events (Fischbacher-Smith, 2010, 2011). Yet, after this initial period of reflection, we often revert to our early position, rendering the event a one-off that will (hopefully) not happen again; a behavioural process that results in a crisis prone culture in many organizations (Mitroff *et al.,* 1989; Pauchant and Mitroff, 1992). As a consequence, organizations often fail to learn from the early warnings or take precautionary action (Turner, 1976, 1978, 1994). Inevitably, managers choose to believe that the controls already in place will do the job that they are designed for and that those responsible for testing those controls do so adequately. The notion of 'it can't happen here' becomes a powerful defence mechanism in shaping the cognitive frames that we use to delimit the boundaries of the risks that we face (Pauchant and Mitroff, 1992).

Hospital management may start with an audit to uncover potential for failure at multiple points in their hospital system and consider the associated implications that exist for their organizations as a consequence. Such an audit represents the first stage in generating the *potential* crisis portfolio, by considering the nature of the vulnerability that exists within the various layers of the organization. The second stage involves an assessment of the networks that the hospital depends upon in order to function – including both human and technical elements – as a means of considering the modes by which those networks can shape failure or serve to help build resilience. Both of these processes will require management to challenge their main assumptions around the nature of vulnerability and the processes by which it can be generated.

The next stage in the process should consider how the hospital's existing defences might cope with the potential threats that have been highlighted in this initial assessment. This needs to be seen as a continuous and iterative process in order to ensure that the organization learns and adapts to the dynamic nature of the threats.

Hospitals specifically need to address several elements of their normal activities if they are to be more robust in the face of potential threats. Hospital boards need to refocus their attention from primarily considering the core business of providing hospital services, to examining potential vulnerabilities, identifying gaps in their systems (strategic and operational) and *testing organizational defences* to ensure that any gaps or weaknesses within the system are addressed. Managers also need to *communicate* the importance of conforming to security protocols in order to raise *awareness* of the potential problems around rogue colleagues or the threats from outsiders. Greater rigour is also needed in relation to *recruitment and selection* of all categories of staff in terms of background checks. Ultimately, the open and permeable nature of health care will remain its main vulnerability. Unless we change the very nature of how we provide care, then such vulnerabilities will be inevitable.

Perhaps one of the greatest challenges to health care managers and to governments, particularly in an evidence-based world, is how to plan for events that have no *a priori* evidence – especially when resource allocation is often contingent on a rational business case. Where there is no evidence for the likelihood of a particular kind of attack, it can be hard for policy-makers or senior managers to engender the kind of serious attention that is required to reshape the thinking within an organization to think of the unthinkable, and to create the capacity to deal with it, and yet to maintain normality in some form of hope for the best but prepare for the worst (Moynihan, 2012). Few organizations have the resource slack for such flexibility.

Finally, a major challenge is for hospital managers and policy-makers to think from the perspective of the attackers when considering emergency planning and organizational security. Attacking a school or hospital seems intuitively objectionable, but such limits may not exist in the mind of the terrorists. Hospital planners need to challenge their own and others' assumptions about where vulnerabilities exist, how (and by whom) they may be exploited and where the vulnerabilities exist within the city system on which the hospital is dependent. In the light of these, and hugely challenging, is their reconsideration of how to ensure security within a health care setting, without compromising freedom, ease of access and the environment and culture of care that such organizations espouse.

A key challenge relates to the timeframe for addressing such concerns in relation to infrastructure investment given that policy-makers must ensure a proportionate response to the risks faced, and yet the timescale for major capital projects is often 10–20 years in a planning cycle. Such a strategic approach to developing resilience will be necessary if government policies in terms of urban protection and health care performance are to have any hope of success. As we noted above, many hospital providers are yet to fully engage in these debates and considerations, both in terms of existing hospital systems and in terms of future hospital service provision, and so further research is also needed to explore managers' and policy-makers' approaches to understand hospital vulnerability to various forms of physical and systems attacks and to the nature of the insider threat.

ACKNOWLEDGEMENTS

The authors thank the editors of this special issue along with the referees for their helpful comments on earlier drafts of this article. The authors acknowledge the funding provided by the EPSRC under grant EPRSC EP/G004889/1 that made this research possible. All errors of omission and commission remain those of the authors.

NOTE

1 In recent years, the focus on radicalized individuals has tended to be associated with Islamic terrorists. However, the term is used here to describe any individual who is inducted into any form of political violence including anti-abortion and animal rights protestors.

REFERENCES

Al-Alawi, I. and Schwartz, S. (2008) Radical Muslim Doctors and What They Mean for the NHS. *British Medical Journal*, 336 pp834.

Amin, A. and Thrift, N. (2002) *Cities. Reimagining the Urban*, Cambridge: Polity Press.

Bishop, R. and Clancey, G. (2008) 'The City-as-Target, or Perpetuation and Death' in S. Graham (ed.) *Cities, War, and Terrorism*. London: Blackwell Publishing.

Bishop, R. and Roy, T. (2009) Mumbai: City-as-Target. *Theory, Culture & Society*, 26 pp263–77.

Boin, A. and Smith, D. (2006) Terrorism and Critical Infrastructures: Implications for Public-Private Crisis Management. *Public Money and Management*, 26 pp295–304.

Boisot, M. (1995) *Information Space: A Framework for Learning in Organizations, Institutions and Culture*, London: Routledge.

Bratton, B. H. (2009) On Geoscapes and the Google Caliphate. *Theory, Culture & Society*, 26 pp329–42.

Brookfield, D. and Smith, D. (2007) Managerial Intervention and Instability in Healthcare Organisations: The Role of Complexity in Explaining the Scope of Effective Management. *Risk Management: An International Journal*, 8 pp268–93.

Calman, K. and Smith, D. (2001) Works in Theory but Not in Practice? Some Notes on the Precautionary Principle. *Public Administration*, 79 pp185–204.

Clarkson, W. (2001) *The Good Doctor – Portrait of a Serial Killer*, London: John Blake Publishing.

Collingridge, D. (1984) *Technology in the Policy Process – The Control of Nuclear Power*, London: Francis Pinter.

—— (1992) *The Management of Scale: Big Organizations, Big Decisions, Big Mistakes*, London: Routledge.

Coupland, R. M. and Meddings, D. R. (1999) Mortality Associated with Use of Weapons in Armed Conflicts, Wartime Atrocities, and Civilian Mass Shootings: Literature Review. *British Medical Journal*, 319 pp407–10.

Cullen, L. (1996) *The Public Inquiry Into the Shootings at Dunblane Primary School on 13th March 1996*, London: HMSO.

Day, M. (2007) Doctors Held for Bombing Attempts, But NHS Defends Vetting Procedures. *British Medical Journal*, 335 p9.

Defoster, R. (2010) American Gun Culture, School Shootings, and a 'Frontier Mentality': An Ideological Analysis of British Editorial Pages in the Decade after Columbine. *Communication, Culture & Critique*, 3 pp466–84.

Donaldson, L. (1994) Doctors with Problems in an NHS Workforce. *British Medical Journal*, 308 pp1277–82.

Durham, M. (1996) Preparing for Armageddon: Citizen Militias, the Patriot Movement and the Oklahoma City Bombing. *Terrorism and Political Violence*, 8 pp65–79.

Field, A. (2009) The 'New Terrorism': Revolution or Evolution? *Political Studies Review*, 7 pp195–207.

Fischbacher-Smith, D. (2010) Beyond the Worse Case Scenario. 'Managing' the Risks of Extreme Events. *Risk Management: An International Journal*, 12 pp1–8.

—— (2011) Destructive Landscapes – (Re)Framing Elements of Risk? *Risk Management: An International Journal*, 13 pp1–15.

—— (2012) 'Spaces of Destruction – Examining the Vulnerabilitiy of Socio-Technical Systems'. Royal Geographical Society-Institute of British Geographers Annual International Conference, 3–5 July, Edinburgh.

Fischbacher-Smith, D. and Calman, K. (2010) 'A Precautionary Tale – The Role of the Precautionary Principle in Policy Making for Public Health' in P. Bennett, K. Calman, S. Curtis and D. Fischbacher-Smith (eds) *Risk Communication and Public Health*. Oxford: Oxford University Press.

Fischbacher-Smith, D., Fischbacher-Smith, M. and Bamaung, D. (2010) 'Where Do We Go from Here? The Evacuation of City Centres and the Communication of Public Health Risks from Extreme Events' in P. Bennett, K. Calman, S. Curtis and D. Fischbacher-Smith (eds) *Risk Communication and Public Health*. Oxford: Oxford University Press.

Fortune, J. and Peters, G. (1995) *Learning from Failure – The Systems Approach*, Chichester: John Wiley and Sons.

Gilbert, P. H., Isenberg, J., Baecher, G. B., Papay, L. T., Spielvogel, L. G., Woodard, J. B. and Badolato, E. V. (2003) Infrastructure Issues for Cities – Countering Terrorist Threat. *Journal of Infrastructure Systems*, 9 pp44–54.

Graham, S. ed. (2008) 'Cities as Strategic Sites: Place Annihilation and Urban Geopolitics' in *Cities, War, and Terrorism*. London: Blackwell Publishing.

—— (2009) The Urban 'Battlespace'. *Theory, Culture & Society*, 26 pp278–88.

Haggerty, K. D. and Gazso, A. (2005) Seeing Beyond the Ruins: Surveillance as a Response to Terrorist Threats. *The Canadian Journal of Sociology/Cahiers Canadiens De Sociologie*, 30 pp169–87.

Hodgetts, T. J. (1993) Lessons from the Musgrave Park Hospital Bombing. *Injury*, 24 pp219–21.

La Porte, T. R. (2007) Critical Infrastructure in the Face of a Predatory Future: Preparing for Untoward Surprise. *Journal of Contingencies and Crisis Management*, 15 pp60–4.

Laraia, W. and Walker, M. C. (2009) 'The Siege in Mumbai: A Conventional Terrorist Attack Aided by Modern Technology' in M. R. Haberfeld and A. Hassell (eds) *A New Understanding of Terrorism*. New York: Springer.

Libicki, M. C., Chalk, P. and Sisson, M. (2007) *Exploring Terrorist Targeting Preferences*, Santa Monica, CA: RAND Corporation.

Matusitz, J. (2007) Improving Terrorism Preparedness for Hospitals: Toward Better Interorganizational Communication. *International Journal of Strategic Communication*, 1 pp169–89.

May, T. and Aulisio, M. P. (2006) Access to Hospitals in the Wake of Terrorism: Challenges and Needs for Maintaining Public Confidence. *Disaster Management & Response*, 4 pp67–71.

Misen, C. (2000) 'Preface – Shipman's Predecessors' in M. Sitford (ed.) *Addicted to Murder – The True Story of Dr Harold Shipman*. London: Virgin Publishing.

Mitroff, I. I., Pauchant, T. C., Finney, M. and Pearson, C. (1989) Do (Some) Organizations Cause Their Own Crises? Culture Profiles of Crisis Prone Versus Crisis Prepared Organizations. *Industrial Crisis Quarterly*, pp269–83.

Moscardino, U., Axia, G., Scrimin, S. and Capello, F. (2007) Narratives from Caregivers of Children Surviving the Terrorist Attack in Beslan: Issues of Health, Culture, and Resilience. *Social Science & Medicine*, 64 pp1776–87.

Moynihan, D. P. (2012) A Theory of Culture Switching: Leadership and Red Tape During Hurricane Katrina. *Public Administration*, 90:4 pp851–68.

Mulinari, D. and Neergaard, A. (2012) Violence, Racism, and the Political Arena: A Scandinavian Dilemma. *NORA – Nordic Journal of Feminist and Gender Research*, 20 pp12–18.

Muschert, G. W. (2007) Research in School Shootings. *Sociology Compass*, 1 pp60–80.

Neuner, T., Hübner-Liebermann, B., Hajak, G. and Hausner, H. (2009) Media Running Amok after School Shooting in Winnenden, Germany! *The European Journal of Public Health*, 19 pp578–9.

Oh, O., Agrawal, M. and Rao, H. (2011) Information Control and Terrorism: Tracking the Mumbai Terrorist Attack Through Twitter. *Information Systems Frontiers*, 13 pp33–43.

Olson, K. B. (1999) Aum Shinrikyo: Once and Future Threat? *Emerging Infectious Diseases*, 5 pp513–16.

Pauchant, T. C. and Mitroff, I. I. (1992) *Transforming the Crisis-Prone Organization. Preventing Individual Organizational and Environmental Tragedies*, San Fransisco, CA: Jossey-Bass Publishers.

Perrow, C. (1984) *Normal Accidents*, New York: Basic Books.

Reader, I. (2001) Consensus Shattered: Japanese Paradigm Shift and Moral Panic in the Post-Aum Era. *Nova Religio: The Journal of Alternative and Emergent Religions*, 4 pp225–34.

Reason, J. T. (1987) 'An Interactionist's View of System Pathology' in J. A. Wise and A. Debons (eds) *Information Systems: Failure Analysis*. Berlin: Springer-Verlag.

— (1990a) The Contribution of Latent Human Failures to the Breakdown of Complex Systems. *Philosophical Transactions of the Royal Society of London, B*, 37 pp475–84.

— (1990b) *Human Error*, Oxford: Oxford University Press.

— (2008) *The Human Condition. Unsafe Acts, Accidents and Heroic Recoveries*. Farnham: Ashgate.

Rosenthal, M. M. (1987) *Dealing with Medical Malpractice: The British and Swedish Experience*, London: Tavistock.

— (1995) *The Incompetent Doctor*, Milton Keynes: Open University Press.

Sagan, S. D. (1993) *The Limits of Safety. Organizations, Accidents, and Nuclear Weapons*, Princeton, NJ: Princeton University Press.

Sassen, S. (2010) When the City Itself Becomes a Technology of War. *Theory, Culture & Society*, 27 pp33–50.

Savitch, H. V. (2003) Does 9-11 Portend a New Paradigm for Cities? *Urban Affairs Review*, 39 pp103–27.

Srivastava, P. (1987) *Bhopal. Anatomy of a Crisis*, Cambridge, MA: Ballinger Publishing Company.

Smith, D. (1992) The Kegworth Aircrash – A Crisis in Three Phases? *Disaster Management*, 4 pp63–72.

— (2000) On a Wing and a Prayer? Exploring the Human Components of Technological Failure. *Systems Research and Behavioral Science*, 17 pp543–59.

— (2002) Not by Error, But by Design – Harold Shipman and the Regulatory Crisis for Health Care. *Public Policy and Administration*, 17 pp55–74.

Sorkin, M. (2008) 'Urban Warfare: A Tour of the Battlefield' in S. Graham (ed.) *Cities, War, and Terrorism*. London: Blackwell Publishing.

Stenkel, S. (2011) *Storming the World Stage. The Story of Lashkar-e-Taiba*, London: Hurst & Company.

Tenner, E. (1996) *Why Things Bite Back. Technology and the Revenge Effect*, London: Fourth Estate.

Turner, B. A. (1976) The Organizational and Interorganizational Development of Disasters. *Administrative Science Quarterly*, 21 pp378–97.

– (1978) *Man-Made Disasters*, London: Wykeham.

– (1994) The Causes of Disaster: Sloppy Management. *British Journal of Management*, 5 pp215–19.

van Eeten, M., Nieuwenhuijs, A., Luijf, E., Klaver, M. and Cruz, E. (2011) The State and the Threat of Cascading Failure Across Critical Infrastructures: The Implications of Empirical Evidence from Media Incident Reports. *Public Administration*, 89:2 pp381–400.

Vidino, L. (2007) The Hofstad Group: The New Face of Terrorist Networks in Europe. *Studies in Conflict & Terrorism*, 30 pp579–92.

Warden, J. A. (2011) Strategy and Airpower. *Air and Space Power Journal*, 25 pp64–77.

Weick, K. E. (1995) *Sensemaking in Organizations*, Thousand Oaks, CA: SAGE.

— (2001) *Making Sense of the Organization*, Oxford: Blackwell.

Wessely, S. (2007) When Doctors Become Terrorists. *New England Journal of Medicine*, 357 pp635–7.

Abstract

Emergency planning and response increasingly involve close interactions between a diverse array of actors across fields (emergency management, public health, law enforcement, etc.); sectors (government, non-profit and for-profit); and levels of government (local, state and federal). This article assesses the temporal dynamics of emergency management networks in two moderately sized communities that have served as large-scale disaster evacuation hosting sites in the past decade. The paper uses two strategies for tracking the evolution of these networks across time. First, we develop a network roster using newspaper and newswire data sources across a decade. Second, we develop a view of the evolution of the networks by analysing emergency operations plans for each community.

Analysis of data reveals a contrast between a core set of consistent (mostly governmental) actors and a peripheral set of rapidly turning over (mostly non-governmental) actors – though the account depends on the mode of data on which one focuses. The article concludes with a discussion of the advantage presented by having a two-tier network for evacuation hosting that mixes core and periphery across multiple sectors.

THE CORE AND PERIPHERY OF EMERGENCY MANAGEMENT NETWORKS

A multi-modal assessment of two evacuation-hosting networks from 2000 to 2009

Scott E. Robinson, Warren S. Eller, Melanie Gall and Brian J. Gerber

Scott E. Robinson
Bush School of Government and Public Service
Texas A&M University
College Station, TX USA

Warren S. Eller
Department of Public Administration
University of North Carolina - Pembroke
Pembroke, NC USA

Melanie Gall
Department of History and Sociology
Claflin University
Orangeburg, SC USA

Brian J. Gerber
School of Public Affairs
University of Colorado
Denver, CO USA

INTRODUCTION

Public administration and political science are currently focusing quite a bit of attention on issues related to political and administrative networks (Lewis, 2011; McGuire and Agranoff, 2011). While attention to collaborative public management and policy networks is high right now, this is by no means a new subject. The classic argument of the dominance of iron triangles or policy whirlpools is a network argument – albeit of a small network (Redford, 1969). The counter-argument that policy tends to involve issue networks is also rather obviously a network construct (Heclo, 1978). More recent work posits changing levels of participation over time and across policy areas suggest that these networks can evolve over time as characteristics of individual policy domains change (McCool, 1998; Sabatier and Jenkins-Smith, 1993).

While attention to administrative networks has been a component of the literature for decades, the dynamics of the networks across time has proven to be a difficult subject to study – especially in the area of emergency management. Given the inherently collaborative nature of emergency management networks, understanding change in this domain is especially important. Due to extraordinary demands on data and the necessity of novel inferential techniques for data involving networks, very little work has engaged issues related to network change.

This article represents an initial step towards assessing the evolution of emergency management networks across time – in this case over a decade involving two major events. The section 'The Evolution of Emergency Management Networks' will discuss the existing literature on the incorporation of new actors into a policy network and the evolution of network characteristics over time. The result will be a series of propositions about the nature of emergency management network change – with particular attention to the differences in volatility between sectors (government, non-profit, private). The section 'Data' will introduce two approaches to measuring membership[1] and relationships within policy networks. The sections 'Brazos County, TX, Results' and 'Caddo–Bossier Parishes, LA, Results' report on the roster of emergency management networks in two communities for each of the two measurements strategies. Finally, the sections 'Lessons for Evacuation Hosting and Emergency Management' and 'Lessons for Network Dynamics' discuss the implications of these results for the management of evacuation networks and the administrative/policy networks generally. The section 'Conclusion' concludes with a summary and discussion of potential avenues for future research.

THE EVOLUTION OF EMERGENCY MANAGEMENT NETWORKS

central question of research into policy and administrative networks is the scope and idity of participation. The key characteristic of policy subsystem approaches to tworks was the emphasis on closed and limited participation by predictable actors g. congressional subcommittees, interest groups and agencies). The principal critique of the argument was that participation in actual policy domains tends to be broad and volatile. It was argued that a large variety of actors may participate within any policy network including representatives of other levels of government and even public interest groups. Furthermore, the participation level of actors is thought to change over time. An issue network represents an extreme version of this open and fluid network (Heclo, 1978). The next subsection will discuss the issue of participation in emergency management networks specifically.

Networks and emergency management

Over the past two decades, the importance of collaborative networks has become clear to scholars specializing in emergency management (Comfort, 2006; Kapucu, 2009). Emergency management represents a wicked problem (O'Toole, 1997). Emergencies tend to cross jurisdictional boundaries due to the geographic scope and the broad range of consequences they present. For example, Hurricane Katrina devastated communities across multiple states, mobilizing a variety of government agencies (emergency management, law enforcement, transportation, public health, housing and Welfare, etc.) and non-governmental agencies (the American Red Cross, Wal-Mart, local religious institutions, etc.) (Simo and Bies, 2007).

Comfort (1994) has argued that emergency management networks are best understood as self-organizing systems. The emphasis in her account is volatile participation and the inability to predict mobilizations *ex ante*. Rather than following documented plans or stable expectations, mobilization tends to involve an unpredictable set of actors that vary in terms of prior disaster experience, organizational sector and other characteristics.

Concluding that mobilization is unpredictable is unsatisfying in a number of ways. First, it suggests planned mobilizations are doomed to failure. If one cannot predict who will be involved then one cannot know whom to involve in emergency planning. While it is important to acknowledge the limitations of attempts to predict participation, predicting all participants may not be essential to emergency planning. Second, to the extent that exercises and other simulations are key preparatory elements of emergency management, knowing whom to include is essential. The limited composition of exercises preceding Hurricane Katrina was a key cause of the eventual problems in evacuating residents of New Orleans with limited access to transportation (Kiefer and Montjoy, 2006). Some stability is essential for the inclusion of actors in pre-event exercises (Kapucu, 2008). A compromise between assuming the ability to predict participation completely (predictability and stability) and the inability to predict any participation (complete chaos) is appropriate.

While Comfort's arguments are an important corrective to the sometimes heroic assumptions of planning, one cannot give up on the process of planning completely. In a study of the mobilization of evacuation-hosting activities in the Dallas/Fort Worth, TX area following Hurricane Katrina, Robinson et al. (2006) found that the mobilization many organizations was predictable given a series of prior relationships. These relationships sometimes had little to do with emergency management but served as a basis for the emergent networks. While there was also evidence of spontaneous mobilization of organizations with no prior relationships with other actors, a good part of the network – particularly the network leadership – involved prior relationships that could easily escape the attention of emergency management scholars.

The complexity of the mobilization of emergency management networks has raised important questions about the management and leadership of these networks. Waugh and Streib (2006) argued that coordination is difficult within emergency management networks despite recent attempts to provide structure to the networks through the National Incident Management System (NIMS) and the Incident Command System (ICS). The difficulties in leadership are accentuated given the diversity of these networks. Recent studies of emergency management from Florida and Louisiana have illustrated this complexity, pointing to diversity across private, public and non-profit sectors (Kapucu, 2006, 2007; Kapucu et al., 2009). Actors from diverse sectors and policy areas bring with them a variety of assumptions about the nature of emergencies and appropriate forms of coordination and communication (Comfort, 2007). It is natural to wonder whether the volatility (the focus of the previous work on issue networks) varies by sector – with some sectors' member participation being more volatile than others.

Propositions for network evolution

Given the importance of network collaboration, research into the evolution of these networks is essential to the improvement of management of emergency preparedness and response networks. The topic of interest is the character of the entire network rather than the actions of specific individuals (or pairs/dyads) within it. While there is valuable research at the dyadic level – investigating issues such as network performance (Meier and O'Toole, 2001) – we seek to investigate questions at the level of the network itself (Provan et al., 2007).

This article focuses on the key characteristic that distinguishes subsystem models from issue network models of policy networks: volatility in network participation (Heclo, 1978). Volatility can take on a number of meanings. In its simplest form, volatility can involve a change in the size of a network (that is, the number of members it has). Assessing the aggregate size of networks would yield limited information, though. If one only knew network size, one could not tell whether a constant size was the result of the lack of change or the result of additions and subtractions of members. For this reason, we are interested in volatility as measured by the number of actors at time t that are not present in the network at time $t + 1$.

Given the strength of prior research suggesting that there is volatile participation in emergency management networks, we start with the following proposition:

Proposition 1: Emergency management network membership will experience significant change from t to $t + 1$.

This proposition contrasts with the expectations of the iron triangle theories of only a small number of unchanging participants. In its strongest form, it could suggest essential unpredictability of network members.

However, the size of a network may be less important than the resources and knowledge contained within that network – its breadth. As a result, involving different organizations may not be as important as increasing representation from diverse types of organizations. Diversity engages a key trade-off in network studies between brokerage and closure (Burt, 2005). Linkages between a particular clique and the rest of the network (like an emergency management network embedded within its broader political community) provide informational advantages to members of the network. Connections to local law enforcement, for example, could provide support during emergency situations. These are advantages to brokerage – connections across cliques or clusters of organizations.

There are advantages also in having a tightly knit group. A tightly knit group expands the opportunities for repeated interaction and trust building. Having the members of a network participate consistently in emergency exercises provides for community building within the emergency management clique. In Burt's (2005) terms, these are advantages to closure. The art of effective network building is to balance the advantages of broad brokerage with the advantages of focused closure.

We focus on the representation of policy sectors (e.g. emergency management, law enforcement, etc.) and non-profit/private sector organizations (Kapucu, 2007). A network may experience brokerage to the extent it represents a broad range of policy and organizational sectors. A network will experience closure to the extent that the network experiences stability in membership.

We propose that these two strategies are not entirely inconsistent. Networks can develop a core of stable actors supplemented by an extended group of actors whose presence in the network is transient. In an approach similar to the notion of hierarchal networks (Moynihan, 2008), emergency management networks may experience closure among its core while taking advantage of access to resources present within a transient periphery of organizations where members change based on the particular nature of the event.

The question remains as to why members are in the core or the periphery. Traditionally, emergency management research has focused almost exclusively on the role of government organizations. With the central role given to governmental organizations,[2] we anticipate that the stable core of the networks will be dominated by government organizations with private and non-profit organizations most often found in the periphery. This results in two more specific propositions:

Proposition 2: There will be an identifiable core of government organizations in emergency management networks.

Proposition 3: There will be an identifiable periphery of non-governmental organizations.

DATA

Disaster evacuations offer an opportunity to understand these networks. In each of the communities we studied, evacuation activities lasted past the basic planning assumption of 48–72 hours of hosting. These activities illustrate to whom emergency managers turn when forced to support activities beyond routines. The activities needed to support evacuation hosting are built into the host communities themselves – ranging from nutrition and feeding to entertainment to basic retail sales.

Disaster evacuation represents one type of disaster response activity – rather than the totality of disaster response. Evacuation hosting provides a useful domain of investigation in that it has historically existed at the intersection of non-profit and government organizational activities. This specific domain of disaster response allowed us to focus attention on practical activities within a narrowly defined domain, analyse a specific set of relevant planning documents (core and mass care plans), while providing a measure of comparability across the communities under study.

Testing our propositions requires data with a particular set of characteristics. The data set must record participation within emergency management networks.[3] Furthermore, the observations must be ordered so that a time path is clear. The data should record participation over a number of years – preferably a decade (Sabatier, 1993). Hypothetically, one could conduct interviews annually over a decade but such efforts are incredibly expensive and rare. The twin needs of comparable measurement and available data across time are best (or at least, most feasibly) served by documentary analysis. This paper will focus on two types of documentary sources: media reports and formal emergency operations plans.

To collect these data, we located six comparable communities. We identified communities that had recent (within the last decade) experiences with evacuation-hosting activities. These communities need to be similar in terms of population size. For this reason we chose moderately sized communities rather than the largest cities where the variances in size are large in absolute terms (populations between 200,000 and 1 million residents when not hosting evacuees). This paper will focus on two Gulf Coast communities: Brazos County, Texas and Caddo–Bossier Parishes, Louisiana.

Media-reported networks

For our first data source, we used a database of media documents. Our goal was to create a single system for collecting coverage of emergency management networks that could be used for a variety of communities across time. For purposes of this study, we are focusing attention on evacuation-related activities. We elected to search within the Westlaw database using the substantive search term evac!. This captured all words that begin with the letters evac including evacuation, evacuate and the like. The Westlaw database allowed us to search all newspapers and news wires – to ensure we captured local as well as national media sources. We added geographic limiters to the substantive search term including the major cities and the county in which the community resides. For example, we looked for articles that included a term starting with evac and also included College Station, Bryan or Brazos County.

Given the varying roles that county and city official play in emergency management, we felt it was essential to search based on city and county. This paper reports the results of document searches related to Brazos County, TX (which includes the cities of College Station and Bryan) and Caddo and Bossier Parishes, LA (including the city of Shreveport). The use of media reports to reconstruct networks was inspired by Comfort's (2006) study of response networks to Hurricanes Katrina and Rita.

These searches of the Westlaw database resulted in hundreds of hits for each year of our sample (2000–2009 – all days in each year included). For the purpose of this analysis, we aggregated the media reports into two periods: 2000–2005 (up to and including Hurricane Katrina) and 2006–2009 (post–Hurricane Katrina through Hurricanes Gustav and Ike). Each of these articles was then read individually to ensure that the article was germane to issues of evacuation. This eliminated many articles. Some articles included references to entertainment or sporting events in the target community (such as Texas A&M University sports teams) and coverage of something having to do with an evacuation in a different community. We only selected articles that involved an evacuation or evacuation-hosting activity within the target community. We then read each of the selected articles to identify all organizations mentioned.

There is reason to believe that relying on media reports can lead to systematic biases in network identification. Media accounts may be sensitive during rare events in ways that make comparisons across communities difficult. Furthermore, internal predispositions within the media organizations may exaggerate the presence of larger organizations and depress the reporting on smaller organizations. These potential biases may relaying on media reports as a sole source of data potentially problematic.

Plan-based networks

To complement the media reports, we have also collected formal emergency operation plans. The emergency operations plan serves as primary coordinating document for variety of actors in emergency management. The document lays out the structure authority and responsibility as well as an assessment of locally prominent hazards and specific annex documents for a variety of detailed functions.

We coded each formal emergency operation plan to create a roster of formal members of the emergency management network within each community. While the media-reported network is a permissive sample that includes a wide variety of actors, the formal plans tend to have much smaller rosters and focus on organizations with legally defined responsibilities within emergency management. Where possible, we have collected historical plans as well as the current plan through the use of the web archive service 'The Wayback Machine' at web.archive.org.

The plan-based data are potentially limited. The threshold for participation may be high because of the reliance on formal planning processes (Robinson and Gaddis, 2012). The result of such a high hurdle may be stable but limited participation. This threshold is most likely to affect organizations with informal roles or members of a peripheral preparedness and response network, resulting in a view of the network that is unrealistically static and small. Additionally, the plans are not likely independently written – but rather evolutionary documents with the more recent plans emerging out of the previous plans. This creates a bias towards consistency within the plans across time. These biases directly offset the disadvantages of the media report network. Rather than employing a single, flawed data collection approach, we have employed two flawed techniques with offsetting flaws – the result of which should be a stronger aggregated view of the networks. This approach is most commonly associated with the multi-method research strategy (Creswell and Clark, 2007).

The collection of these two sources of data is not novel (e.g. Comfort et al., 2009). However, many studies aggregate the two data sources to create an inclusive list (cf. Kapucu and Demiroz, 2011). We will maintain the separation of the data sources to better contrast their strengths and weaknesses.[4] All lists are available from the corresponding author but do not appear here due to the limited space available for publication.

BRAZOS COUNTY, TX, RESULTS

Brazos County has been involved in two major evacuation efforts in the time period of our study: one in 2005 (including Hurricanes Katrina and Rita) and one in 2008 (including Hurricane Ike). Additionally, there was a notable local evacuation in 2009 stemming from a release from a chemical plant. This local evacuation was limited in duration but resulted in an evacuation order for most of the city of Bryan.

Media-reported networks

The media-reported networks for Brazos County are diverse and extensive. This section compares the media-reported networks for the early (2000–2005) and the late (2006–09) period. We will discuss each of these rosters in turn.

2000–2005

The media-reported network roster for 2000–2005 for Brazos County included 52 participants. Of the 37 government organizations, 24 appeared only once and 13 were persistent actors (appearing also in the latter time period). Of the 15 non-governmental actors, only one, the American Red Cross, appeared in both time periods, with all other organizations appearing only once. This indicates a great deal of volatility in membership between the two time periods.

The diversity of policy domains and organization types is remarkable. Organizations oriented towards public health, transportation, environmental quality and housing are all part of the media-reported networks. Among the actors who persist in the network, there are many educational and health care organizations (e.g. Texas A&M University and the Texas A&M School of Rural Public Health) along with transportation (e.g. Texas Department of Transportation) and traditional emergency management organizations (e.g. the Federal Emergency Management Agency). Among the actors who do not persist, there is a wider array of policy areas including law enforcement management (e.g. the Federal Bureau of Investigation and the Department of Justice), environmental management (e.g. Texas Natural Resources Conservation Committee and the Environmental Protection Agency (EPA)), and housing (e.g. the Department of Housing and Urban Development), among other policy areas. This roster represents a broad range of participants with significant change over time – in support of Proposition 1. While there is a set of actors present in both time periods (which represents candidates for core actors in the network), there is a great deal of change across time – even among government actors, challenging Proposition 2.

The roster of non-governmental organization experiences even more change over time. While there was significant turnover among governmental organizations, there was almost total turnover among the non-governmental organizations with the notable exception of the American Red Cross (ARC). The difference in the turnover rate between government and non-governmental actors supports Proposition 3.

It is also interesting that emergency management organizations, while present, are not particularly prominent on the list. Curiously missing are the county and city emergency management organizations. State and federal emergency management organizations are present, but not the local offices. It is hasty to conclude from this exclusion that the county and city emergency management offices were not active and important. However, their operations were missing from media accounts of the activities.

2006–2009

The second time period covers the post-Katrina/Rita period that included another major hurricane evacuation (related to Hurricane Ike in the east Texas area) and a local evacuation related to a chemical release (at the El Dorado Chemical Plant). Media analysis indicates the governmental network membership was fairly evenly distributed between single- and multi-appearance organizations, with 14 actors appearing only in the late period and 15 appearing as persistent actors. In contrast, only one non-governmental entity appeared in both the 2000–2005 and 2006–2009 time periods.

In the government organization roster, university units are again prominent and persistent along with a handful of other organizations. In the latter period, local fire and emergency management organizations make it into the media-reported network. The diversity of policy domains is still present though the specific representatives often change. For example, the EPA drops out during this time period but the Texas Center for Environmental Quality (the state equivalent of the EPA) enters.

The specific members of the non-governmental organization roster changed considerably in this period. We already saw that only one non-governmental actor is on both rosters. The new non-governmental actors include a number of private sector companies specific to the context of the chemical release event – mirroring Comfort's argument for spontaneous networks. In the media-reported networks, various sectors and policy fields are consistently represented but by different organizations.

Plan-based networks

We also collected rosters for the emergency management and mass care/sheltering organizations from official emergency plans. This data source provides a quite different view of the relevant policy networks. The emergency plans include those who are formally responsible for emergency management and a variety of tasks related to evacuee sheltering. For each plan, we identified all of the actors named as responsible parties in the general emergency management network within the core emergency operations plan.

For Brazos County, we were able to locate two general (core) emergency operations plans that covered the sample time period. The first plan is from 2004 while the second was approved in 2009. These plans provide a pre-Katrina view and an update following the lessons of the various hurricanes.

004

The Brazos County 2004 plan includes 18 governmental organizations responsible for various emergency management activities, with 13 of these entities also present in the later 2009 plan. Of the two non-governmental organizations named in the 2004 plan, both were also included in the 2009 plan.

The emergency operations plans provide a starkly different view of the local emergency management networks. Most obviously, the roster of the network is much shorter than the media-reported network rosters. The rosters are focused almost entirely on governmental organizations (with the notable exception of the Red Cross) and the actors are largely persistent across the plans. This view of the emergency management network supports Propositions 2 and 3.

2009

The roster looks largely similar in the more recent emergency plans. Although there are fewer governmental organizations named in the 2009 plan, 13 out of the 14 named were also present in the plan's previous iteration. In terms of non-governmental entities, the 2009 plan included three members (an increase of one from 2004), of which two were persistent.

Here again the roster is stable and focused almost exclusively on governmental organizations. From the perspective of the emergency operations plans, the network includes little volatility over time. There was some consolidation between the two time periods, but most of the actors involved through the decade were in both plans. The actors stay largely the same – contradicting Proposition 1. A few actors drop out (e.g. Radiological Officer) and a couple of actors emerge (notably, the Salvation Army). A diversity of policy domains are represented but the range is not as large or the membership as diverse as in the media-reported networks. There is some turnover (in support of Proposition 1) but not as much as seen in the media data – particularly among the non-governmental actors. Instead there seems to be a core of persistent actors within the plan consisting of government (notably, emergency management organizations) with the persistent addition of the ARC and utility companies. If one had looked only at this data source, one could reach a different conclusion regarding our propositions related to network evolution – certainly about the strength of Proposition 2 and little support for Proposition 3.

CADDO–BOSSIER PARISHES, LA, RESULTS

The second community in our study consists of the Caddo–Bossier Parishes in northwest Louisiana. These twin parishes include Shreveport and were a major evacuation site during Hurricane Katrina (and for months afterward). The key is to compare the networks for these two communities.

Media-reported networks

Caddo and Bossier Parishes experienced a tremendous influx of evacuees – including tens of thousands of residents for their shelters. These parishes are located far enough away from the coast to miss most of the extreme elements of incoming hurricanes. It is a natural location for intra-state evacuee hosting for Louisiana.

2000–2005

The media-reported network for Caddo–Bossier Parishes from 2000 to 2005 indicates a governmental network membership of 30 entities, with 12 of these actors also appearing in the later media analysis. The media-reported network of non-governmental organizations was vast, with 36 organizations named, only six of which also appeared in the 2006–2009 media analysis.

As in the case of Brazos County, there is tremendous instability in the participants in the media-reported network. In the government organization roster, the persistent components include local fire and law enforcement organizations along with state and federal emergency management organizations. About half of the governmental actors are persistent. This represents evidence for Proposition 1 and mixed evidence regarding Proposition 2.

The ARC is again a persistent actor. This is not a surprise given its role in sheltering activities in most communities. However, it is one of a small number of persistent non-governmental organizations. Here we see more support for Proposition 3.

As to policy domain representation, we see a similar array in this community as the last one. Transportation and health care organizations are present and persistent. There are other policy areas present (e.g. nutrition support, parks and recreation, and agriculture) but in a more intermittent way.

2006–2009

The media-reported network for Caddo–Bossier Parishes from 2006 to 2009 indicate somewhat fewer governmental organizations, with only 24 mentions during the time period, half of which also appeared in the 2000–2005 period. There was a significant decline in the number of mentions of non-governmental entities as network members, with 14 organizations reported in total, of which eight appeared for the first time.

As in the previous community, there is diversity in terms of policy domain and organization sector. Some of the instabilities are artefacts of name changes through the period (the state shifted to the title of 'Office for Homeland Security and Emergency Preparedness'). However, representation by local and state emergency preparedness offices seems light compared to what one might expect. Propositions 1 and 3 find strong evidence in the media-reported networks for the Caddo–Bossier Parishes. There is inconclusive evidence related to Proposition 2.

Plan-based network

Again we will contrast the media-reported network with the official emergency plan for the jurisdiction. In the case of the Caddo–Bossier Parishes, we were not able to collect a historical plan. We only have access to the current plan from 2009. In seeking older versions of the plan, we were assured that the previous versions of the plan operative from 2000 were largely the same as the current plan. When we explained that we were most interested in the actors present and the relationships between actors within the plan, one representative of the emergency management office said that there would be very few changes. Given the few changes in the Brazos County plans discussed previously, this seems credible though we were unable to confirm it with an old version of the document.

2009

Analysis of the Caddo–Bossier Parishes emergency plan reveals a total of 20 governmental entities named as network participants, seven of which were unique to Caddo–Bossier and 13 also appeared in Brazos County's plan. The roster of non-governmental network members for Caddo–Bossier also broadly matched that of Brazos County – of the four organizations named, only the Salvation Army was unique (and it also appeared in the 2009, but not 2004, version of the Brazos County emergency plan).

The plan-based roster for this community is larger than the plan-based roster for Brazos County and includes a broader range of organizations. This plan includes a broader range of government actors (including code enforcement and agriculture extension offices). Even with this diversity, though, the diversity of the plan network is still quite limited compared to the media-reported networks.

We cannot directly evaluate the propositions in the absence of a formal plan from the earlier time period. However, given the similarities between the Caddo–Bossier plan and the Brazos County plan, we are confident that the plans experienced similar changes over time. The Caddo–Bossier plan represents the plan after the dramatic evacuation-hosting events associated with Hurricane Katrina. It still represents only small number of sectors and policy domains.

The conclusion one would draw in relation to our network evolution proposition would be quite different if you looked only at the formal plan. Looking at the plan, there is little evidence of variability or diversity. A small number of closely knit actors dominate the network from the perspective of the formal plan. The network looks more like narrow policy subsystem than a broad and volatile issue network. The government actors are similar to those in the persistent core in the Brazos County plans but the few non governmental actors are also the persistent actors in the Brazos County plan. The transient actors seen in the media data are absent from the plan-based data.

Based on the Caddo–Bossier plan, we have support for Proposition 2 but mixed evidence for Proposition 3. We are unable to directly assess Proposition 1 given the absence of an earlier plan.

LESSONS FOR EVACUATION HOSTING AND EMERGENCY MANAGEMENT

These data confirm that evacuation hosting is a complex and evolving enterprise. The media networks identify a large and ever-changing network of participants representing a range of policy domains and sectors. The formal plans do not indicate the same level of diversity. There is no convergence on a single image of the respective networks. Instead, the different data sources tell somewhat different stories.

One could seek to declare one method more reliable or otherwise better than the other. A pessimistic reading of the discrepancy between the results, for example, is that the plans ignore the volume and nature of activities within the community. We are not convinced that this is the case. Instead, we see the plans as serving a specific purpose. The plans provide for a framework of formal responsibilities. They do not prevent the emergence of new participants. The media reports are consistent with this interpretation. The limited networks represented in the formal plans existed within large and diverse informal networks.

What is not clear is whether the plans would be better off with a more inclusive vision of their communities. Including a broad range of actors risks diluting and confusing the core plan with references to participants who may come and go over time. The broadly inclusive media networks also included a great deal of volatility. Some of the actors who dropped out may have stayed if included in the core plan; but some may have dropped out anyway leaving vestigial references to clot up the formal plan. The inclusion of the brokerage components of the periphery directly competes with the closure of the core network. While further research is needed on the balance of inclusiveness and focus in formal plans, we encourage great care in creating formalized relationships between non-traditional actors within the core emergency plan. It may be ideal to balance the vision advantage of brokerage with the reliability advantage of closure by bifurcating the network into core actors (identified within the formal plans) and peripheral actors (identified within the media coverage – but absent from the formal plans). The results may be a hierarchical network (Moynihan, 2008).

Engagement of non-traditional actors can work without including those actors in the formal plans themselves. This may be possible through a hybrid plan that makes clear distinctions (possibly with the Emergency Support Function (ESF) framework, as has been done in some communities) between core and peripheral participants. An approach that includes a broad range of actors from the periphery into the ESF appendices may appropriately balance the needs for a coherent core and the inclusion of the periphery.

One theme that emerges clearly from the data is that evacuation hosting is a community event that calls upon the resources of a broad range of actors. Emergency management professionals (including consistent participants like the ARC) do not manage this process by themselves. Communities, not just agencies, host evacuees. Whether or not the formal plans include the broad range of actors engaged in evacuation-hosting activities, emergency management professionals must be aware of the range of organizations that one may potentially recruit to assist in hosting activities.

LESSONS FOR NETWORK DYNAMICS

The lessons for network dynamics, more generally, depend entirely on which approach to network measurement one prefers. The formal plans provide an image of the networks as limited in scope and stable over time. A small number of participants in these networks tend to stay in the network. The network provides little evidence of permeability to changes – even in what may be seen as a remarkable challenge to the network. These were networks that operated below the radar of public media attention. Despite the high salience, there is little evidence of change in the participants as viewed through the formal plans.

The media-reported networks tell quite a different story. Within these two communities, we see dynamic networks that change size and membership. Each network includes participants from diverse policy domains and sectors. This view suggests participation by the broad civil society in issues of evacuation hosting. Religious organizations provide a broad range of services as well as serving as evacuee hosts. Similarly, private sector organizations are involved in services ranging from providing supplies and meals (sometimes at a remarkable discount). Government organizations represent a broad range of policy domain, including – most obviously, public health and transportation; but also social services, education and environmental quality.

This equivocation within the data does not help us to resolve the fundamental question related to policy networks. Whether networks are diverse (as issue networks) or limited (as iron triangles) depends to a great extent on the data one uses to view the network. The formal plans provide an image of limited participation that is larger than the most strict iron triangle models, but still limited largely to a steady group of government organizations.

Our conclusion is that neither data source is (independently) accurate – and that both are (partially and jointly) accurate. Each data source views the networks in different ways and from different perspectives. The formal plans focus on participant with specific legal authority and responsibility. This is a narrow range of participation - but an important one. The number of actors with legal authority and responsibilitie related specifically to emergency management activities is small and there is littl variation in this network. At the same time, there is a larger network of actors withou specific authority and responsibilities who may participate in evacuation hosting i informal capacities. These informal participants are important but they play a differer role. The informal actors are more likely to disappear from the network (or appea only in a later time period). They are the components of a network that is volatile an diverse. The data suggest that we need to move away from looking for a single networ – even within single policy areas. Policy networks involve overlapping memberships various networks including core and periphery actors, those with and those witho formal authority, and those whose presence is consistent and those whose presence not consistent. Narrow and broad images of networks are both correct – though of different networks within a policy area.

A possible frontier for additional work would be to include additional modes of data collection. The most obvious is After Action Reports. These documents may provide a balance of some of the biases present in plan and media-based accounts while being subject to their own biases (recall biases and biases towards official/formal partici-pants). We leave this work to future research though the justification for multi-modal research is now clear.

In the end, it is clear the networks are both diverse and homogeneous – both stable and volatile. There is an inner-core of actors whose membership is steady over time. Interestingly, this group operates without significant media attention. There is an outer-periphery of actors who enter and leave the network quickly, represent a broad range of interests, and draw the attention of the media. This combination may prove to be a strength of emergency management networks. This may create the potential for both reliable operations from a formalized core and rapid reorganization of the supporting informal ring (Moynihan, 2008).

From the standpoint of the measurement of networks, this leaves an important question. The pooling of these two methods of actor identification presumes that they contribute to a vision of a single network. It may be more telling to avoid such pooling and instead talk about the sub-networks separately. This is especially the case with the non-governmental actors and the media networks. In volume, the media network members outnumber those actors that are only present in the formal plans. If one pooled the rosters and then performed statistical tests or summaries on the aggregate pool, the dynamics of the media pool would drive the results. Separate analysis of the formal rosters might be appropriate if one's theoretical interest involved the core set of actors. Based on the lack of a convergent image of the networks in this study, we recommend choosing a pooling strategy carefully depending on the theoretical interest of one's own study.

CONCLUSION

Network analysis is an emerging and potentially powerful perspective for the study of policy implementation generally and emergency management networks specifically. The results of studies of two emergency and shelter management networks that have been presented here provide some insight into the dynamics of these networks over time – but raise substantial questions about the nature of data collection for network analysis.

Two different methods of data collection provide contrasting portraits of the emergency and shelter management networks. The media-reported networks provide vision of a broad issue network including an ever-changing roster representative of various policy domains and organizational sectors. The plan-based networks are much smaller and focus almost exclusively on government partners and a handful of longstanding non-profit partners. The resulting image of the networks is of an inner-core of players surrounded by a volatile periphery of actors.

This raises important questions in regard to the study of emergency management networks. Is the division of actors into such tiers efficient? Does it effectively focus attention on the most important actors without distractingly cluttering the formal plan? Does the informal role played by so many actors create a disincentive for those actors to continue to participate or to contribute as much as they could to the hosting effort? How many domains within emergency management or in other policy areas deliberately create and formalize such core and periphery distinctions? There is clearly a great deal still to be learned about the structure and dynamics of emergency management networks.

ACKNOWLEDGEMENT

This research was supported by a National Science Foundation grant (award number CMMI-1143922, Brian J. Gerber, Warren S. Eller, Melanie Gall and Scott Robinson, Investigators); the authors thank the NSF for this support. All opinions, findings and conclusions or recommendations expressed in this material are those of the author(s) and do not necessarily reflect the views of the National Science Foundation.

NOTES

1 Here membership only means co-participation in a community effort. It does not imply formal membership or acknowledgment. Given our interest in organizations that may act in the periphery of the network, a restriction to formal or self-acknowledged membership would exclude potentially interesting actors.

2 But see Robinson and Gerber (2007) and Kapucu (2007).

3 It is important to note that the resulting lists of participants are rosters and include no indications of relations between actors. This means that there can be no formal assessment of brokerage relations within the data. We return to the issue of brokerage in the conclusion.

4 Even with the combination of these two sources, measurement error is possible. The media and plan roles were confirmed individually through the context of each document to ensure that actors had a specific role in emergency management. It is possible that an actor has escaped coverage by the media or inclusion in the plans. The justification for combining modes of measurement is to reduce this measurement error through the adoption of contrasting methods by which the likely sources of error are offset. The combination of the methods, then, should provide a strong basis for inference – if, still, not a perfect one. Any roster method (surveys, interviews, field research, etc.) encounters the same issue.

REFERENCES

Burt, R. S. (2005) *Brokerage and Closure: An Introduction to Social Capital*, New York: Oxford University Press.

Comfort, L. K. (1994) Self-Organization in Complex Systems. *Journal of Public Administration Research and Theory* 4:3 pp393–410.

——. (2006) 'The Dynamics of Policy Learning: Catastrophic Events in Real Time'. Presented at the 2006 Annual Meeting of the American Political Science Association, August 31–September 3, Philadelphia, PA.

——. (2007) Crisis Management in Hindsight: Cognition, Communication, Coordination, and Control. *Public Administration Review*, 67:s1 pp189–97.

Comfort, L. K., Oh, N. and Ertan, G. (2009) The Dynamics of Disaster Recovery: Resilience and Entropy in Hurricane Response Systems 2005–2008. *Public Organization Review*, 9:4 pp309–23.

Creswell, J. W. and Clark, V. L. P. (2007) *Designing and Conducting Mixed Methods Research*, Thousand Oaks, CA: Sage Publications, Inc.

Heclo, H. (1978) 'Issue Networks and the Executive Establishment' in A. King (ed.) *The New American Political Establishment*. Washington, DC: American Enterprise Institute, pp87–124.

Kapucu, N. (2006) Public-Nonprofit Partnerships for Collective Action in Dynamic Contexts of Emergencies. *Public Administration*, 84:1 pp205–20.

——. (2007) Non-Profit Response to Catastrophic Disasters. *Disaster Prevention and Management*, 16:4 pp551–61.

——. (2008) Collaborative Emergency Management: Better Community Organising, Better Public Preparedness and Response. *Disasters*, 32:2 pp239–62.

——. (2009) Performance under Stress: Managing Emergencies and Disasters. *Public Performance and Management Review*, 32:3 pp339–44.

Kapucu, N., Augustin, M. E. and Garayev, V. (2009) Interstate Partnerships in Emergency Management: Emergency Management Assistance Compact in Response to Catastrophic Disasters. *Public Administration Review*, 69:2 pp297–313.

Kapucu, N, and Demiroz, F. (2011) Measuring Performance for Collaborative Public Management Using Network Analysis Methods and Tools. *Public Performance & Management Review*, 34:4 pp549–79.

Kiefer, J. J. and Montjoy, R. S. (2006) Incrementalism before the Storm: Network Performance for the Evacuation of New Orleans. *Public Administration Review*, 66 p122.

Lewis, J. M. (2011) The Future of Network Governance Research: Strength in Diversity and Synthesis. *Public Administration*, 89:4 pp1221–34.

McCool, D. (1998) The Subsystem Family of Concepts: A Critique and a Proposal. *Political Research Quarterly*, 51:2 p551.

McGuire, M. and Agranoff, R. (2011) The Limitations of Public Management Networks. *Public Administration*, 89:2 pp265–84.

Meier, K. J. and O'Toole, L. J. (2001) Managerial Strategies and Behavior in Networks: A Model with Evidence from U.S. Public Education. *Journal of Public Administration Research and Theory*, 11 pp271–94.

Moynihan, D. P. (2008) Learning under Uncertainty: Networks in Crisis Management. *Public Administration Review*, 68:2 pp350–65.

O'Toole, L. J. Jr. (1997) Treating Networks Seriously: Practical and Research-Based Agendas in Public Administration. *Public Administration Review*, 57:1 pp45–52.

Provan, K. G., Fish, A. and Sydow, J. (2007) Interorganizational Networks at the Network Level: A Review of the Empirical Literature on Whole Networks. *Journal of Management*, 33:3 pp479–516.

Redford, E. S. (1969) *Democracy in the Administrative State*, NewYork: Oxford University Press.

Robinson, S. E., Berrett, B. and Stone, K. (2006) The Development of Collaboration of Response to Hurricane Katrina in the Dallas Area. *Public Works Management & Policy*, 10:4 p315.

Robinson, S. E. and Gaddis, B. S. (2012) Seeing Past Parallel Play: Survey Measures of Collaboration in Disaster Situations. *Policy Studies Journal*, 40:2 pp256–73.

Robinson, S. E. and Gerber, B. J. (2007) A Seat at the Table for Nondisaster Organizations. *The Public Manager*, 5 p4.

Sabatier, P. (1993) 'Policy Change Over a Decade or More' in P. Sabatier and H. Jenkins-Smith (eds) *Policy Change and Learning: An Advocacy Coalition Approach*, 13–40. Boulder, CO: Westview Press.

Sabatier, P. A. and Jenkins-Smith, H. C. (1993) *Policy Change and Learning: An Advocacy Coalition Approach*, Boulder, CO: Westview Press.

Simo, G. and Bies, A. L. (2007) The Role of Nonprofits in Disaster Response: An Expanded Model of Cross-Sector Collaboration. *Public Administration Review*, 67 pp125–42.

Waugh, W. L. and Streib, G. (2006) Collaboration and Leadership for Effective Emergency Management. *Public Administration Review*, 66:s1 pp131–40.

Abstract

This article studies a disaster management network in the state of Gujarat, India. Through social network analysis and interviews, the article examines the governance structure of a disaster management network and identifies factors that affect its effectiveness. Four factors – trust, number of participants in the network, goal consensus and the need for network-level competencies based on the nature of the task – were examined. The article concludes by discussing how the dynamics of these factors affected this particular disaster management network.

MANAGING DISASTER NETWORKS IN INDIA

A study of structure and effectiveness

Triparna Vasavada

Triparna Vasavada
School of Public Affairs
Pennsylvania State University
Harrisburg, PA
USA

INTRODUCTION

Governments and non-profit organizations (NPOs) typically form partnerships, alliances and networks to manage a disaster (Moynihan, 2008; Kapucu, 2009; Ansell *et al.*, 2010; Garrow, 2011). Scholars have begun to study these networks (Comfort and Kapucu, 2006; Kapucu and Van Wart, 2006; Birkland, 2009; Boin and 't Hart, 2010). We know that a network governance approach can improve service delivery to clients and, by using resources efficiently, provides advantages when dealing with complex problems (Provan and Milward, 2001; Ferlie *et al.*, 2011; Steijn *et al.*, 2011). Networks also present challenges concerning coordination and resource management (Agranoff and McGuire, 2001, 2003; Lewis, 2011; McGuire and Agranoff, 2011). The governance of a disaster management network requires multi-organizational coordination and collective action.

In this exploratory study, I examine a disaster management network in Gujarat, the western state of India. Because of its geography and its underdeveloped infrastructure, Gujarat has experienced natural disasters with depressing regularity. Gujarat suffered from the Morbi flood (1978); the Surat plague (1994); the Kandla cyclone (1998); floods sweeping across Ahmedabad, Baroda, Surat and Mehsana in 2000 and the historical 2001 Gujarat earthquake, to name but a few disasters.

The article's theoretical contribution is two-fold. First, by using network governance and resource dependence theory as a framework, this research attempts to understand disaster management networks by focusing on the structure of the network. Social network analysis is conducted to study the structural form of the network. Second, by using data from follow-up interviews, this study identifies the factors that impact the effectiveness of network governance.

The following section provides an overview of disaster management activities in the state of Gujarat, India. The article then presents the theoretical explanation for network governance and discusses various models of governance structure. In the following sections, the data and methods are discussed. Analysis of the network structure and key predictors of effectiveness are examined. This is followed by a discussion of the research implications.

DISASTER MANAGEMENT IN THE STATE OF GUJARAT, INDIA

The Gujarat earthquake of 26 January 2001, killed at least 20,000 people, injured 3,00,000 and destroyed more than a million homes. The Government of Gujarat quickly began emergency rescue operations to restore lost communication links, electricity, water supply and civil supplies. The state and central government mobilized thirty-six units of army engineers, thirty-four companies of paramilitary personnel, over 3,000 police officers, 2,600 home guards, 480 engineers, over 120 senior administrative officers and 11,000 employees from various departments in the relief operations (UNDP, 2001).

However, because of the magnitude of the earthquake, government required support from the non-governmental sector and the international community. The government of Gujarat initiated the formation of the Gujarat State Disaster Management Authority (GSDMA) to implement rehabilitation programmes.[1] The GSDMA, as an agency, coordinated the comprehensive earthquake recovery programme. The Gujarat Earthquake Rehabilitation and Reconstruction Project (GERRP) was conducted under the authority of GSDMA. The implementation of the GERRP stimulated a collaborative networking among governmental agencies, non-governmental organizations (NGOs), the private sector and international organizations, replacing the government' sole efforts with cross-sector collaborations.

Gujarat is home to hundreds of NPOs. A report by the United Nations Development Programme (UNDP) noted that over 300 NGOs were involved with relief operations after the 2001 Gujarat Earthquake (National Crisis Management Committee (NCMC) 2001). NPOs play an active and important role in local disaster management.

To assess the recovery needs, the international community responded by sending a five-member United Nations (UN) Disaster Assessment and Coordination team after the disaster. The UN Disaster Management Team (UNDMT), supplemented by staff from the UNDP Emergency Response Division, was deployed immediately to coordinate the UN response. The team established an On-Site Operations Coordination Center (OSOCC) that enabled the development of a close working relationship and a continuous exchange of information between the Chief Relief Coordinator, the collector and the UN system. The OSOCC also included the World Health Organization Disease Surveillance Team to offer medical services and the World Food Programme to provide relief food provisions. The World Bank and the Asian Development Bank jointly undertook a preliminary assessment of damage and reconstruction needs. The assessment called for close collaboration with the Indian Government, the Government of Gujarat and the service agencies of the Government of Gujarat (Asian Development Bank, 2008).

A variety of NGOs conducted the recovery programmes. With the assistance of the GSDMA, NGOs were immediately mobilized to help the community in the recovery project. The state government encouraged extensive collaboration between international and local NGOs. Thus, NPOs developed rehabilitation projects and proposed a financial partnership with the government. The government facilitated and monitored the projects, alongside conducting their own projects. Financial support for these partnerships was largely provided by funding from international agencies, such as the World Bank, the Asian Development Bank, the European Commission, the Government of Netherlands, the UN and the central ministry of India along with various other donors through the Government of Gujarat, via GSDMA.

According to Provan and Kenis (2008), network effectiveness is 'the attainment of positive network-level outcomes that could not normally be achieved by individual organizational participants acting independently' (Provan and Kenis, 2008: 230). In this regard, the network governance in Gujarat was effective – the network effectively achieved network-level outcomes of successful disaster management.[2]

THEORETICAL FRAMEWORK

Network governance

Cross-sector collaborative networks have been shown effective in dealing with disasters (Kapucu et al., 2009; Moynihan, 2009; Comfort et al., 2010). A process-oriented point of view assumes that actors are interdependent and find solutions to common problems by constructively dealing with differences through the joint ownership of decisions and collective action during the emergent process of collaboration (Gray, 1989; Ostrom, 1990; Alexander et al., 2011).

Research on networks includes examinations of variations in the structures of networks (Uzzi, 1997), factors associated with the origins of networks (Ebers, 1997) and the ways in which networks have evolved (Human and Provan, 2000). Networks have been analysed by studying 'nodes' and 'relational ties', to understand the function of the network (Huxham and Vangen, 2000). These scholars are mainly focused on the 'nodes' or 'relationships' as the unit of analysis. They seldom focus on the entire network (see, e.g. Provan and Milward, 1995; Provan et al., 2007). Scholars argue that more empirical research is necessary to understand networks as a form of governance structure (Kilduff and Tsai, 2003; Provan et al., 2007; Provan and Kenis, 2008) and what makes them effective in times of disasters (Boin and Rhinard, 2008; Boin and 't Hart, 2010). To better understand the dynamics of collaborative networks and the factors that influence goal-directed performance (Kilduff and Tsai, 2003), we focus on the forms of governance (Milward and Provan, 2006; de Bruijn and Heuvelhof, 2008; Provan and Kenis, 2008; Robins et al., 2011).

Provan and Kenis (2008) identify three types of network governance: participant-governed networks, lead-organization-governed networks and network administrative organizations (NAOs). The networks are ordered along a dimension that gauges whether the structure is centralized, decentralized or somewhere in between.

Participant-governed networks embody the decentralized form; participants in the network share the responsibility of managing internal and external relationships on a relatively equal basis. Power is also distributed equally among participants. In this form no single organization or actor represents the network as a whole. *Lead-organization-governed networks* are highly centralized; a single lead organization plays a key role in coordinating and managing all network governance activities. This lead organization also oversees the activities associated with, and makes decisions related to, internal and external relationships to achieve network-level goals aligned with the goals of the lead organization. One feature of this network governance form is that power is distributed asymmetrically among participating members. The third type is the NAO, which is centralized. In this typology, a separate administrative group governs the network and its activities. The administrative group serves as a mediator role in the coordination of relationships in the network. Power is relatively centralized in this form of network governance (Moynihan, 2009).

The effectiveness of these three models of network governance is based on four contingencies: trust, number of participants in the network (size), goal consensus and the need for network-level competencies based on the nature of the task (Provan and Kenis, 2008). I try to capture the patterns of interaction among networked actors. These patterns of interaction are influenced by resource dependence and the power it brings to the actors. To unravel these dynamics, resource dependence theory is employed, alongside the network governance perspective, as a framework for this study.

Resource dependence theory is based on the assumption that no organization is completely self-reliant for its survival and existence. Organizations depend on their environment for (i) material resources, including monetary and human resources, (ii) information and (iii) social and political support (Aldrich and Pfeffer, 1976). In a disaster, the government and other organizations seek a collaborative strategy to manage external dependencies to facilitate disaster recovery.

Three mechanisms are important for effective networked responses for disaster management – (i) high levels of trust among key actors in the network, (ii) high coordination with clearly defined authorities and (iii) configurations of the right type of organizations in the network (Moynihan, 2007, 2009; Boin and 't Hart, 2010). Trust building takes an inordinate amount of time and nurturing (de Bruijn and ten Heuvelhof, 2008; cf. Tummers et al., 2012). Therefore, building and maintaining mutual trust between various actors is important for networked governance.

Network analysis provides a variety of indicators to grasp the structure and effectiveness of the network. Centrality is one of the concepts used frequently to study the structure in social networks (Choi and Brower, 2006; Kapucu et al., 2009; Shea, 2011). centrality measure indicates who is at the centre of the network. Centrality is measured by degree, closeness and betweenness.

Degree centrality can be measured by how well-connected an actor is to other nodes the network. High degree centrality indicates where the most activity in the network occurs. An actor with high degree centrality is in direct contact with many other members in the network. As a result, this actor is considered a crucial channel for information flow. Closeness centrality is based on the distance between actors. In networked governance, the flow of information is the key. Actors with a high level of closeness centrality are very productive in communicating information to other actors the network (Comfort and Haase, 2006; Kapucu, 2006). Closeness centrality indicates who has short communication paths to other actors. Another measure of centrality is betweenness centrality. Non-adjacent actors might depend on actors who adjacent to both of them for interaction. Actors who lie between other actors, therefore, have some control over the paths. As a result, these actors play the role of a mediator in the network. Actors with high betweenness centrality have more 'inter-personal influence' (Freeman, 1979) on other actors.

METHODS

This study has two purposes. The first purpose is to understand the structure of disaster management networks from a network governance perspective; the second goal is to explore the key factors that influence the effectiveness of the network governance form. This research was conducted in two phases: phase one and phase two. Phase one focused on collecting relational data for network analysis and phase two included follow-up qualitative interviews with participants of the network.

The purpose of phase one was to capture information on inter-sector collaboration by identifying the actors involved in disaster management for the recovery phase and mapping their connections with one another. A boundary was specified by employing Laumann et al.'s (1989) 'realist' approach. The 'realist' approach focuses on actors' memberships and boundaries, as perceived by the members themselves. The three-step process included: (i) generating the master list, (ii) influence rating and (iii) informant nomination during interviews. In step one, the initial list was generated by analysing archival sources such as websites, newspapers and reports. The list contained 10 organizations that were considered 'influential' in disaster management.

To define the network, five individuals known in the state in the field of disaster management (but who were not in the studied network), such as retired officers from the disaster management agency completed a process of influence rating using the list. These individuals were asked to rate the actors on the list from zero to five, with five being the most important actor for disaster management in Gujarat. These individuals were provided two criteria for evaluation – the actors' level of influence in decision making and breadth of role in planning and implementation of disaster management activities. To increase the internal reliability, description of these two criteria was provided to the individuals before they conducted the ratings. To ensure that the network was not missing any important actors, informants were asked to nominate any missing actors during a follow-up interview. The social network data on communication ties were collected using structured interviews; these data were then analysed using the UCINET network analysis software program to draw the network of the disaster management and analyse the relational ties structure.

Phase two of the data collection process was to identify the factors influencing the effectiveness of network management. Semi-structured interviews were conducted with actors in the disaster management network. The non-probability sample consisted thirty-four individuals – nineteen from the government, eight from NPOs, two from accounting firms, one from an academic organization, one from a business organization and three from funding agencies. The government sample consisted of the municipal commissioner, District Collectors, District Development Officers and officers and staff of the GSDMA task force. To obtain the NGO perspective, NGO directors, programme managers/leaders and team members were included. The interview transcripts were coded for analysis. Open coding and selective coding techniques were used (Strauss and Corbin, 1998).

The quantitative and qualitative data were analysed by focusing on the following concepts: trust, number of participants in the network, level of goal consensus among the network partners and the network-level competencies to meet the internal and external needs and demands of the network. Qualitative network analytics were used to assess these concepts at the network level. Data on these items were collected in the follow-up qualitative interviews after the quantitative relational data were recorded in a pre-designed questionnaire. More specifically, the linkages between organizations for trust were established by reviewing in-depth qualitative narratives about relationship dynamics questions (e.g. 'Whom do you trust in this network? And why?' 'What level of trusting relationship do you have with the organizations? And why?'). These in-depth accounts provided for a rich database of information that went beyond the superficial level of 'yes/no' categories, as interview questions were aimed at the process of building trust and encountered challenges.

The findings are organized in two sections. In the first section, the findings from the social network analysis are presented. In the second section, findings from both the qualitative interviews and social network analysis provide insights about the factors that influence the effectiveness of network governance structure.

STRUCTURE OF THE NETWORK GOVERNANCE

An analysis of disaster recovery in the state of Gujarat indicates that the recovery phase was characterized by networked governance. The network consisted of international funding agencies, government organizations, NPOs and experts from academic institutions. Government actors included policy-makers, state leaders, state-level service agencies and district- and village-level administration offices. NPOs included both local and international NPOs. Figure 1 provides a graphic presentation of the sectors and actors involved in the disaster management network. Table 1 contains a description of the members of Gujarat's disaster management network.

Figure 2 provides a visual representation of the Gujarat disaster management network. In Figure 2, the network appears dense, with a network density (the proportion of actual ties to possible ties in the network) of 0.627. This measure does not provide specific information about the prominence of a given actor.

To identify the prominent actors in the network, centrality measures were calculated. Table 2 presents the centrality measures for the members of the network. The analysis of the data in Table 2 suggests that actors A1 (past disaster management agency leader and personal secretary to state political leader), A3 (current disaster management agency), IF1 and IF2 (international funding agencies), NPO1w (urban non-profit

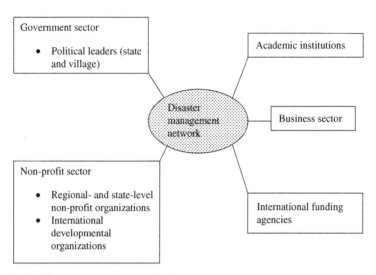

Figure 1: Sectors in disaster management networks

with rural outreach), NPO3w (urban non-profit with rural outreach), LA1 (top government official at district level), LA2 (district-level development officer) and NPO6r (religious NPO) have relatively high levels of degree centrality. A high degree centrality indicates 'where the action is' (Wasserman and Faust, 1994: 179) in the network. These results suggest that these actors are in direct contact with many other actors in the network, and thus occupy a central location in the network. Hence, other actors in the network consider these actors important members.

The same actors also have a high level of closeness centrality, which indicates that these actors are relatively close to other members in the network. As a result, they are not dependent on many other actors for communicating information and can efficiently relay information to other members. The data in Table 2 reveal that members S1 (the government unit that deals with revenue), S9 (unit that used to deal with disaster management activities in the past) and A2 (Representative of State) also have relatively high closeness centrality compared to the remaining members in the network.

However, the analysis of betweenness centrality (the 'brokerage measure') reveals that only actors A1, A3, NPO1w, NPO3w and NPO6r have high betweenness levels. This result implies that these actors are located between many of the other members; therefore, the interaction between the two non-adjacent members may depend on these actors facilitating communication. As a result, they might control the interaction between two non-adjacent members when they serve as the 'actor in the middle' (Wasserman and Faust, 1994: 188).

Actor A3 (current disaster management agency), which has the highest score on all three centrality measures, requires special attention. The centrality measures indicate that A3 is the most central actor in the network and acts as a leader, thus, holding the

Table 1: List of actors in disaster management

Number	Actor code	Actor description
1	P1	Political leader of the state
2	A1	Secretary to political leader of the state and appointed leader of A3 for 2 years
3	S1	The government unit that deals with revenue
4	S2	The government unit that deals with finance
5	S3	The government unit that deals with home affairs
6	S4	The government unit that deals with urban housing development
7	S5	The government unit that deals with roads and building
8	S6	The government unit that deals with health-related issues
9	S7	The government unit that deals with irrigation-related issues
10	S8	The government unit that deals with education and related issues
11	A2	Representative of the State
12	A3	The government unit that deals with disaster management
13	S9	Revenue-related matters/office that used to deal with disaster relief
14	S10	The government unit that deals with law and order
15	INO1	International developmental organization
16	INO2	International developmental organization
17	IF1	International funding organization
18	IF2	International funding organization
19	C1	Consulting company
20	C2	Consulting company
21	S11	Semi-government organization working in housing development
22	NPO1w	Non-profit organization led by woman
23	BO1	Business organization
24	ACDM	Academic institution
25	LA1	Top local (district)-level government administrator
26	NPO2	Non-profit organization created by a prominent industry
27	NPO3w	Umbrella non-profit organization led by a woman
28	NPO4	Non-profit organization
29	NPO5	Non-profit research and training institute
30	LA2	District-level development officer
31	LA3	District-level representative
32	P2	Village-level representative
33	S12	Government unit that deals with the water supply
34	NPO6r	Faith-based non-profit organization

rongest position in the network. An understanding of why A3 is prominent in the network requires further insight into the nature of the actors and the dynamics of the resource dependence among them.

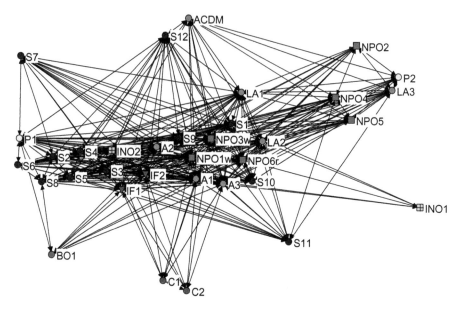

Figure 2: Disaster recovery networks of the Gujarat State in India

The role of the agency is to plan for disaster management, manage both domestic and international disaster management funds and coordinate and monitor disaster management efforts. These responsibilities will be performed by 'utilizing the resources and expertise of relevant Government departments, district administration, local authorities, NGOs, the public sector, the private sector, international development agencies, donors and the community' (Government of India, 2001: 4). Due to the important role of A3, its leadership role in the network seems obvious. Furthermore, the history of A3's leader and the organization's role in politics puts A3 in an even stronger position. The head of A3 held two positions, one as a leader (appointed by political officials) of A3 and another as A1 – the secretary of the political leader of the state (P1). The strategy behind dual positioning was to keep decision-making in A3 under the control of the political leader of the state. The leader of A3 oversees the administration and politics of disaster management activities and balances the two when required. Such dynamics brings A3 to a powerful central position in the network.

The network closely resembles the 'lead-organization governed' form of a network The network centrality analysis indicates that A3 plays the role of the lead organization in the disaster management network, makes key decisions and coordinates all network level activities. Having A3 as a central agency for disaster management facilitates, the disaster relief and rehabilitation activities are performed by the network members because A3 conducts regular meetings with other member organizations. Consequently A3 plays an important role in relaying information to the network members and also

Table 2: Centrality measures

Actors	Degree	Closeness	Betweenness
P1	69.69	76.74	0.513
A1	96.96	97.05	4.806
S1	75.75	80.48	1.531
S2	66.66	75	0.334
S3	69.69	76.74	0.529
S4	66.66	75	0.387
S5	63.63	73.33	0.171
S6	57.57	70.21	0.025
S7	45.45	64.70	0.025
S8	60.60	71.73	0.259
A2	78.78	82.5	1.240
A3	100	100	5.576
S9	78.78	82.5	1.016
S10	51.51	67.34	0.153
N01	15.15	54.09	0
N02	72.72	78.57	1.370
F1	81.81	84.61	2.240
F2	84.84	86.84	2.356
1	24.24	56.89	0.027
2	21.21	55.93	0
11	45.45	64.70	0.172
P01w	93.93	94.28	3.320
D1	27.27	57.89	0
CDM	42.42	63.46	0.234
A1	84.84	86.84	1.858
P02	39.39	62.26	0.092
P03w	93.93	94.28	3.627
P04	57.57	70.21	0.544
P05	48.48	66	0.307
2	84.84	86.84	2.599
3	48.48	66	0.350
	33.33	60	0.034
2	57.57	70.21	0.228
06r	93.93	94.28	3.642

ministers the financial resources provided by the international funding agencies. In summary, the Gujarat state disaster management network is a highly centralized and mediated network led by A3.

The leadership role of A3 emerged for two primary reasons. First, as a government agency with a mission of disaster management in the state, A3 had the legitimacy to play a leadership role in recovery activities. Second, external international funding agencies channel their funding for disaster relief through A3 to other organizations. With considerable oversight, external international funding agencies allow A3 to make decisions about how much funding each agency receives for various activities. This combination of power, legitimacy and resource dependence of other actors allows A3 to play a leadership role in the network.

FACTORS THAT INFLUENCE THE EFFECTIVENESS OF NETWORK GOVERNANCE STRUCTURE

Using the Provan and Kenis (2008) typology as a framework, the findings about factors that influence the effectiveness of network governance structure are organized, with a focus on four contingencies: trust, number of participants in the network, goal consensus and the need for network-level competencies based on the nature of the task.

Provan and Kenis (2008: 241) presented the following proposition for a lead organization-governed network: 'Lead-organization network governance will be most effective for achieving network-level outcomes when trust is narrowly shared among network participants (low-density, highly centralized trust), when there are relatively moderate number of network participants, when network-level goal consensus is moderately low and when the need for network-level competencies is moderate'. Let us now analyse the four factors in reference to this proposition.

Trust

The analysis of interview data was conducted keeping two factors in mind: the level distribution of trust in network-level interactions and the level of reciprocity of trust among members. The analysis indicates that the diffusion of trust is not very high among participants at the network level. Rather, trust is distributed narrowly among small group of actors that are central to the network. Trust is reciprocated in two ways: (i) in dyadic or clique relationships with peripheral actors and (ii) within the small group of actors in the central positions – A1, A3, IF1 and IF2, NPO1w, NPO3, LA1, LA2 and NPO6r. Although there is no complete lack of trust among network members, the density of trust seems moderate to low at the network level among members. Notably, though, there are two groups with a moderately high level of trust – the central actors of the network and the peripheral actors.

An understanding of the dynamics underlying the seemingly low density of trust among the members of the network is important. During the interviews, the lack trust between members from two different sectors, the government and NPO, was apparent. All nineteen individuals from the government sector provided the following reasons for their low level of trust in non-profit members: (i) a lack of transparency in NPOs' motives for collaboration with the government, (ii) the existence of fraudulent NPOs used to divert black money, (iii) an opportunistic attitude of NPOs seeking to obtain financial resources, even if they lacked the capacity and knowledge required and (iv) a lack of respect for the government.

The following statement from a government official is illustrative:

> There are many fraud[ulent] NGOs. It is hard to trust all who come to us for joint actions. NGOs are very enthusiastic about the project proposal, but in many instances, they do not have the same enthusiasm about the follow-up.

According to a government leader, non-profit leaders should strategically opt for projects in their field of specialization:

> Otherwise it becomes hard to get the desired output from networked collaboration. In most of the cases, government is always to blame for the failure, and falsely labeled as not responsive to the needs of victims. But that is not always the real reason; NGOs could be the reason, too.

A local-level government official mentioned the following reasons for the low level of trust government officers have in NGOs:

> NGOs in the village claim that they are the ones who think about betterment for the village. They do not share the credit for success with the government. Villagers see only NGO workers working on site. However, in most of the cases [the] government is a financial partner for a project.

Conversely, five individuals from NPOs expressed little trust in the government and its sincerity in cross-sector collaboration. Non-profit members stated following reasons for his lack of trust: (i) no commitment to the timeline of the project, (ii) too many layers of bureaucracy to manage as well as a lack of transparency and (iii) a lack of respect for NPOs. For example, when asked about transparency and the lack of trust, the leader of an NPO responded:

> At times, government prefers to leave the deadline portion of the contract blank. We have to pursue hard to get it on paper and even after doing that there is no guarantee that the timeline will be observed.

Later, another leader reported:

> The experience of working with government and bureaucracy is very frustrating. If given a choice, I would wish to escape from such partnerships.

The proposition that lead-organization network governance will be most effective for achieving network-level outcomes when trust is narrowly shared among network participants seems partially true in this case. Trust is centralized, but there is a high density of trust among the central actors and among the peripheral actors. Those at the centre of the network share a high level of trust among themselves. Their interdependence for financial resources and outreach efforts existed prior to the disaster. Similarly, trust is moderately higher among the peripheral actors, as they are more primarily local-level actors that worked together prior to the disaster, and hence, have established trusted relationships. However, there are peripheral actors that have a low level of trust in the central actors.

Number of network participants

The magnitude of the earthquake required a large number of organizations to come together for recovery efforts. The network size presented a challenge in coordinating the activities of various NPOs for the implementation of policies and projects and attending to the network-level needs of information sharing and resource management.

The lead-organization structure of the disaster management network provided effective outcomes in this situation, as the majority of the decision-making about recovery planning was centrally conducted by actor A3. Thus, participants did not have to interact directly with each other, but were able to rely on A3 for coordination.

The proposition that the lead-organization network governance will be most effective for achieving network-level outcomes when there are relatively moderate to large number of network participants seems to be true in the case of the Gujarat state disaster management network.

Network goal consensus

Goal consensus at the network level plays an important role in the effective governanc of networks. Networks consist of many different organizations, each with individua goals. Each organization is in the network for a specific reason and to achieve specifi goals. These goals may be similar or different to the collaborative network goal. For network to function effectively, there must be some degree of goal consensus at th network level.

The goal of this disaster management network was to conduct the recovery oper. tion for the community affected by the earthquake. Actors in the network also had the own organizational goals. More specifically, the majority of the NPOs in the networ had development as a primary goal; disaster response and mitigation were seconda goals. Similarly, government agencies have their primary goals to build the infrastru ture; however, due to the disaster-prone nature of the region, disaster management w also one of their goals. Therefore, the goal consensus was moderate to high. Why moderate? Because some NPOs were not involved in the disaster management-related activities prior to this earthquake. Due to the magnitude of the calamity, NPOs decided to enter the disaster management network and be part of the recovery efforts. One NPO leader stated that: 'The communities we are serving were hit hard by devastation and [participation] wasn't an option. We have to participate and help them build their life again. We cannot say that we were here only for teaching the kids or women'!

Such organizations entered the network with little or no experience of disaster management. In this sense, there was moderate goal consensus. The network efforts were effective in this situation, primarily because of the NPO dependence on A3 for financial resources, monitoring and the oversight of their rehabilitation efforts. In addition, A3 was in charge of making sure that the projects met the regulations required by the international funding agencies. The power dynamics were clear, due to the NPOs' financial dependence. Consequently, the lead organization A3 was in charge of making network-level decisions.

The proposition that lead-organization network governance will be most effective for achieving network-level outcomes when network-level goal consensus is moderately low is not validated in this case. This is because the majority of the organizations in the network have disaster management as their secondary organizational goal since they always operated in the disaster-prone region. Therefore, the overall level of goal consensus was moderate to high.

Resource dependence theory helps to explain this change. Even though the level of commonness of the goal of networked organizations is high, there is a lead organization (A3). This lead organization holds the majority of the resources and the powers of decision-making. The majority of the other organizations, except for the international funders, are dependent on A3 for financial resources. Additionally, only A3 has the power to make decisions about who gets resources and how the resources are allocated.

Need for network-level competencies

Organizations become a member of a network and bring specific competencies to a network to help meet network-level goals. Members of the disaster management network have specific competencies that were useful in achieving the network-level goal of disaster recovery. More specifically, NPOs provided grassroots connections and access to the communities that had been devastated by the earthquake. International funding agencies (IF1 and IF2) provided financial resources. Government service agencies (actors indicated with an 'S') helped regain utility services.

I considered two characteristics discussed by Provan and Kenis (2008) to analyse the level of need for network-level competencies: (i) the nature of the task being performed at the network level and (ii) external demands and needs faced by the network. Resource dependence theory provides clarity in understanding these two characteristics. The disaster management network's task was to conduct recovery efforts. The nature of the task required a moderate-to-high level of interdependence between actors. For example, the government was dependent on international funding agencies to acquire the necessary resources and relied on NPOs to build housing. International agencies were dependent on the government to facilitate, coordinate and monitor the relief operation and manage the financial resources they provided for recovery projects. NPOs depended on the government to fund rebuilding projects and provide subsidized building materials. In this manner, the lead-participant network structure of the disaster management network enabled the integration of specialty skills at the network level – which was required to achieve the network goal – by facilitating interdependent relationships.

Because the network evolved during the turbulent aftermath of the earthquake, it had to deal with external pressures related to the dependence of the government on international funding for recovery efforts. The network received funding from several international and national actors, including the central government of India. These entities imposed strict rules and required monitoring of the recovery efforts. Additionally, NPOs were required to adhere to the building codes for earthquake-resistant structures as they rebuilt houses in the earthquake-affected region. To deal with the external pressure, actor A3, the lead organization, took the responsibility of monitoring the building codes and issued procedural mandates to all network members. Because A3 was a government entity, the external legitimacy of the network was already established. Thus, the need for network-level competencies to deal with the external environment was moderate.

Resource dependence theory helps explain these dynamics further. In the disaster management network, each member – NPOs, government service agencies, funding agencies and accounting consulting agencies – brought their individual skills to the network to help meet the network-level goal. Each member worked in their specialty area and applied their expertise. Any other required skills were met primarily by the lead organization, A3. It is clear that networked actors are dependent on other organizations for resources. They are also accountable to the external environment for the use of these resources. However, because of the power and legitimacy of the A3, the need for network-level competency for other organizations is reduced. Thus, the proposition that lead-organization network governance will be most effective for achieving network-level outcomes when the need for network-level competencies is moderate seems to be true in this particular situation.

DISCUSSION AND CONCLUSION

This empirical study examines the governance structure of the disaster management network in the state of Gujarat, India. Research indicates that the NAO form of governance is the most commonly applied structure in crisis situations (see, e.g.

Moynihan, 2009). However, the findings here indicate that the disaster management network evolved as a lead-organization-governed structure. Unlike the NAO, the state disaster management agency exists independently of the network and its sole purpose was not just to provide network governance. Its role in disaster management was to provide its own services in addition to leading the disaster management network.

There are two reasons for this. First, unlike in a developed country, the government did not have any agency that was solely devoted to disaster management. As an immediate response to the earthquake, the state disaster management authority was formed. Therefore, it played a broader role of a formal authority leading disaster management efforts as a whole in addition to managing the network for disaster recovery activities. Second, international funding agencies provide funding for relief efforts to a government. Hence, the government is the lead organization in managing the funding and implementation of the projects. Consequently, it makes sense for the agency to build a disaster management network and play a lead role.

This article also explored the factors that affect the effectiveness of the network governance. The findings indicate partial divergence from the propositions about trust and goal consensus offered by Provan and Kenis (2008). In this case, the level of trust was moderate to low and trust is narrowly shared among two groups – the central group of actors and the peripheral group of actors – with an overall low density of trust in the network. In addition, goal consensus at the network level was moderately high. This divergence can be attributed to the resource dependence dynamics in the developing country setting. The role of the state government is considered primary in disaster recovery. However, due to the magnitude of the disaster, the government was dependent on international funding agencies, while the NPOs were dependent on the government for funding. In return, international funding agencies were dependent on the government agency for monitoring and the oversight of the funded projects. The government is also dependent on NPOs to conduct the recovery efforts at the grass-roots level. This interdependence was managed by the pragmatic leadership of the disaster management agency.

This research has several theoretical implications. This research presents empirical evidence about a lead-organization-governed network and provides insights about contingencies related to effective network governance. It contributes to the literature on networks by analysing the entire network, as encouraged by scholars (O'Toole, 1997; Provan et al., 2007). Finally, this study provides an analysis of disaster management in a developing country.

This study has three specific implications for practice. First, the findings will help a lead organization of a network to better understand its role by focusing on the predictors of network effectiveness for disaster management efforts. Second, network members can learn how the dynamics of the network relationships can be managed by focusing on trust and goal consensus as factors necessary for effective recovery efforts. Third, by recognizing the need to identify and respond to both the external and the internal demands of the network, the findings will help lead organizations to effectively manage their networks.

NOTES

1 It is important to note that the agency was not created specifically to administer the disaster management network. Rather, it was established as a government agency with a specific mission to deal with disasters, as there was no government authority designated to disaster management at the state level.
2 The state was awarded the 2003 UN Sasakawa Award for its outstanding work in the field of disaster management and risk reduction as well as the Gold Award by the Commonwealth Association for Public Administration & Management (CAPAM) for initiatives undertaken in governance.

REFERENCES

Agranoff, R. and McGuire, M. (2001) Big Questions in Public Network Management Research. *Journal of Public Administration Research and Theory*, 11 pp295–326.

—— (2003) *Collaborative Public Management: New Strategies for Local Governments*, Washington, DC: Georgetown University Press.

Aldrich, H. and Pfeffer, J. (1976) Environments of Organizations. *Annual Review of Sociology*, 2 pp79–105.

Alexander, D., Lewis, J. M. and Considine, M. (2011) How Politicians and Bureaucrats Network: A Comparison Across Governments. *Public Administration*, 89:4 pp1274–92.

Ansell, C., Boin, R. A. and Keller, A. (2010) Managing Transboundary Crises: Identifying Building Blocks of an Effective Response System. *Journal of Contingencies and Crisis Management*, 18:4 pp205–17.

Asian Development Bank. (2008) *India: Gujarat Earthquake Rehabilitation and Reconstruction Project*. Available at http://www.adb.org/Documents/PCRs/IND/35068-IND-PCR.pdf (accessed 23 March 2011).

Birkland, T. (2009) Disasters, Catastrophes, and Policy Failure in the Homeland Security Era. *Review of Policy Research*, 26:4 pp423–38.

Boin, A. and 't Hart, P. (2010) Organizing for Effective Emergency Management: Lessons From Research. *Australian Journal of Public Administration*, 69:4 pp357–71.

Boin, R. A. and Rhinard, M. (2008) Crisis Management in Europe: What Role for the Union? *International Studies Review*, 10 pp1–26.

Choi, S. O. and Brower, R. S. (2006) When Practice Matters More Than Government Plans: A Network Analysis of Local Emergency Management. *Administration and Society*, 37:6 pp651–78.

Comfort, L. K., Boin, R. A. and Demchak, C. eds. (2010) *Designing Resilience: Preparing for Extreme Events*. Pittsburgh, PA: Pittsburgh University Press.

Comfort, L. K. and Haase, W. T. (2006) Communication, Coherence, and Collective Action: The Impact Hurricane Katrina on Communication Infrastructure. *Public Works Management and Policy*, 10:4 pp328–4.

Comfort, L. K. and Kapucu, N. (2006) Inter-Organizational Coordination in Extreme Events: The World Trade Center Attack. *Natural Hazards*, 39:2 pp309–27.

de Bruijn, H. and ten Heuvelhof, E. (2008) *Management in Networks: On Multi-Actor Decision Making*, New York: Routledge.

Ebers, M. (1997) *The Formation of Interorganisational Networks*, Oxford: Oxford University Press.

Ferlie, E., Fitzgerald, L., McGivern, G., Dopson, S. and Bennett, C. (2011) Public Policy Networks and 'Wicked Problems': A Nascent Solution? *Public Administration*, 89:2 pp302–24.

Freeman, L. C. (1979) Centrality in Social Networks: Conceptual Clarification. *Social Networks*, 1 pp215–39.

Garrow, E. E. (2011) Receipt of Government Revenue Among Nonprofit Human Service Organizations. *Journal of Public Administration and Theory*, 21:3 pp445–71.

Government of India. (2001) *Gujarat State Disaster Management Policy Overview*, Gandhinagar: GSDMA.

Gray, B. (1989) *Collaborating: Finding Common Ground for Multiparty Problem*, San Francisco, CA: Jossey-Bass.

Gujarat State Disaster Management Authority. (n.d.). *GSDMA: An Initiative of Govt. of Gujarat*. Available at http://www.gsdma.org/

Human, S. E. and Provan, K. G. (2000) Legitimacy Building in the Evolution of Small-Firm Networks: A Comparative Study of Success and Demise. *Administrative Science Quarterly*, 45 pp327–65.

Huxham, C. and Vangen, S. (2000) Leadership in the Shaping and Implementation of Collaboration Agendas: How Things Happen in a (Not Quite) Joined-up World. *Academy of Management Journal*, 43 pp1159–76.

Kapucu, N. (2006) Interagency Communication Networks During Emergencies: Boundary Spanners in Multi-Agency Coordination. *The American Review of Public Administration*, 36:2 pp207–25.

—— (2009) Interorganizational Coordination in Complex Environments of Disasters: The Evolution of Intergovernmental Disaster Response Systems. *Journal of Homeland Security and Emergency Management*, 6:1 Article 47.

Kapucu, N., Augustin, M. and Garayev, V. (2009) Interstate Partnerships in Emergency Management: Emergency Management Assistance Compact in Response to Catastrophic Disaster. *Public Administration Review*, 69:2 pp297–313.

Kapucu, N. and Van Wart, M. (2006) The Evolving Role of the Public Sector in Managing Catastrophic Disasters: Lessons Learned. *Administration & Society*, 38:3 pp279–308.

Kilduff, M. and Tsai, W. (2003) *Social Networks and Organizations*, Thousand Oaks, CA: Sage.

Laumann, E. O., Marsden, P. V. and Prensky, D. (1989) 'The Boundary Specification Problem in Network Analysis' in L. C. Freeman, D. R. White and A. K. Romney (eds) *Research Methods in Social Network Analysis*. Fairfax, VA: George Mason University Press.

Lewis, J. (2011) The Future of Network Governance Research: Strength in Diversity and Synthesis. *Public Administration*, 89:4 pp1221–34.

McGuire, M. and Agranoff, R. (2011) The Limitations of Public Management Networks. *Public Administration*, 89:2 pp265–84.

Milward, H. B. and Provan, K. G. (2006) *A Manager's Guide to Choosing and Using Collaborative Networks*, Washington, DC: IBM Center for the Business of Government.

Moynihan, D. P. (2007) *From Forest Fires to Hurricane Katrina: Case Studies of Incident Command Systems*, Washington, DC: IBM Center for Business and Government.

—— (2008) Learning Under Uncertainty: Networks in Crisis Management. *Public Administration Review*, 68:2 pp350–65.

—— (2009) The Network Governance of Crisis Response: Case Studies of Incident Command Systems. *Journal of Public Administration Research and Theory*, 19:4 pp895–915.

National Crisis Management Committee. (2001) *Strategic Framework for Disaster Risk Management and Capacity Building After the Gujarat Earthquake*. State of Gujarat's Emergency Management Commission, Government of Gujarat.

Ostrom, E. (1990) *Governing the Commons: The Evolution of Institutions for Collective Action*, London: Cambridge University Press.

O'Toole, L. J. (1997) Treating Networks Seriously: Practical and Research-Based Agendas in Public Administration. *Public Administration Review*, 57 pp45–52.

Provan, K. G., Fish, A. and Sydow, J. (2007) Interorganizational Networks at the Network Level: A Review of the Empirical Literature on Whole Networks. *Journal of Management*, 33 pp479–516.

Provan, K. G. and Kenis, P. (2008) Modes of Network Governance: Structure, Management, and Effectiveness. *Journal of Public Administration Research and Theory*, 18:2 pp229–52.

Provan, K. G. and Milward, B. H. (1995) A Preliminary Theory of Interorganizational Network Effectiveness: A Comparative Study of Four Community Mental Health Systems. *Administrative Science Quarterly*, 40 pp1–33.

—— (2001) Do Networks Really Work? A Framework for Evaluating Public-Sector Organizational Networks. *Public Administration Review*, 61:41 pp4–23.

Robins, G., Bates, L. and Pattison, P. (2011) Network Governance and Environmental Management: Conflict and Cooperation. *Public Administration*, 89:4 pp1293–313.

Shea, J. (2011) Taking Nonprofit Intermediaries Seriously: A Middle-Range Theory for Implementation Research. *Public Administration Review*, 71:1 pp57–66.

Steijn, B., Klijn, E.-H. and Edelenbos, J. (2011) Public Private Partnerships: Added Value by Organizational Form of Management? *Public Administration*, 89:4 pp1235–52.

Strauss, A. and Corbin, J. (1998) *Basics of Qualitative Research: Techniques and Procedures for Developing Grounded Theory*, Thousand Oaks, CA: Sage Publications.

Tummers, L., Steijn, B. and Bekkers, V. (2012) Explaining the Willingness of Public Professionals to Implement Public Policies: Content, Context and Personality Characteristics. *Public Administration*, 90:3 pp716–36.

United Nations Development Programme. (2001) *From Relief to Recovery: The Gujarat Experience*. Available at http://www.undp.org/cpr/disred/documents/regions/asia/gujarat_report.pdf (accessed 23 March 2011).

Uzzi, B. (1997) Social Structure and Competition in Interfirm Networks: The Paradox of Embeddedness. *Administrative Science Quarterly*, 42 pp35–68.

Wasserman, S. and Faust, K. (1994) *Social Network Analysis: Methods and Application*, New York: Cambridge University Press.

Abstract

While evacuation behaviour and shelter choice have been extensively studied in developed countries, very limited research exists on the challenges faced by disaster survivors from developing countries. This is especially critical in countries where there is an absence of pre-designated shelters, lack of staging capacities and most importantly an inability of public sector entities to manage catastrophic events, independent of local and international non-profit organizations. This article aims to fill this gap by investigating on evacuation, decision-making and shelter choice in the wake of the 2004 Indian Ocean tsunami. We present our findings from a survey of 1,000 randomly selected households from 15 villages and one urban settlement in the Nagapattinam District (Tamil Nadu, India). Our research suggests that approximately 79.6 per cent of displaced households selected permanent public buildings and religious or community buildings as their first choice of shelter. Our analysis suggests that these decisions were affected by the severity of damage to homes, whether families were separated while evacuating and taking shelter, and their socio-economic characteristics.

MANAGING THE IMPACT OF DISASTER

Patterns of post-tsunami sheltering and duration of stay in South India

Simon A. Andrew, Sudha Arlikatti and Marina Saitgalina

Simon A. Andrew
Department of Public Administration
University of North Texas
Denton
TX 76203
USA

Sudha Arlikatti
Department of Public Administration
University of North Texas
Denton
TX 76203
USA

Marina Saitgalina
Department of Public Administration
University of North Texas
Denton
TX 76203
USA

77

INTRODUCTION

Immediately after a major disaster, a common though troubling phenomenon is the displacement of households. The uprooting of individuals from their permanent homes and physical damage often forces them to take refuge in emergency or temporary shelters. Most studies in the developed world have focused on the challenges of temporary sheltering in the United States, where a formalized selection and network of pre-identified shelters exist (Davis, 1978; Mileti *et al.*, 1992; Quarentelli, 1995; Oliver-Smith, 2005; Peacock *et al.*, 2006; Robinson *et al.*, this issue). Studies in the developing world, however, demonstrate the problems Internally Displaced Populations (IDPs) face due to a lack of formalized shelter networks and shelter planning (Gall, 2004). Moreover, problems in decision-making and planning in countries fraught with political instability, scarce resources, poverty and lack of land tenure documents have also been highlighted (Ritchie and Tierney, 2011). There have been calls to public agencies to take into account planning for temporary shelters that preserve human dignity and choice through collaborative efforts, continued assessment and involvement of displaced households (Babister and Kelman, 2002).

Aside from a large-N study conducted by Lindell *et al.* (2001) in 22 coastal counties of the Gulf coast region, there are few empirical studies examining evacuation behaviours associated with various types of temporary shelters. To fill this gap, we examine the evacuation behaviour of tsunami affected households, their duration of stay in temporary shelters and factors explaining these decisions. Based on the social vulnerability perspective (Cutter *et al.*, 2003; Phillips *et al.*, 2010), we argue that the decision to stay longer in a temporary shelter is partly a function of existing social structures and partly the physical environment in which displaced households must muddle through during the process of recovery. A household's ability to translate tangible resources into a functional asset is susceptible to multiple stressors that hinder them from meeting their basic needs, thereby influencing their sheltering patterns (Peacock *et al.*, 1997).

The following section briefly reviews the disaster literature on evacuation behaviour, displaced populations and temporary sheltering. Based on the social vulnerability perspective, we develop a set of hypotheses to explain the duration of stay in temporary shelters. Following this, a description of the research site in the Nagapattinam District of Tamil Nadu (India), the research design and data collection methodology are presented. The article then discusses key findings and limitations of the study and concludes with opportunities for future research.

EVACUATION BEHAVIOUR, DISPLACEMENT AND SHELTERING

Studies have shown that the type of hazard, speed of onset, amount of lead time and forewarning, the extent of casualties and the degree of damage to structures collectively affect the displacement (Lindell, 1994; Yelvington, 1997). When building structures are deemed unsafe or uninhabitable, the demolition of houses may force households to seek alternative living arrangements prolonging the time they spend in shelters (Babister and Kelman, 2002; Ritchie and Tierney, 2011). We refer to temporary displacement of households to mean households that were displaced from their pre-disaster homes for a short period of time, ranging from a day to about 6 months.

Disaster survivors in the United States typically pass through four stages of housing recovery (Quarentelli, 1982).[1] The first stage is *emergency shelter* which is unplanned and spontaneous. Such shelters are typically open yards or cars after earthquakes (Bolin and Stanford, 1998) or upper floors of homes during a flood, usually lasting only one night. The second stage is *temporary shelter,* which could be second homes, the house of a friend, a motel or public buildings identified as shelters by local governments and non-profits in host communities where evacuees could potentially stay for a week to a month. A temporary shelter often provides basic necessities, such as food and water and other routine activities on a modified basis (e.g. bathing/washing clothes on rotation). The next stage is *temporary housing,* which allows victims to re-establish household routines in non-preferred locations or structures such as mobile homes and rented apartments. The final stage is *permanent housing,* which is the long-term solution to housing disaster survivors in safer, sustainable and permanent homes. These may be at their original locations and include repairing and/or rebuilding the home to better building standards or relocating households to new and safer sites.

Households vary in their progression from one stage to the next depending on unpredictable circumstances such as aftershocks after earthquakes (Bolin and Stanford, 1998). Particularly significant are the problems faced by socially vulnerable populations including the elderly, disabled, widows, female-headed households, children, racial and ethnic minorities and economically disadvantaged groups (Fothergill et al., 1999; Tierney et al., 2001; Suar and Khuntia, 2004; Arlikatti et al., 2010). Emergency shelters can take on a permanent character even if the conditions are not suitable for long-term living because of difficulties in finding alternative housing arrangements (Arlikatti and Andrew, 2012), or the inability to return home due to severity of damage (Levine et al., 2007; Ritchie and Tierney, 2011).

While emergency and temporary shelters help displaced individuals perform basic household functions and offer them immediate physical protection, given a choice, households temporarily displaced are generally reluctant to stay in mass emergency shelters (Quarentelli, 1982; Peacock et al., 2006). Many who stay in temporary shelters do so after exhausting every other option and often find themselves competing with the homeless and disaster responders for housing (Davis, 1978). Studies have also shown that, when displaced households spend considerable amount of time in close confinement, coupled with lack of privacy, the environment can provoke ethnic and class tensions, unsocial behaviour and psychological stress among survivors (Peacock al., 2006).

A study of 559 residents from 22 counties in the Texas Gulf Coast region, from the Louisiana State line to the Texas–Mexico border in the United States, found that about

46.3 per cent of the respondents planned to stay with friends and relatives, only 32.9 per cent expected to stay in hotels and motels, 4.3 per cent of evacuees expected to stay in trailers or campers, 3.2 per cent in second homes, 9.8 per cent did not know where they would stay and only 3.4 per cent were expected to stay in public shelters (Lindell et al., 2001).

Most of the temporary shelters in the developed world are partially organized and stocked with food, drinking water and medicine for evacuees (Peacock et al., 2006). Despite the best of intentions by response agencies, recurrent problems persist in choosing culturally and climatically appropriate construction materials, handling of anti-social problems within the proximity of temporary camps, resolving operational delays associated with the procurement of shelters, suitable land sites and a lack of organizational capacities (Davis, 1978; Bolin and Stanford, 1990). Because of the spontaneity of setting shelters, getting households to comply with shelter rules can be difficult, adding to stress and hopelessness among displaced households (Lizarralde et al., 2010).

A spatial analysis conducted by Gall (2004) suggests that in developing countries with no sheltering plan or pre-staging areas, temporary shelters are often set up ad hoc by governmental agencies, domestic and international faith-based organizations. Temporary sheltering in temples, mosques or churches are at times sought by grieving survivors to meet their spiritual needs (Koeing, 2006; Holcombe, 2007; Pant et al. 2008). Additionally, scarcity of resources intensifies discriminatory attitudes and behaviour, which suggests that government efforts to provide social services can lead to exclusion of certain households. For example, an empirical study conducted in Andhra Pradesh, India, highlights that social institutions matter in explaining households' access to physical public resources (Bosher, 2007). Households from a lower social caste may lack access to resources because they live in a multi-caste village where decisions are dominated by the higher social caste.

THEORETICAL FRAMEWORK

In disaster research, the concept of social vulnerability has been defined as 'characteristics of a person or group in terms of their capacity to anticipate, cope with, resist and recover from the impacts of a natural hazard' (Wisner et al., 2004: 11). Social vulnerability refers to various factors including demographic, political and psychological that vary across communities and households. These factors affect their ability weather disaster impacts, and thereby their response. The decision to stay in temporary shelters may vary because of social conditions that force the households to adapt to the circumstances through different sets of priorities, highlighting not only their dependence on public assistance but also their differing coping strategies.

Disasters have two dimensions: natural and human (Wisner et al., 2004). The dimensions are inextricably bound together making certain households more vulnerable than others. The relationships between the physical environment and social structure (i.e. norms and cultures) affect displaced households' sets of priorities and recovery processes (Bolin and Stanford, 1998; Cutter *et al.*, 2003; Wisner *et al.*, 2004).

At the most general level, the social vulnerability perspective assumes that certain groups of households are disproportionally impacted by disasters (Dash *et al.*, 1997; Wisner *et al.*, 2004; Phillips *et al.*, 2010). For example, poorer households with little financial resources lack opportunities to protect themselves against external environmental shocks. They are removed from familiar surroundings and social support structures that protect their livelihoods. This has prompted scholars to argue that displaced households seeking temporary shelters are conditioned by social, economic and political forces (Peacock *et al.*, 1997; Wisner *et al.*, 2004).

Research hypotheses

The literature based on the social vulnerability perspective suggests that gender is a good predictor of evacuation behaviour (Peacock *et al.*, 1997). Situating the gender perspective in the context of developing countries, we hypothesize that the duration of stay for female-headed households in temporary shelters will be longer than their male counterparts for several reasons. First, women and particularly female-headed households are often powerless to seek alternative shelters due to social norms and societal expectations (Enarson and Morrow, 1998). Second, female-headed households have different capacities to act on their choice or preferences due to their competing obligations (Enarson, 2010), evacuation preparation and greater physiological risks (Richter and Flowers, 2010).

H1: Female-headed households stay longer in temporary shelters than male headed households.

The vulnerability perspective also posits that segments of the population historically discriminated against tend to be poorer and of a lower social class. They are also likely to live in an evacuation zone or hazard-prone locations (Peacock *et al.*, 2006; Dash, 2010; cf. Phillips, 1993), and less likely to have political and economic power to garner necessary resources that would allow them to avoid public shelters.

H2: Households from a lower social class stay longer in temporary shelters.

Disaster scholars have noted that government regulations and mitigation policies can lead to involuntary displacement of socially disadvantaged groups (Oxfam, 2005). A study conducted in Sri Lanka found that the post-tsunami coastal buffer zone policy hastily designed by the Sri Lankan government failed to be sensitive to the availability of livelihood choices (Ingram *et al.*, 2006). A similar problem was observed in India, where stricter building codes and land-use and coastal zoning regulations delayed displaced households' return to their permanent homes and livelihoods (Arlikatti *et al.*, 2010; Arlikatti and Andrew, 2012). Although the government had good intentions of keeping the populace safe from future disasters, it caused a massive relocation of fisher folk, miles away from their only means of livelihood. This caused them to inadvertently stay longer in temporary shelters, while seeking alternative livelihoods.

H3: Households whose occupations are directly impacted by a disaster stay longer in temporary shelters.

Another factor influencing displaced households' decisions to stay in temporary shelters is the severity of damage to homes and whether these can be easily repaired (Dash, 2010). When the physical integrity of the built environment is compromised and unsuitable for living, people take refuge in the safety of temporary shelters. Babister and Kelman (2002:7) remind us that 'Often but not always, those affected worst by disasters are the poor who have the least resources to rebuild ... If people need to be temporarily accommodated, the length of time they stay is usually directly related to the practical task of rebuilding of their homes'.

H4: Households whose homes are severely damaged stay longer in temporary shelters.

When there is a sudden onset of disaster, the communities and response agencies face the challenges of improvising and adapting their response strategies. Oftentimes, households may be separated during evacuation, especially large families with children, elderly and disabled household members (Prater *et al.*, 2006). Empirical studies are limited on the impacts of family members being separated during evacuation and how this affects a households' decision on where to shelter and how long to stay. According to Quarentelli (1980: 46), '...instead of responding as separate individuals, family members act as collective units at times of evacuation. Household members will try to respond to warnings together, to withdraw together and to find shelter together .. [They] will try to reunite at home, and if not possible, to go to a place where they think others will converge'. This leads us to the final hypothesis:

H5: Households with no missing or separated family members tend to stay longer in temporary shelters.

THE TSUNAMI

An earthquake of magnitude 9.0 occurred off the coast of Sumatra in Indonesia on 2 December 2004 (Chadha *et al.*, 2005) . It set-off huge tsunami waves, which travelled throughout the Indian Ocean claiming over 250,000 lives in 11 countries. Most severe affected were Indonesia, Thailand, Sri Lanka, India and Somalia. In India, the Distri

Nagapattinam was one of the hardest-hit areas: about 6,000 lost their lives, 196,000 people were displaced and over 28,000 were sheltered in temporary relief camps (Prater et al., 2006).[2] Given the high population density along the Tamil Nadu coastline, the bulk of the damage was within 500 m (0.31 miles) from the High Tide Line (HTL) (Kumaran and Negi, 2006). As the tsunami was an unfamiliar hazard and hit the Indian coastline suddenly, in the early morning hours, the coastal communities were not prepared to take protective measures.

In the immediate aftermath of the tsunami, the local government agencies under the direction of the Nagapattinam District Collector set up temporary shelters at 45 different locations. About 1,931 units were sponsored by the State Government of Tamil Nadu (GoTN) and 9,540 units by numerous non-governmental agencies (Prater et al., 2006). The GoTN also provided temporary emergency aid for communities involved in fishing and agricultural activities. The combined efforts of the local government agencies, nongovernmental organizations (NGOs) and international non-governmental organizations (INGOs), under the leadership of the District Directorate,[3] was crucial in turning the reconstruction and rehabilitation process into development opportunities for the survivors (Shaw, 2006).

Some affected households took refuge in makeshift temporary shelters while repairing and rebuilding their damaged homes, while others with homes damaged beyond repair waited for over 2 years to be allocated permanent housing. Initial reports after the tsunami were quick to note that public agencies underestimated the assistance needed for continued support of marginalized groups and overlooked households with children, elderly and women in southern India (Srinivasan and Nagaraj, 2006). Allocation of permanent housing for displaced households was also complicated by government land-use regulations. An updating of land-use and zoning regulations (the Coastal Regulation Zone Notifications) and a requirement for households living within 1 km of the coastline to be in compliance with the existing zoning regulations impacted households' living arrangements and their recovery processes (Arlikatti and Andrew, 2012).

DATA ANALYSIS

A survey was conducted among 1,000 households selected randomly from fifteen coastal villages and one urban settlement in Nagapattinam district between June and August of 2005 (Table 1). The selection of coastal villages was based on information provided by the NGO Coordination and Resource Centre (n.d.) set up by the Nagapattinam District Collectorate's office, which identified eighty-one villages as being severely impacted by the tsunami and requiring relief aid. The sampled communities comprised the urban centre Akkaraipettai, located in the coastal zone of Nagapattinam city, as well as nine communities to the north of Akkaraipettai and six to the south (Table 2). For each community, a detailed listing of households was

Table 1: Nagapattinam District and sample demographics

Demographic characteristics	Number of persons	% of district total	Sample
Total population	1,487,055	–	1,000 households
Male	738,287	49.65	46.5%
Female	748,768	50.35	53.5%
Rural	1,157,714	78	74.9%
Urban	329,341	22	25.1%
Literate	1,010,488	68	–
Individuals below poverty line	405,912	27	–
Demographic characteristics	Number of households	% of district total	
Total households	317,000	–	–
Households below poverty line	101,500	32	–

Source: Information on population characteristics was retrieved from Nagapattinam District Website (n.d.).

Table 2: Surveyed communities

Surveyed communities	Frequency	%
Urban centre		
Akkaraipettai	251	25.1
North of urban centre		
Madavamedu	47	4.7
Vellakulam	15	1.5
Koolaiyar	34	3.4
Thoduvai	87	8.7
Vapanchery	25	2.5
Thalampettai	36	3.6
Chandrapadi	47	4.7
Kottaimedu	22	2.2
Chinnagudi	69	6.9
South of urban centre		
Seruthur	52	5.2
Kameswaram	107	10.7
Kovilpathu	60	6.0
Vanavanmahadevi	71	7.1
Mottandithoppu	10	1.0
Pushpavanam	67	6.
Total	1,000	100

generated from the electoral rolls, which had been revised by the Nagapattinam District's Revenue Division Office in 2004 (Arlikatti *et al.*, 2010). The lists represented the most accurate enumeration of households residing in each village at the time of the tsunami and a proportionate random sample of households was drawn from each of the villages. The actual size of the resulting sample was proportionate to the number of households in each of the fifteen villages and one urban centre.

A local research organization headed by two social scientists was contracted to conduct the household surveys in *Tamil*, the native language of the region. Two members of the US research team and the principals of the organization trained the interviewers. The translated survey instrument (English to Tamil) was pre-tested in three villages and then modified slightly to address translation problems. The structured questionnaire requested information about a household's main occupation, types and levels of government assistance, emergency and temporary housing, types of damage to primary dwelling and household assets, impacts to livelihoods, psychological impacts, as well as households' demographic characteristics, injuries and fatalities.

To ensure the reliability of information reported about the household experiences, up to three visits were made to each selected household to conduct interviews with the head(s) of the household. Nearly 78 per cent of the interviews were conducted in damaged homes of the respondents, and at other times the interviews were conducted in temporary shelters or relatives' homes that tended to be either near original homes or in central locations in or near the respondent's village, yielding a response rate of 100 per cent.

Identifying temporary shelters

We identified household shelter choice by using household responses in our survey instrument to the following question: 'Where was the first place you and your household sought shelter after you left your home?' Based on our field work and recurrent household responses, we categorized temporary shelters as follows: (1) mass public shelters temporarily provided by government or non-governmental agencies such as relief camps and emergency shelters, (2) public buildings converted into temporary shelters such as school buildings, university compounds, hospitals and sports complexes, (3) improvised shelters such as religious buildings or community centres and (4) private homes offered by close friends, relatives, neighbouring communities or even strangers. Households that took shelter in their own home were classified as taking refuge in a private home.

Evacuation behaviour

In our survey instrument, respondents were also asked (1) the number of days they stayed in each type of temporary shelter, (2) the number of times they moved from one shelter to another before moving back to their home or being allocated permanent housing, and (3) whether they stayed together as a family while taking shelter or were separated.

Severity of damage to home

The severity of damage to a home was computed as an index by asking heads of households a number of questions related to the extent to which the roof, walls and floors of their primary dwelling was damaged by the tsunami. The items were aggregated and trans-formed on to an index ranging from 0 (No Damage) to 1 (Completely Damaged/ Destroyed). The procedure provides a single overall score of damaged home with a Cronbach's alpha reliability coefficient of 0.96. The higher the index, more severe is the damage caused by the tsunami to respondents' homes ($M = 0.48$, SD$= 0.42$).

Socio-economic characteristics

Consistent with the social vulnerability perspective, the socio-economic characteristics of respondents were operationalized by capturing the effect of gender on duration of stay in a temporary shelter, by coding female-headed households as 1, otherwise 0. In our sample, about 53 per cent of households were headed by females.

The household annual income before the tsunami was measured as an ordinal scale of 8 categories, with 1 being a low income household earning less than Rs. 4,999 per year, and 8 being the highest income category with households earning above Rs. 85,000. About 64 per cent of the households earned less than Rs. 10,000 per year. While 27 per cent had an annual income less than Rs. 4,999 per year, about 8 per cent of households in our survey fell in the highest income category of above Rs. 56,000 (conversion rate: 1 US dollar = 45 Indian rupees).

The number of family members per household varied from a single member to maximum of ten with the average household size being four. In addition, because most of the respondents living in this coastal region are predominantly involved in fishing activities, we classified their general occupation into two categories as either involved in fishing activities or not. Households not involved directly in fishing activities are either farmers or labourers working in the urban centre. About 61 per cent of the respondents were involved in primary fishing activities. Three social castes responded to our survey: the backward, most-backward and scheduled caste.[4] Although, broadly speaking, they are referred to as *Dalit*, scholars have noted subtle differences in terms of their social functioning and thus their economic activities (John et al., 2007). Because this is a categorical variable, the backward caste was used as the reference group in the final analysis. Of the total respondents, about 11 per cent of the households identified themselves as scheduled caste, 12 per cent as backward caste and 77 per cent as the most-backward caste.

FINDINGS

Of the 1,000 households surveyed, about 7.6 per cent of the respondents reported that at least one of their family members was either killed or missing and presumed dead. About 11.7 per cent of them reported at least one family member injured by the tsunami. Consistent with media and some NGO reports (Oxfam, 2005), based on our sample, about 62.5 per cent of the fatalities were females, while males were more likely to be among the injured (i.e. 65.6%). The percentages of fatalities and injured were also associated with social castes. For instance, the majority of the deaths and injuries were reported among the most-backward caste.

We first examined the number of days households stayed in different types of temporary shelters and the extent to which they moved from one shelter to another over a period of six months. Findings suggest that households that moved more than once generally spent a maximum of 150 days (5 months) in government shelters, before moving to the home of a relative or close friends (Table 3). Most households spent

Table 3: Descriptive statistics: Duration of stay by type of temporary shelters

Temporary shelter type	Total (households)	Median (days)	Standard deviation	Minimum	Maximum
First shelter					
Temporary Govt./NGOs shelters	131 (13.4%)	7	8.57	1	36
Permanent public buildings	346 (35.3%)	7	6.27	1	45
Religious/Comm. buildings	435 (44.3%)	10	8.26	1	60
Private homes**	69 (7%)	6	8.95	1	45
Second shelter					
Temporary Govt./NGOs shelters	47 (37.6%)	15	51.26	2	150
Permanent public buildings	30 (24.0%)	7	6.84	2	30
Religious/Comm. buildings	26 (20.8%)	8.5	8.65	2	30
Private homes	22 (17.6%)	10	35.70	2	150
Third shelter					
Temporary Govt./NGOs shelters	17 (39.5%)	120	47.75	1	150
Permanent public buildings	13 (30.2%)	7	5.83	3	20
Religious/Comm. buildings	4 (9.3%)	2	1.50	2	5
Private homes	5 (11.6%)	10	4.39	5	15
Overall*	981 (100%)	8	24.65	1	183

Notes: *excluding days after households returned to permanent homes; ** excluding households that stayed at their primary dwelling during the tsunami, the analysis only included households taking refuge.

about 8 days in their first temporary shelter. The maximum number of days in the first choice of shelter varied from 36 days to 60 days for households that took refuge in religious buildings or marriage halls. The median length of stay in religious buildings and marriage halls was 10 days and 15 days, respectively. Those who took refuge in government shelters and permanent public buildings stayed for relatively shorter periods (7 days). Households that sheltered in their own homes stayed for about 6 days before moving.

We found that about 79.6 per cent of the households sought shelter in permanent public or community and religious buildings (Table 3). Only 13.4 per cent of the households stayed in government/NGO-sponsored emergency shelters highlighting the lack of a formal mass-care sheltering plan with previously identified government-sponsored facilities immediately available to the disaster survivors. Only 7 per cent sheltered with relatives or homes of close friends suggesting the large-scale geographical impact of the tsunami that adversely affected the social support systems of evacuees.

The patterns of temporary sheltering were further analysed by examining the characteristic differences between households that were separated during the disaster and those that stayed together as a family unit. Table 4 shows that most households evacuated to one temporary shelter during the disaster. While 85.5 per cent of households stayed in their first shelter, a few households moved more than once. About 8.6 per cent of the households reported having moved twice and 5 per cent reported having moved to three or more different locations.

When we compared households that were separated and those that stayed together, during temporary sheltering, there was no evidence to suggest that there were significant variations on how many times each group moved. However, by utilizing the difference of mean test, we found that most households that were separated had a lower annual household income than households that stayed together. The difference is

Table 4: Number of times household relocated

Number of times moved (relocation)	Household unit				Number of observations	
	Separated		Stayed together			
0	–	–	19	(2.3%)	19	(1.9%)
1	127	(80.9%)	725	(86.4%)	855	(85.5%)
2	19	12.1%)	66	(7.9%)	86	(8.6%)
3	–	–	1	(0.1%)	1	(0.1%)
4	–	–	–	–	–	–
5	1	(0.64%)	3	(0.4%)	4	(0.4%)
6	6	(3.8%)	23	(2.7%)	29	(2.9%)
7	4	(2.5%)	2	(0.2%)	6	(0.6%)
Total	157	(100%)	839	(100%)	1,000	(100%)

statistically significant suggesting that the households that were separated were from the lower socio-economic groups (M_{diff} = 0.35, t = 5.50, p < 0.01). Not surprisingly, households that separated during evacuation and sheltering had suffered extensive damage to their primary dwelling unit compared to households that stayed together (M_{diff} = 0.16, t = 4.47, p < 0.01). The results suggest that survivors from the lower socio-economic groups were also ones that stayed in substandard housing in high risk areas, closer to the coastal HTL.

To examine the extent to which socioeconomic factors influenced the length of time households stayed in temporary shelters, a semi-log regression analysis was conducted (see Table 5). The total number of days that households spent in temporary shelters (log-transformed) was used as the dependent variable. The explanatory variables included social caste, household income categories, composition of household members and household livelihood, which explained about 31 per cent of the total variation in the duration of stay in temporary shelters. The diagnostic tests suggest no serious multi-collinearity and heteroscedasticity problems after log transformation, which is appropriate given the skewness of the data.

We found no evidence to support Hypothesis 1 that female-headed households' length of stay in temporary shelters was longer than male-headed households. Hypothesis 2, when operationalized by household's annual income before the tsunami, was also not supported. However, the analysis in Table 5 asserts that households from the backward caste stayed for relatively shorter time in temporary shelters compared to

Table 5: Semi-log regression analysis: Factors explaining duration of stay

Dependent variable: duration of stays (logged)	Coefficient	Standard error
Female-headed households	−0.018	0.051
Social caste (ref: backward caste)		
- Most-backward caste	0.337***	0.093
- Scheduled caste	0.543***	0.108
Household annual income (1 low, 8 high)	0.018	0.027
Household engaged in fishing	0.371***	0.074
Home damages: floor, wall and roof	0.647***	0.072
Household stayed together	0.122*	0.069
Household size (number of family members)	0.001	0.015
Constant	1.239***	0.121
No. of observations	980	
Adjusted-R^2	0.24	
F value (7,973)	38.8***	

Notes: *p < 0.10, **p < 0.05, ***p < 0.01. Mean VIF value is 1.50, suggesting no serious multicollinearity problem; the Breusch–Pagan/Cook–Weisberg test suggests no serious heteroscedasticity problem (Chi^2 = 0.08; p = 0.779).

households from the most-backward caste ($\beta = 0.337$, $p < 0.01$) and schedule caste (i.e. $\beta = 0.543$, $p < 0.01$). Our findings support the hypothesis that, because of different opportunities and historically discriminatory experiences, households from a lower social group would stay longer in temporary shelters. Even in terms of household livelihood, there were marked differences. For example, as suggested by Hypothesis 3, most households that were not involved in fishing activities only spent 5 days in temporary shelters compared to households dependent on fishing. The difference was statistically significant at a 0.01 level, i.e. between households involved in fishing activities compared to those that were not (i.e. $\beta = 0.371$, $p < 0.01$).

As predicted by Hypothesis 4, we found that households who suffered severe damage to their homes stayed longer in temporary shelters. The result highlights that the length of time displaced households stayed in temporary shelters was affected by their ability to rebuild their damaged home, which was indirectly influenced by the GoTN's coastal zoning regulations. Hypothesis 5 was also supported, i.e. households that had no missing members and were not separated during evacuation stayed longer in temporary shelters. Our analysis extends and validates Quarentelli's (1980) argument in the context of a developing country, by showing that households that stayed together tend to take refuge longer in temporary shelters.

DISCUSSIONS AND LIMITATIONS

Our analysis supports the social vulnerability perspective, which argues that households' length of stay in temporary shelters can be partly explained by existing social structures and partly by their physical environment. Our findings highlight three important contributions: First, a majority of households that were temporarily displaced stayed in a single emergency shelter. They generally preferred to converge in permanent public buildings such as schools and marriage halls and religious buildings such as temples and churches. Although there is no evidence to suggest that households had to move multiple times, the decision to stay relatively longer in these temporary shelters reflects the familiarity and strong existence of strong social bonding.

Second, temporarily displaced households generally stayed fewer days in government/NGO-sponsored shelters compared to other types of temporary shelters, which could be explained by the unsatisfactory conditions of many of these facilities, their distance from a household's damaged home or lack of transportation in accessing them. These findings are also consistent with previous studies that suggest many government and NGO-sponsored shelters are not culturally or climatically appropriate, and lack organizational capacities to handle the procurement and dispensing of relief packets making them unattractive to disaster survivors (Bolin and Stanford, 1990; Babister and Kelman, 2002; Gall, 2004).

Third, households with severely damaged homes or involved directly in fishing activities tend to stay longer in temporary shelters. As expected, the tsunami had greater impact on those involved in fishing activities simply because fishing households lived closer to the shore with their fishing boats and equipment. Their homes and families were thus exposed to higher and stronger surge levels, while agricultural households that resided inland and closer to agricultural fields were relatively safer (De Silva and Yamao, 2007).

Although our analysis provides a greater understanding of the duration of stay of displaced households and factors that might explain displaced household decisions, the study does have a few limitations. We only examined the first three shelter choices of respondents. While the distinctions between the first, second and third choice may reflect the availability and accessibility of different types of temporary shelters (especially in a developing country like India), additional studies could confirm the generalizability of our findings. Moreover, the factors explaining duration of stay were based on the social vulnerability perspective with a strong emphasis on the characteristics of households. Other factors may also explain households' decisions to stay for prolonged periods in shelters including the political climate or form of government, availability and disbursement of disaster relief aid, disaster management agencies and protocols and type of civil society.

Another limitation is that, in our final analysis we did not take into account the inability of households to plan to evacuate voluntarily, especially during sudden onset events. While households in our research site were familiar with cyclones and floods, they were unfamiliar with tsunamis (only 1.2% of the total households in our survey were aware of what a tsunami was), thus affecting their evacuation behaviour and shelter choice. While the research was framed specifically as temporary displacement caused by the tsunami, we also recognize that the immediate implementation and enforcement of the GoTN's coastal zoning regulations impacted survivors' abilities to return to their homes to start repairing or rebuilding. This is also likely to explain their need to prolong their stay in temporary shelters.

CONCLUSIONS AND RESEARCH NEEDS

Our research makes important theoretical and empirical contributions to temporary sheltering literature. It demonstrates that the number of days a household chooses to spend in a temporary shelter depends on whether the family stayed together during evacuation. Our findings also emphasize that households from a lower social class or those who have experienced severe damage to their homes tend to take refuge in temporary shelters for longer periods of time (about 6 months). Most notable finding in our expectation is that, before transitioning into permanent housing, the majority of displaced households stayed longer in permanent public buildings such as community halls, schools and religious buildings, rather than government and NGO-sponsored temporary shelters, camps, or homes of friends and relatives.

Our analysis confirms the general view that the decision to take refuge in temporary shelters varies in certain segments of the population. The findings underscore the need for community disaster response and recovery activities to focus not only on the direct structural and economic damage, but also the limited capacities and diverse sets of priorities of the survivors (Lindell et al., 2006; Green et al., 2007). In the first instance, multi-sector agencies should take charge in working towards not only providing temporary shelters as a safe physical space for a couple of days, but also the accessibility of living arrangements for a longer period of time. The need to pre-plan, identify and communicate which community halls, schools and religious buildings are suitable for conversion into temporary shelters is critically important while planning for future disasters.

Our study has several implications for future research. Because we only examined displaced households' length of stay in temporary shelters, it leaves open the questions of what factors affected a survivor's choice of one shelter over another and the long-term implications of shelter choice on recovery. Future research should also examine the decisions of displaced households from a social linkages perspective. If displaced households' familiarity with their built environment can influence their decisions to choose certain types of shelters over another, then it would be worthwhile to study how transient populations such as university students, tourists and pilgrims to an area might respond to sheltering needs. Another area of research is to examine households perceptions of shelters and their actual experiences when taking refuge in these sheltering facilities. Finally, it would be worthwhile to investigate the challenges and impediments of creating shelter hubs or pods within coastal villages and the strategies adopted by state and local governments to disseminate the information to the public.

NOTES

1 Similar patterns of sheltering behaviour have been observed in Guatemala after the 1976 earthquake (Peacock et al., 1987; Bates and Peacock, 2008).

2 In the state of Tamil Nadu, the response and restoration of infrastructure was quick and decisive (Arya et al., 2006; Srinivasan and Nagaraj, 2006). About 1,000 district staff and 380 staff members from other district were involved in the response efforts. Together with volunteers from the local communities, they were joined by 200 military officers, the Deputy Inspector General of Police, and numerous superintendents and almost 1,500 officers. Within a week, the government of Tamil Nadu (GoTN) announced initial relief package issuing numerous number of Government Orders (G.Os.) dealing with emergency relief (Prater et al., 2006). A week after the tsunami, on 6 January 2005, the GoTN authorized the District Collector to construct temporary shelters through Government Order Ms 10 (i.e. G.O. Ms 10) at a cost of Rs. 8,000 (conversion rate: 1US Dollar = 45 Indian rupees) per family for 50,000 households.

3 In the Nagapattinam District, about 193 NGOs were registered with the NGO Coordination and Resource Centre (NCRC). Due to under-reporting on most activities conducted by non-registered NGO, the full extent of NGO assistance during the recovery phase of disaster is difficult to determine.

4 The scheduled castes (SCs), also known as the Dalit, and the scheduled tribes (STs) are two groupings historically disadvantaged people that are given special recognition in the Constitution of India. The SCs STs make up around 15% and 7.5%, respectively of India's population.

REFERENCES

Arlikatti, S. and Andrew, S. A. (2012) Housing Design and the Long-Term Recovery Processes in the Aftermath of the 2004 Indian Ocean Tsunami. *Natural Hazards Review*, 13:1 pp34–44.

Arlikatti, S., Peacock, W. G., Prater, C. S., Grover, H. and Sekar, A. (2010) Assessing the Impact of the Indian Ocean Tsunami on Households: A Modified Domestic Assets Index Approach. *Disasters*, 34:3 pp705–31.

Arya, A. S., Mandal, G. S. and Muley, E. V. (2006) Some Aspects of Tsunami Impact and Recovery in India. *Disaster Prevention and Management*, 15:1 pp51–66.

Babister, E. and Kelman, I. (2002) The Emergency Shelter Process with Application to Case Studies in Macedonia and Afghanistan. *Journal of Humanitarian Assistance*. Available at http://sites.tufts.edu/jha/files/2011/04/a092.pdf (accessed 19 July 2011).

Barenstein, J. D. (2010) 'Who Governs Reconstruction? Changes and Continuity in Policies, Practices, and Outcomes' in G. Lizarralde, C. Johnson and C. Davidson (eds) *Rebuilding After Disasters: From Emergency to Sustainability* 149–76. New York, NY: Spon Press.

Bates, F. L. and Peacock, W. G. (2008) *Living Conditions, Disasters, and Development: An Approach to Cross-Cultural Comparisons*, Athens: University of Georgia Press.

Bolin, R. and Stanford, L. (1990) 'Shelter and Housing Issues in Santa Cruz County' in R. Bolin (ed) *The Loma Prieta Earthquake: Studies of Short-Term Impacts* 99–108. Program on Environment and Behavior Monograph #50. Boulder, CO: Institute of Behavioral Science, University of Colorado.

Bolin, R. C. and Stanford, L. (1998) *The Northridge Earthquake: Vulnerability and Disaster*, London: Routledge.

Bosher, L. S. (2007) A Case of Inappropriately Targeted Vulnerability Reduction Initiatives in Andhra Pradesh, India. *International Journal of Social Economics*, 34:10 pp751–71.

Chadha, R. K., Lata, G., Yeh, H., Peterson, C. and Katada, T. (2005) The Tsunami of the Great Sumatra Earthquake of M 9.0 on 26 December 2004–Impact on the East Coast of India. *Current Science*, 88:8 pp1297–307.

Cutter, S. J., Boruff, B. J. and Shirley, W. L. (2003) Social Vulnerability to Environmental Hazards. *Social Science Quarterly*, 84:1 pp242–61.

Dash, N. (2010) 'Race and Ethnicity' in B. D. Phillips, D. S. K. Thomas, A. Fothergill and L. Blinn-Pike (eds) *Social Vulnerability to Disasters* 101–22. Boca Raton, FL: CRC Press.

Dash, N., Peacock, W. G. and Morrow, B. (1997) 'And the Poor Get Poorer: A Neglected Black Community' in W. G. Peacock, B. H. Morrow and H. Gladwin (eds) *Hurricane Andrew: Ethnicity, Gender and the Sociology of Disaster* 206–25. London: Routledge.

Davis, I. (1978) *Shelter After Disaster*, Oxford: Oxford Polytechnic Press.

De Silva, D. A. M. and Yamao, M. (2007) Effects of the Tsunami on Fisheries and Coastal Livelihood: A Case Study of Tsunami-Ravaged Southern Sri Lanka. *Disasters*, 31:4 pp386–404.

Enarson, E. (2010) 'Gender' in B. D. Phillips, D. S. K. Thomas, A. Fothergill and L. Blinn-Pike (eds) *Social Vulnerability to Disasters* 123–54. Boca Raton, FL: CRC Press.

Enarson, E. and Morrow, B. H. (1998) 'Women Will Rebuild Miami: A Case Study of Feminist Response to Disaster.' in E. Enarson and B. H. Morrow (eds) *The Gendered Terrain of Disaster: Through Women's Eyes* 185–99. Westport, CT: Praeger.

Fothergill, A., Maestas, E. G. M. and Darlington, J. D. (1999) Race, Ethnicity, and Disasters in the United States: A Review of the Literature. *Disasters*, 23:3 pp156–73.

Gall, M. (2004) Where to Go? Strategic Modeling of Access to Emergency Shelters in Mozambique. *Disasters*, 28:1 pp82–97.

Green, R., Bates, L. K. and Smyth, A. (2007) Impediments to Recovery in New Orleans' Upper and Lower Ninth Ward One Year After Hurricane Katrina. *Disasters*, 31:3 pp311–35.

Holcombe, E. (2007) 'Understanding Community-Based Disaster Response: Houston's Religious Congregations and Hurricane Katrina Relief Efforts.' in D. L. Brunsma , D. Overfelt and J. Picou (eds) *The Sociology of*

Katrina: Perspectives on a Modern Catastrophe 107–23. Lanham, MD: S. Rowman & Littlefield Publishers, Inc.

Ingram, J. C., Guillermo, F., Rumbaitis-del Rio, C. and Khazai, B. (2006) Post-disaster Recovery Dilemmas: Challenges in Balancing Short-term and Long-term Needs for Vulnerability Reduction. *Environmental Science and Policy*, 9:7–8 pp607–13.

John, P. B., Russell, S. and Russell, P. S. S. (2007) The Prevalence of Posttraumatic Stress Disorder Among Children and Adolescents Affected by Tsunami Disaster in Tamil Nadu. *Disaster Management & Response*, 5:1 pp3–7.

Kates, R. W., Colten, C. E., Laska, S. and Leatherman, S. P. (2006) Reconstruction of New Orleans After Hurricane Katrina: A Research Perspective. *Proceedings of the National Academy of Sciences of the United States of America*, 103:40 pp14653–60.

Koenig, H. G. (2006) *In the Wake of Disaster: Religious Responses to Terrorism and Catastrophe*, West Conshohocken, PA: Templeton Foundation Press.

Kumaran, T. V. and Negi, E. (2006) Experiences of Rural and Urban Communities in Tamil Nadu in the Aftermath of the 2004 Tsunami. *Built Environment*, 32:4 pp375–86.

Levine, J. N., Esnard, A. M. and Sapat, A. (2007) Population Displacement and Housing Dilemmas Due To Catastrophic Disasters. *Journal of Planning Literature*, 22:1 pp3–15.

Lindell, M., Prater, C. and Perry, R. (2006) Fundamentals of Emergency Management. Available at http://training.fema.gov/EMIWeb/edu/fem.asp (accessed 19 July 2011).

Lindell, M. K. (1994) Perceived Characteristics of Environmental Hazards. *International Journal of Mass Emergencies and Disasters*, 12:3 pp303–26.

Lindell, M. K., Prater, C. S., Sanderson Jr, W. G., Lee, H. M., Yang, Z., Mohite, A. and Hwang, S. N. (2001) *Texas Gulf Coast Residents' Expectations and Intentions Regarding Hurricane Evacuation*, College Station, TX: Hazard Reduction & Recovery Center, Texas A&M University.

Lizarralde, G., Johnson, C. and Davidson, C. (2010) *Rebuilding After Disasters: From Emergency to Sustainability*, New York, NY: Spon Press.

Mileti, D., Sorensen, J. and O'Brien, P. W. (1992) Toward an Explanation of Mass Care Shelter Use. *Disasters*, 10:1 pp25–42.

Nagapattinam District Website (n.d.) *Nagapattinam District*. Available at http://www.nagapattinam.tn.nic.in/default.htm (accessed 20 December 2005).

NGO Coordination and Resource Centre, Nagapattinam (n.d.) *Snapshot of Damages Due to Tsunami: Village-wise in Nagapattinam District*. Available at http://www.ncrc.in/Publications/NCRC/SnapshotofdamagesEnglish pdf (accessed 1 August 2009).

Oliver-Smith, A. (2005) 'Communities after Catastrophe: Reconstructing the Material, Reconstituting th Social.' in S. Hyland (ed.) *Community Building in the 21st Century*. Santa Fe: School of America: Research Press.

Oxfam (2005) *The Tsunami's Impact on Women*. Available at http://www.oxfam.org.uk/what_we_do/issues conflict_disasters/downloads/bn_tsunamiwomen.pdf (accessed 1 June 2009).

Pant, A. T., Kirsch, T. D., Subbarao, I. R., Hsieh, Y. H. and Vu, A. (2008) Faith-Based Organizations ar Sustainable Sheltering Operations in Mississippi After Hurricane Katrina: Implications for Inform Network Utilization. *Prehospital and Disaster Medicine*, 23:1 pp48–54.

Peacock, W. G., Dash, N. and Zhang, Y. (2006) 'Sheltering and Housing Recovery Following Disaster.' in F Rodriquez, E. L. Quarentelli and R. R. Dynes (eds) *Handbook of Disaster Research* 258–74. New Yor NY: Springer US.

Peacock, W. G., Killian, C. D. and Bates, F. L. (1987) The Effects of Disaster Damage and Housing Aid Household Recovery Following the 1976 Guatemalan Earthquake. *The International Journal of M Emergencies and Disasters*, 5:1 pp63–88.

Peacock, W. G., Morrow, H. B. and Gladwin, H. (1997) *Hurricane Andrew: Ethnicity, Gender, and the Sociology of Disaster*, London: Routledge.

Phillips, B. D. (1993) Culture Diversity in Disasters: Sheltering, Housing and Long-Term Recovery. *International Journal of Mass Emergencies and Disasters*, 11:1 pp99–110.

Phillips, B. D., Thomas, D. S. K., Fothergill, A. and Blinn-Pike, L. eds. (2010) *Social Vulnerability to Disasters*, Boca Raton, FL: CRC Press.

Prater, C. S., Peacock, W. G., Arlikatti, S. and Grover, H. (2006) Social Capacity in Nagapattinam, Tamil Nadu after the December 2004 Great Sumatra Earthquake and Tsunami. *Earthquake Spectra*, 22(Special Issue III) ppS715–S730.

Quarentelli, E. L. (1980) Evacuation Behavior and Problems: Findings and Implications from the Research Literature. Report No. 27. Columbus, OH: The Ohio State University, Disaster Research Center.

Quarentelli, E. L. (1982) *Sheltering and Housing After Major Community Disasters: Case Studies and General Observations*, Washington, DC: Final Report for the Federal Emergency Management Agency.

Quarentelli, E. L. (1995) Patterns of Sheltering and Housing in US Disasters. *Disaster Prevention and Management*, 4:3 pp43–53.

Radhakrishnan, J. (2005) 'Tsunami Relief in the State of Tamil Nadu, India: The Nagapattinam Experience,' Presentation to the Indian Ocean Tsunami Conference, Colombo, Sri Lanka, March.

Richter, R. and Flowers, T. (2010) Gender Aware Disaster Care: Issues and Interventions in Supplies, Services, Triage and Treatment. *International Journal of Mass Emergencies and Disasters*, 28:2 pp207–25.

Ritchie, L. and Tierney, K. (2011) Temporary Housing Planning and Early Implementation in the 12 January 2010 Haiti Earthquake, *Earthquake Spectra*, 27:S1 ppS487–S507.

Shaw, R. (2006) Indian Ocean Tsunami and Aftermath: Need for Environment-Disaster Synergy in the Reconstruction Process. *International Journal Disaster Prevention and Management*, 15:1 pp5–20.

Srinivasan, K. and Nagaraj, V. K. (2006) The State and Civil Society in Disaster Response: Post-Tsunami Experiences in Tamil Nadu. In N. T. Tan, A. Rowlands and F. K. O. Yuen (eds) *Asian Tsunami and Social Work Practice: Recovery and Rebuilding. Journal of Social Work in Disability & Rehabilitation*, 5:3/4 pp57–80.

Suar, D. and Kunthia, R. (2004) Caste, Education, Family and Stress Disorders in Orissa Supercyclone. *Psychology and Developing Societies*, 16:1 pp77–91.

Tierney, K. J., Lindell, M. K. and Perry, R. W. (2001) *Facing the Unexpected: Disaster Preparedness and Response in the United States*, Washington, DC: Joseph Henry Press.

Wisner, B., Blaikie, P., Cannon, T. and Davis, I. (2004) *At Risk: Natural Hazards, People's Vulnerability and Disasters* (2nd edn), London: Routledge.

Yelvington, K. (1997) 'Coping in a Temporary Way: The Tent Cities.' in W. Peacock, B. Morrow and H. Gladwin (eds) *Hurricane Andrew: Ethnicity, Gender, and the Sociology of Disaster* 92–115. New York, NY: Routledge.

Abstract

A heatwave in 2003 caused 15,000 deaths in France. This article examines the impact of the public health crisis on French public management, considering how government actors across various state institutions, including central and decentralized tiers of public administration, have been engaged in reform. It studies how these actors in the post-crisis reform process established responsibility and drew lessons. The paper shows that solidarity was used discursively in a game of political blameshifting and experimentation. It also points to the politics behind the framing of crisis enquiries.

SOLIDARITY AS POLITICAL STRATEGY

Post-crisis reform following the French heatwave

Paul Stephenson

Paul Stephenson
Department of Political Science
Faculty of Arts and Social Sciences
Maastricht University
P.O. Box 616 Maastricht 6200
The Netherlands

INTRODUCTION

A decade ago, in the summer of 2003, a heatwave struck. In France, 22,000 deaths are normally registered every month. Throughout August, two-thirds of weather stations across France reported temperatures in excess of 35°C (15 per cent registered 40°). There were 15,000 additional deaths in a 2-week period – an increase of 70 per cent on normal annual figures. As much as 82 per cent of the excess deaths were people over 75 years old (Grynszpan, 2003: 1169). While the excess mortality rate was just 4 per cent in the northern city of Lille, it increased by 142 per cent in Paris (Vandentorren et al., 2004: 1518). Three thousand of the 7,000 district councils (communes) declared a state of emergency.

Most crises are followed by promises of political reform. But not every crisis actually leads to an overhaul of existing practices (Boin et al., 2008). Political elites may talk about the need for a change, and they also have a tendency to forget their promises when the immediacy of the crisis dissipates and other issues rise up the political agenda.

The fate of announced reforms depends to a considerable extent on so-called issue-framing contests. Politicians, policymakers, stakeholders, victims and media describe the crisis from different angles in a competition to define the situation (Boin et al., 2005; Masters and 't Hart, 2012). This article seeks to understand the politics of reform following the French heatwave. It sets out to examine how central state actors framed the crisis to implement institutional, administrative and financial changes. The article is based on qualitative research and relies on primary data drawn from parliamentary enquiries, legislation, official government records, press releases, international newspaper coverage and political speeches by key political figures.[1]

The article argues that political actors at the central state level used the reform process to distinguish between their own strategic decision-making powers and the operational obligations of lower-level administrative units, thereby insulating themselves from (future) blame. After an introduction on key concepts and theoretical insights, the 2003 heatwave is contextualized with regards to what happened during the crisis. Thereafter, the post-crisis period is analysed for examining responsibility, lesson-drawing and experimentation afterwards. The conclusion discusses what we can learn from the French case and what it tells us about the behaviour of public managers in implementing post-crisis reform.

Dealing with the aftermath of a heatwave

The institutional dynamics of the post-crisis period – which can play out over several years – can seal the fate of political actors and institutions (Fischer, 2012). The processes of establishing responsibility and accountability ('looking back and judging the performance of people') and drawing lessons from the event ('looking forward and improving the performance of structures and arrangements') both present ample room for political manoeuvre to secure support for an official account of events or an endorsement of a preferred solution (Boin et al., 2010: 707).

Post-crisis reform is about political and social *catharsis*: for elites, it is about restoring confidence in leadership; for institutions, about re-establishing trust and confidence in effectiveness; for society, about getting over the shock or disbelief of what occurred. There is usually much questioning, scrutiny and self-examination, with actors using discourses to distance themselves from the crisis. Academics and think tanks may ruminate, recommending 'intelligent solutions', while politicians may try to sell personal visions or make symbolic gestures.

After a crisis has died down, at least operationally, political leaders have to manage its 'fallout', which implies rebuilding damaged reputations and restoring trust and public confidence. Political leaders tend to deflect responsibility, engaging in drawn-out blame games. They can point out that it is difficult to pin the blame on any single actor. Political leaders may exert 'discursive power' by linking the crisis to values that were absent or missing. They may employ 'restorative rhetoric' that draws on societal values in an attempt to convey to pre-empt a public apology.

Political elites use discourse to legitimate the need for action, apportion responsibility and demand collective action (Edelman, 1967, 1985). However, with emotions aroused, struggle and resistance may ensue by those ambivalent or by those who remain unconvinced by claims as to where responsibility lies and where (from whom compensation should be sought (Brändström and Kuipers, 2003).

When it comes to *drawing lessons* from crisis, organizations are not particularly gifted students (Stern, 1997). One can distinguish between 'fine tuning' (incremental adaptation of policies and practices without affecting core political values), 'policy reform' (important policy principles and institutional values normally hard to change are fundamentally adapted) and 'paradigm shifts' (when basic underlying aspects of political system are drastically altered or destroyed) (Boin et al., 2008: 16–17).

In practice, deeply embedded institutional cultures and practices often inhibit the capacity to absorb new ways of doing. In fact, political learning may not be about 'getting to the heart of the matter' in terms of what went wrong (Boin et al., 2008 14), but instead making sure that such a crisis – for elites and executive institutions does not happen again. Reform may thus be more about media rhetoric than purposive action; a commitment to drastic measures is often followed by little action of an substance.

FRENCH PUBLIC MANAGEMENT AND THE HEATWAVE CRISIS

The response of the French government to the heatwave can be characterized in terms of 'Deny, Deflect, Defend' (Klinenberg, 2002; Lagadec, 2004: 160) – it was very much a 'mismanaged crisis' (Boin et al., 2008: 290). With directors on holiday and reduced staff numbers, there was no manpower to respond effectively. Hea organizations were unable to detect the relevant signs or disseminate knowledge effectively. Lagadec (2004: 162) paints a general picture of unread dossiers building up, statistics slow to be collated and data and signals 'lost in corridors'. He argues that it was not in the nature of French state officials to seek extra information, organize meetings or take decisions, because a complex administrative culture favoured passivity. Moreover, complex structures meant a laborious mobilization of staff, with divisions, partitions and demarcations ('wait-and-see policies'), vertical isolations (each layer protects itself), communications errors and an immediate search for scapegoats (Lagadec, 2004: 164). Even well-adapted services proved inept: 'our exclusive and curative medical culture prohibited effective preventive action' (Thirion *et al.*, 2005: 154).

Sense making proved a slow and iterative process, with the full extent of the event as 'catastrophe' emerging only through the successive build-up of images, during a 'critical period' of several days. Only when temperatures lowered in late August did the full picture begin to emerge. The French government was heavily criticized for its media handling. Its news management strategy was inept, not in any way tailored to the 'demands of a 24-hour rolling news media culture […] it got it signals woefully wrong' (Kuhn, 2005: 256). Media coverage was persistent and 'therapeutic', meaning any public action was based on a response to recorded deaths, rather than targeted broadcasts promoting preventative action. TV debates revolved around the great burden on hospitals and the failure of geriatric wards to cope.

Efforts to frame the crisis began immediately, however. The French president, Jacques Chirac, finally spoke on 21 August 2003 as the heat died down. He called for sympathy from the Republic's citizens, his rhetoric imbued with pleas for solidarity and calls for the nation to 'collaborate'. Expressing compassion towards the victims, he underlined fraternity, respect and neighbourliness, calling for action by public institutions at the local level rather than the central state. He pushed for a 6-week review, promising that the French government would make vital proposals to 'make solidarity stronger, more active and effective'. Likewise, the French prime minister, Jean-Pierre Raffarin, made the immediate claim that the underlying cause was 'a weak social fabric', which could be strengthened through an 'increase in solidarity'; implicit in this framing of the event was that society at large should be held to account for the fiasco. He called upon society to 'repair itself', to take responsibility for its own weakness by becoming directly involved in administering a solution. Employing words like 'together', 'we fight', 'our country' and 'solidarity', he sought to share the government's burden with the population. He organized a conference to bring together around thirty key stakeholders from public bodies in the field of medicine, health care and gerontology in an attempt to calm the media and to draw up an 'Old Age and Solidarity Plan'.

Establishing responsibility

The Lower House's (National Assembly) Committee for Cultural, Family and Social Affairs launched an information-gathering exercise on 26 August 2003 without waiting for parliament to reconvene on 1 October. The Committee invited the minister for health, family and handicapped persons, Jean-Françis Mattei and, on 11 and 19 September, conducted thirty-three hearings involving ninety one people from social services, emergency services, the medical profession and paramedics. The minutes of the meeting reveal that the committee found the issue 'too serious and too complex to claim to have identified any definite causes of the crisis' (Assemblée Nationale, 2003a). The Committee wondered if the 'catastrophe could have been foreseen', questioning the quality and effectiveness of the surveillance system for public health and recognizing the massive challenge for hospitals and social care in terms of their ability to cope. It plainly stated that the heatwave had been just as much a social crisis as a public health one (*'La canicule a révélé une crise au moins autant sociale que sanitaire'*). Here we can see the roots of the issue being framed in terms of a breakdown of the social fabric.

Analysing the parliamentary committee process reveals how post-crisis reform was constructed. It was not the case that a committee enquiry was simply set up, rather different 'fields of investigation' were put forward for consideration (Assemblée Nationale, 2003a). The politics behind proposals to set up a committee enquiry, its name and formal tasks ultimately influenced the approach to the crisis. The information report 'on the public health and social crisis resulting from the heatwave' (59 pages), carried out by the committee and submitted to parliament on 24 September 2003, grew out of the information gathering exercise led by an MP (Denis Jacquat) to first determine what the scope and focus of the committee enquiry should actually be. The committee in fact evaluated four different proposals for an enquiry.

The first proposal (n. 1056, 20 August 2003) was made by the current French prime minister (since May 2012), socialist Jean-Marc Ayrault (*PS*), who referred to 'the breakdown of the health system in coping with the heatwave' and called for 'an analysis of the chain of command that led to the failure of the public managers to react'. His proposal [for an enquiry focused on the public health dimension while also addressing problems of geriatric care in hospitals and care homes. The parliamentary committee found the proposal 'too restrictive' The second and third proposals focusing on 'the public health, economic, social and environmental of the heatwave and on the State's management and its effects' (n.1057, 20 August 2003, Alain Bocquet) and on the 'human, political, economic and environmental consequences' (n. 1062, 11 September 2003) were deemed to be 'too broad'. It was the fourth proposal by conservative, Jacques Barrot (UMP) (n. 1059, 9 September 2003), 'on the public health and social consequences of the heatwave' – which is relatively generic and appears to infer no causal linkages *a priori* between the crisis and public mismanagement – that the parliamentary committee felt 'fully corresponded to the questions raised by this essential human drama' (Assemblée Nationale, 2003b).

In short, political actors manoeuvred to submit proposals to the committee, following party political consultation. The significance of the parliamentary committee's rejection of the first proposal, which explicitly referred to a chain of responsibility (*'la chaîne de responsabilité à l'origine du manque de réactivité des pouvoirs publics'*), which would have placed political post holders under the spotlight, clearly shows how the initial framing of an enquiry, in terms of name and tasks, had consequences for the process of identifying causes and establishing responsibility. Intriguingly, a parliamentary majority did not prove significant in determining which proposal is supported – the proposal from a right-wing MP being accepted in a right-wing majority-held chamber. Moreover, the case shows how the focus and direction of reform was determined by the committee first appropriating the issue as being part of their parliamentary remit; arguably, the former Committee for Economic Affairs, Environment and Territory could have had grounds to hold a similar emergency meeting and take the lead in the reform process.

The resolution creating an enquiry committee on the public health and social consequences of the heatwave was adopted on 7 October 2003, with the first weekly meeting on 21 October. The enquiry underlined the need for transparency, yet reserved the right to exclude the press. Adopted 5 months later on 25 February 2004, the d'Aubert report (235-pages, plus 577 pages of hearings) reveals the complexity of the issue and the difficulty of establishing any singular responsibility given the many stakeholders involved (Assemblée Nationale, 2004). Nonetheless, the second part of the report (pages 59–101) does place blame with French public services, finding that the Institute for Public Health Surveillance (IdVS) 'hadn't played its role at all', that the French Agency for Environment Health Safety was 'absent', while the decentralized Department Management of Health and Social Affairs (DDASS) had not passed on sufficient information. The emergency services (fire and ambulance) had not been kept informed of the scale of situation. Moreover, hospital emergency departments raised the alarm, but their messages went unheard by the Ministry of Health. Blame was also apportioned on the central state: the Department of Health was criticized for being 'hermetically sealed off'; the inter-ministerial crisis management centre (COGIC) and certain prefectures had 'under-estimated the acuteness of the situation'; the Department of Social Affairs, Work and Solidarity was considered too distant from health and social services on the ground, with only twelve people at ministerial level working on services for the elderly.

The third part of the report (pages 81–171) identified structural problems in the French health care system, identifying under-capacity and organizational ambiguity in public sector agencies and hospitals. The fourth part (pages 172–212) looked ahead to find ways to improve surveillance and warning systems, better coordinate public administrations and open up the debate on an ageing population. The fifty-two proposals, subsequently voted on by the Parliament, can be seen as the basis for political action.

Drawing lessons

Political learning implies that elites and public institutions recognize that fundamental problems may be structural, even culturally specific both to public organizations and the state's own machinery. However, politicians and public administrations are often thought to be less willing to confront endemic structural causes and more concerned by short-term threats, such as preventing a repeat of events, given the risk to their political career and length of term in office.

In the post-crisis period, French central state actors faced with accusations of blame focused their attention on decentralized state actors. Recognizing considerable ambiguity in the demarcation of responsibility between multilevels of public administration, government sought to secure an explicit legal transfer of responsibility to *other* lower-level strategic administrative actors and to operational actors. It employed a discursive plea of solidarity to accomplish its aims.

The most immediate result was the passing of a new law on solidarity toward the elderly and disabled (*Projet de loi relatif à la solidarité pour l'autonomie des personnes âgées et des personnes handicapées*, n° 1350) in January 2004 to ensure better warning systems were in place and give more power to social services. In May 2004, the new post of 'Minister for Solidarity, Health and Family' was established. Minister Philippe Douste-Blazy presented a 'Heatwave Plan' to a network of healthcare professionals (*Circulaire 219*), defining actions to be put into place at the local level (Premier ministre, 2005). The minister stated that 'we have been able to draw lessons from the crisis' and that 'the services of the central state administration are now better organized to act quickly and effectively to alarms'. Strategic actors at the central state level would give the green light to decentralized strategic actors, who would then – in a kind of relay – engage local, operational actors. The minister made explicit mention of solidarity:

> The service of the state's central administration are henceforth organized to react to alerts effectively and without delay; medical services and police forces have been strengthened and coordinated; the value of grass roots solidarity has been recognized and organized. (Douste-Blazy, 24 June 2004)

The minister argued that the new constellation offered strategic decision making, speed and effectiveness, since it could be tailored to meteorological, geographic and human conditions in the form of a Departmental Heatwave Management Plan. He even boasted to having tested it personally to check that the national meteorological service (*Météo France*) and the National Health Surveillance Survey were responsive. As the minister stated to departmental prefects, operational management was now legally enshrined as the responsibility of the departments:

> It's up to you to put the mechanisms of the plan into effect, quickly and efficiently, without error mechanisms that characterize the body which you belong to, and of which we are all proud. It's up t

you to interpret them and adapt them to local realities, specific climates, geographies, and human settlement of each department. It's up to you, in a word, to make of this national instrument, theoretically well-oiled and articulated, a real rampart against the pain and death that ravaged the weaker among us last summer. (Douste-Blazy, 24 June 2004)

The plan rested on threeaxes: 'prevention, responsibility and solidarity'. First, four levels of alert were established to enhance prevention. Summer monitoring was initiated (*La Vigilance*, level 1). If a problem arises, the ministry of health will be notified and a crisis cell is brought together (*L'Alerte*, level 2). If public health is threatened, the minister launches four 'coloured' responses – blue for retirement homes, white for hospitals and emergency services, red for police and fire services, and silver/gold for voluntary organizations (*L'Intervention*, level 3). If the heatwave looks as if it might incite public disorder, the minister of health informs the defence minister, minister of the interior and prime minister (*La Réquisition*, level 4). District councils (*communes*) and their town halls (*mairies*) conduct censuses of the local population, allowing the local administration to visit, and even detain, those felt to be at most risk.

Second, responsibilities for future crises were defined. The National Health Surveillance Survey would collect data, drawing on information from the national weather station *Météo France* and the emergency services. Its director was charged with communicating information to the minister and making recommendations regarding the level of alert. Responsibility for decision making remained at the ministerial level where the crisis team would meet – then, and only then, could action be taken at lower levels. After official authorization from Paris, the departmental prefect (*préfet*) would be charged with coordinating the response at the departmental level.

A summer emergency commission was set up in 2004 to ensure hospitals received sufficient additional financial provisions to cope with the demands of the summer period (extra patient beds, additional temporary staff). Minister Douste-Blazy proposed to the trade unions to increase the ceiling on overtime for nurses and hospital staff most affected (in need) during a public health crisis. Directors of retirement homes could call in temporary workers to avoid affecting the legal holiday rights of their staff, and public residential homes were officially permitted by the state to take on two extra people per 100 beds as a preventative measure. The minister recognized the 'collective conscience' of well-informed and responsible citizens, while reiterating that the plan would be implemented at ground level since the French departments were deemed to be the most suitably designed politico-administrative entities. The hierarchy and personal accountability (for achievement) are evident:

And on the ground, to put the plan into action, you alone will take charge, as the President of the Republic, Jacques Chirac, reminded you [...] Our organization has sometimes suffered certain confusion in terms of responsibilities. In this respect I had the honour of bringing about a fundamental innovation. Steering the plan at national level is up to the government. And nobody else. Putting it into place is up to the departments, which is you. And nobody else. This concentration of responsibility, if you accept it, is vital so that no French department is ever in a position to fall through the safety net – hence the real originality of my plan [...] You are undoubtedly the best equipped within the Republic to take up the challenge of this key task. (Douste-Blazy, 24 June 2004)

Raffarin's successor, prime minister Dominique De Villepin (May 2005 to May 2007), saw through the implementation of his 'Old Age and Solidarity Plan', which promised to provide nursing care, home visits, day care, night nurses and monitoring; assist carers to take breaks and help families; increase the number of trained professionals with a target ratio of one professional per resident; improve quality of life; place greater research focus on prevention; provide free consultations by a prevention expert for all persons over 70 years old; and new research into diseases afflicting the elderly such as Alzheimer's and Parkinson's. Estimated to cost 2.3 billion euros, the plan promised lower charges, better infrastructure for geriatric care and stronger links between home and residential care establishments. It guaranteed financial independence for the elderly, a degree of purchasing power that would allow choice in the services required and a 40 per cent increase over 5 years in the number of home-visit carers.

All this was greeted with scepticism by public bodies representing the elderly, including the National Federation of Associations and Directors of Elderly Care Institutions (FNADEPA) and the National Union of Private Retirement Home (SYNERPA). Traditional professional organizations such as federations of welfare organizations used the formal space of post-crisis reform as a window of opportunity to advance their own interests, highlighting the link between the severity of the disaster and their lack of funds.

With a subsequent budget of 40 million euros, the government promised to pay up to 40 per cent of the cost of equipping all retirement homes with 'cool rooms' (*espace de fraîcheur*), where the temperature will not exceed 25°C. Hospitals were to be modernized to the sum of 20 million euros. For the emergency and hospital services 489 million euro was released (*débloqué*) within the Emergency Plan (*Plan Urgences*) for the 5-year period 2004–2008. In addition, 10,000 new jobs would be 'created', as well as 15,000 extra or redeployed beds for patients originally admitted to hospital Accident and Emergency wards (*Urgences*).

Responsibilities for the public provision of emergency and medical services were then conferred to lower-level state actors by increasing financial provisions and reinforcing legal mechanisms to improve their effectiveness. The heatwave plan is updated annually and made available by the ministry of health (Ministère de la Santé, 2012).

Experimenting

Reform was packaged in terms of solidarity, building on the Raffarin's initial rhetoric a 'broken social fabric.' His proposal to abolish a May public holiday to finan retirement homes and care for the handicapped should be understood in the context of a decade of attempted pension reform (Schludi, 2003). The idea was that employees would work an extra day but without loss to their earnings, while employers would contribute employee costs to a special fund. Workers would be encouraged to use up a personal holiday or compensation days accumulated, known as '*réduction de temps de travail*' (RTTs), a mechanism for employees working over 35 hours a week to receive extra days off work. The most active would thus help the most vulnerable – a social contract of one's day's duration, supposedly a painless way to raise the required funds. The state effectively placed a moral dilemma upon the workforce, testing its solidarity (*fraternité*) toward the elderly generation. Following the law of 30 June 2004 (article L.212-16 of the labour law), a national day of solidarity toward the elderly aimed at raising 2 billion euros (8,00,000 euros for the handicapped and 1.2 billion euros for the elderly).

The first experiment with the Pentecost holiday on 16 May 2005 was highly confusing. With 1 and 8 May falling on Sundays, abolishing the bank holiday left none in May. Despite a huge communication campaign costing 3 million euros, there were abstentions in schools and public transport. The unions called the day a 'fiasco' and a 'provocation', with demonstrators nationwide asserting that working for free as a gesture of solidarity was a contradiction in terms ('*le travail gratuit c'est l'anti-solidarité*') (Le Monde, 2005a). A fifth of teachers and a half of postal workers went on strike. Traffic was paralyzed in many towns, with delays at Paris airports. An answering machine at the European aircraft manufacturer Airbus said the office was closed because 'Monday is a holiday in France' (Associated Press, 16 May 2005). The press satirized the chaos in cartoons, such as in *Le Parisien*, in which Chirac asks Raffarin: who will actually be at work in France today? Raffarin answers: 'Well, so far, four Polish plumbers and three Romanian plasterers' (BBC, 16 May 2005). The French railways (SNCF) was asked to operate a normal weekday service but requested that employees work an extra 1 minute 52 seconds a day over the whole year to contribute – staff refused (International Herald Tribune, 30 April 2005). On 21 May 2005, the petrol company Total reinstated a day's salary to those who had worked or taken an RTT, as did Sanofi-Aventis and Shell.

The government insisted that 'the spirit of responsibility had won the day' (Libération, 17 May 2005; Le Monde, 2005b), though prime minister Raffarin admitted that the organization of the event would need some adjusting (*aménagement*) in the years to come. Nonetheless, the 'solidarity day' was criticized as a knee-jerk initiative launched before the real causes of the crisis had been identified. It was inconsistent: first, although it sought to raise 2 billion euros, Chirac had meanwhile reduced personal income tax by 3 billion euros; second, while the state was cancelling a public holiday, it was at the same time trying (in vain) to establish a new Muslim festival; third, it allowed those who disagreed on political grounds not to take part (or pay their tax); and fourth, it discriminated against those who were unable to work and who, on such terms, could not show solidarity (Argoud, 2006). The government was criticized for its obsession with obsolete Marxist principles, namely the labour theory of value, whereas in modern post-industrial France, output in many professions, particularly for civil servants and office workers, was no longer felt to be directly related to the amount of time worked (Larané, 2005) – what would an extra day's work, for the sake of it, really achieve? Raffarin resigned 2 weeks later on 31 May 2005, though reportedly as a result of France's rejection of the referendum on the EU draft constitution.

After 3 years of 'solidarity days', a 2007 report by the ministry for work, social relations and solidarity deemed the measure 'a real success'. It proposed three scenarios: sticking with the obligatory day of work but shifting it to a new date; reinstating the public holiday and leaving it open to firms to decide upon their day or keeping it but improving child care on the day (Libération, 18 December 2007). A month before municipal elections on 4 February 2008, the holiday was effectively reinstated but as a solidarity day à la carte, be it an RTT, two half RTTs or 7 hours during the year. In 2011, former prime minister Raffarin sought to resurrect his political hobby horse (Le Figaro, 16 June 2011). The Constitutional Court even formally investigated whether it contravened the other Republican value of equality (égalité) by discriminating against those who cannot work, but in July 2011, it upheld the legal basis (Journal Officiel, 2011).

CONCLUSION: RHETORIC AS A POLITICAL TOOL

Over 5 years, the reactions of political elites can be characterized as *deflecting* responsibility, *insulating* themselves from future responsibility, and *diluting* lingering notions of responsibility, beyond politics to the social partners (cancelling a public holiday to raise funds) and the wider population. Crisis preparedness was undoubtedly improved and public awareness raised.

The French heatwave crisis illustrates how political leaders can use the post-crisis political space to revise legislation. Reform consisted of a new financial commitment to under-sourced public managers, and also of taking steps to improve coordination between public administration and public agencies. The process serves to reinforce hierarchies, strengthen command chains, reiterate sequences for action, and clarify the distinction between the roles of strategic (decision-makers) and operational (implementers) actors. Emotive, often emphatic, political discourse was used to convince of the functional logic of appropriateness of decentralized actors operationalizing decision from Paris.

Political leaders were engaged in a discursive strategy whereby 'solidarity' was political tool used in the 'evolving game of crisis exploitation' (Boin et al., 2008: 28) based on emotive, identity-based appeals lying at the cultural heart of the politic system. State actors sought to regain control by perpetuating the frame initiated during the crisis, implying that a fundamental societal value was missing or broken. The sta sought to orchestrate an 'apology' that would share the moral burden of the crisis among the social partners (employer organizations and employees) and test their political obligation. Solidarity was thus 'reduced' to promoting state-driven collective action through tax collection.

Discourse changed over time: with an initial focus on repairing the social fabric and questioning basic societal attitudes toward the elderly, reform was about 'rescuing' solidarity. But it soon came to be about caring for 'dependant people', articulated through proposals aimed at reinforcing welfare provisions by financing hospitals and care institutions, that is 'reforming' solidarity by reinforcing the sanitary over the social (Argoud, 2006). In short, solidarity *evolved* to highlight the difficulties faced by public managers in the field of gerontology, rather than those commonly experienced by the elderly. Reform was translated into 'operational administrative language' with the 'politico-administrative treatment of a social problem' (Argoud, 2006).

Lessons for public managers

One implication of this paper is that, post-crisis, public managers can find themselves obligated by commitments made emotively during the crisis. Politicians do not wait for official scientific reports but make their own diagnosis based on a hunch or political whim. Blame is often wielded in a knee-jerk reaction based on no evidence and before any enquiry. The pressure of media scrutiny has political leaders deflecting blame away from the state and its handling of the crisis.

The fact that such acute public health crises can occur in developed countries with well-financed healthcare systems is difficult to accept. With competing narratives of responsibility circulating in the media, and practitioners and the public wondering what went wrong, public managers may be tempted courses of action that have the potential to restore trust and 'bury' blame.

The whole process of post-crisis reform is determined very early on as political actors determine *the shape of enquiry*. Any conclusions into crisis responsibility cannot be separated from the initial naming of these temporary structures, and therein their scope of investigation, that is, the framing game begins by determining what the issue is, how a committed should focus, and therein, who should be investigated. It even suggests opportunities very early on for parliaments to politically 'exploit' the enquiry into crisis.

One must act quickly to fulfil any such political commitments in the immediate aftermath of the crisis. The timing of crisis greatly influences the ability of the public managers to react. Heatwaves often occur during parliamentary recess and require the creation of emergency commissions to engage in immediate data gathering and investigation. These bodies can determine the focus of investigation.

This case shows how time lags bring complications and dissensus among the social partners. Large-scale fund-raising exercises may meet with opposition, distrust and rebellion. Post-crisis reform must be compatible with the politico-administrative culture of state institutions – it must be *doable* – but also consistent with the discourse of the earlier crisis period and accepted by the larger population. If experimentation is felt to be coercive, contradictory or to exclude certain groups, then it is likely to fail.

ACKNOWLEDGEMENT

The author is grateful to three anonymous peer reviewers as well as the special issue editors for their patience and encouragement to pursue my research further into the parliamentary debate.

NOTE

1 It also draws on in-depth studies of heatwaves in France and the US. All translations are the author's own.

REFERENCES

Argoud, D. (2006) 21 août 2003–14 janvier 2004: de la canicule au projet de loi – histoire d'une réforme express, 26 November 2006. Available at http://www.cleirppa.asso.fr/SPIP-v1-8/imprimer.php3?id_article=140 (accessed 30 July 2010).

Assemblée Nationale. (2003a) Rapport d'Information sur la crise sanitaire et sociale déclenché par la canicule, M. Denis Jacquat (rapporteur), 24 September 2003. N.1091.

Assemblée Nationale. (2003b) Rapport sur les propositions de résolution tendant à la création d'une commission d'enquête, M. Denis Jacquat (rapporteur), 24 September 2003. N.1090.

Assemblée Nationale. (2004) Rapport sur les conséquences crise sanitaire et sociale de la canicule, M. François d'Aubert (rapporteur), 24 February 2004. N.1455.

Associated Press. (2005) France Protests End of National Holiday. By Jocelyn Gecker. Available at http://www.usatoday.com/news/world/2005-05-16-france-holiday_x.htm (accessed 16 May 2005).

BBC. (2005) French Unions Strike over Holiday. Available at http://news.bbc.co.uk/1/hi/world/europe/4550353.stm (accessed 16 May 2005).

Boin, A. McConnell, A. and 't Hart, P. eds. (2008) *Governing After Crisis – The Politics of Investigation, Accountability and Learning*, Cambridge: Cambridge University Press.

Boin, A., 't Hart, P., McConnell, A. and Preston, T. (2010) Leadership Style, Crisis Response and Blame Management: The Case of Hurricane Katrina. *Public Administration*, 88:3 pp706–23.

Boin, A., 't Hart, P., Stern, E. and Sundelius, B. (2005) *The Politics of Crisis Management – Public Leadership Under Pressure*, Cambridge: Cambridge University Press.

Brändström, A. and Kuipers, S. (2003) From Normal Incidents to Political Crises: Understanding the Selective Politicization of Policy Failures. *Government and Opposition*, 38:2 pp279–305.

Douste-Blazy, P. (2004) Présentation du Plan Canicule devant les préfets. Speech of the Cabinet of the minister of health and social protection. Paris, 24 June 2004. Available at http://lesdiscours.vie-publique.fr/pdf/043001968.pdf (accessed 15 September 2010).

Edelman, M. (1967, 1985) *The Symbolic Uses of Politics*, Urbana and Chicago: University of Illinois Press.

Fischer, J. (2012) '… I Take Political Responsibility!': The Theoretical and Empirical Relation Between Ministerial Responsibility and Ministerial Resignations in Germany. *Public Administration*, 90:3 pp600–21

Grynszpan, D. (2003) Lessons from the French Heatwave – Commentary. *The Lancet*, 362:11 pp1169–70.

International Herald Tribune. (2005) Workers Counting the Minutes. By Thomas Fuller. Available at http://www.highbeam.com/doc/1P1-108267221.html (accessed 30 April 2005).

Journal Officiel. (2011) Decision 2011-148/154 QPC of 22 July 2011. Available at http://www.conseil-constitutionnel.fr/conseil-constitutionnel/francais/les-decisions/acces-par-date/decisions-depuis-1959/2011/2011-148/154-qpc/decision-n-2011-148-154-qpc-du-22-juillet-2011.98975.html (accessed 10 October 2011).

Klinenberg, E. (2002) *Heatwave, A Social Autopsy of Disaster in Chicago*, Chicago and London: The University of Chicago Press.

Kuhn, R. (2005) The Raffarin Premiership: A Case of Failed Political Leadership. *South European Society and Politics*, 10:2 pp245–61.

Lagadec, P. (2004) Understanding the French 2003 Heatwave Experience: Beyond the Heat, a Multi-Layered Challenge. *Journal of Contingencies and Crisis Management*, 12:4 pp160–9.

Larané, A. (2005) Août 2003: Une canicule 'historique', Sacrée solidarité. Available at http://www.herodote.net/articles/article.php?ID=27 (accessed 2 February 2010).

Le Figaro. (2011) Raffarin pour une seconde journée de solidarité, 16 June 2011. Available at http://www.lefigaro.fr/vie-entreprise/2011/06/11/09008-20110611ARTFIG00411-raffarin-pour-une-seconde-jour-nee-de-solidarite.php (accessed 27 July 2011).

Le Monde. (2005a) Succès mitigé pour le premier lundi de Pentecôte travaillé, 17 May 2005. Available at: http://www.lemonde.fr/societe/article/2005/05/17/succes-mitige-pour-le-premier-lundi-de-pente-cote-travaille_650554_3224.html (accessed 5 June 2010).

Le Monde. (2005b) Le gouvernement se satisfait du bilan du premier lundi de Pentecôte travaillé, 18 May 2005. Available at: www.lemonde.fr (accessed 6 June 2010).

Libération. (2005) Raffarin satisfait de la non-paralysie générale. Available at http://www.liberation.fr/evenement/0101529304-raffarin-satisfait-de-la-non-paralysie-generale (accessed 10 June 2010).

Libération. (2007) Lundi de Pentecôte: trois scénarios pour sortir du «désordre», 10 December 2007. Available at http://www.liberation.fr/politiques/010116485-lundi-de-pentecote-trois-scenarios-pour-sortir-du-desordre (accessed 10 June 2010).

Masters, A. and 't Hart, P. (2012) Prime Ministerial Rhetoric and Recession Politics: Meaning Making in Economic Crisis Management. *Public Administration*, 90:3 pp759–80.

Ministère de la Santé. (2012) *Plan Canicule 2012*. Available at http://circulaires.legifrance.gouv.fr/pdf/2012/05/cir_35274.pdf (accessed 22 September 2012).

Premier ministre, Service d'information du Gouvernement. (2005) *Présentation du Plan national canicule 2005*, 22 June 2005. Available at http://www.archives.premierministre.gouv.fr/villepin/information/actua-lites_20/presentation_plan_national_canicule_53352.html (accessed 15 June 2010).

Naludi, M. (2003) Politics of Pension Reform – The French Case in a Comparative Perspective. *French Politics*, 1:2 pp199–224.

Stern, E. K. (1997) Crises and Learning: A Balance Sheet. *Journal of Contingencies and Crisis Management*, 5:2 pp69–86.

Thirion, X., Debensason, D., Delarozière, J.-C. and San Marco, J. L. (2005) August 2003: Reflections on a French Summer Disaster – Why Were Its Medical Consequences So Serious? Are We Sure to Do Better Next Time? *Journal of Contingencies and Crisis Management*, 13:4 pp153–8.

Vandentorren, S., Florence, S., Medina, S., Pascal, M., Maulpoix, A., Cohen, J.-C. and Ledrans, M. (2004) Mortality in 13 French Cities during the August 2003 Heatwave. *Research and Practice*, 94:9 pp1518–20.

Abstract

As the floodwaters of 2005 receded from New Orleans, a new city emerged – rotting and fetid. The guidepost of living in New Orleans had been altered, in many cases, beyond recognition. Public officials tasked with leading the recovery had to come to terms with the unfamiliar and renegotiate a sense of place. Residents faced the same tasks of recovery and making meaning. This article examines the leadership of one organization, Market Umbrella, that used farmers markets as spaces of community gathering to help facilitate the ongoing recovery of the familiar and restoring one meaningful context of New Orleans – food. The study suggests that informal leadership can use 'free spaces' of community gathering to recreate fractured relationships between people and places affected by disaster. The study shows the key roles that informal leadership and the spaces of food played in redressing the anomie brought about by the flooding of New Orleans.

MAKING GROCERIES

Leadership, free spaces and narratives of meaning in post-Katrina New Orleans

Claire Menck and Richard A. Couto

Claire Menck
The International Culinary School at the Art Institute
of Wisconsin
Milwaukee
Wisconsin 53202
USA

Richard A. Couto
Union Institute and University
Cincinnati
OH 45206
USA

INTRODUCTION

On Tuesday, 6 September 2005, a week after Hurricane Katrina hit the Gulf Coast and sent a backlash of water over the levees of New Orleans, the United States Army Corps of Engineers began pumping water out of the submerged city (Brookings Institute, 2010). As the floodwater receded, a new landscape emerged. The city was missing key landmarks. What had been there on 28 August 2005 was now gone or altered in such a way that, as a whole, it was not what it had been – this was a new New Orleans. Water had covered approximately 80 per cent of the city following the failure of the federal levee system, scattering residents of the city as their homes and property languished in the tepid floodwaters and smouldering heat. To many, it appeared as if New Orleans had drowned.

At the very centre of a disaster like the flooding of New Orleans is the destruction of the spaces people know and communities inhabit. These spaces include physical structures and mental frameworks that in combination provide schemas by which we make meaning of our world and the activities that take place within it. Durkheim and Simpson (1997) referred to the removal of mental frameworks as a state of anomie, an unmooring of the self from the environment that prevents individuals from making sense of their place in the world.

This article focuses on one aspect of disaster response: meaning-making (Boin et al., 2010). Drawing on research carried out in the city 5 years after Katrina, the authors suggest that both formal and informal leadership developed narratives of meaning that helped citizens to adapt. The article highlights the changing role of food in recovery and meaning-making from the provision of emergency supplies of food in the immediate aftermath of disaster to the restoration of production, provision, preparation and consumption of food.

The article presents a case study of Market Umbrella, a local non-profit organiza-tion that operates several farmers markets in New Orleans. It was one of the first markets to reopen following the flooding and evacuation of the city. The market was social hub for residents who reconnected with each other while 'making groceries'. Using this case as lens, the authors investigate how the informal leadership of this organization used social space as the stage upon which to develop narratives of meaning as a part of recovery. We use the term informal leadership to distinguish non-constituted leadership, which occurs in civil society and social change efforts, from constituted leadership, the realm of public officials and authority (Tucker, 1995). The article further suggests that normalizing structures such as markets, restaurants, bars and cafes are part of a long-term response to disaster that extends past the immediate response, allowing formal and informal leaders and ordinary citizens a space in which they can digest critical change, and envision a new, more resilient future.

DISASTER, MEANING MAKING AND FOOD

Scholarship on disaster recognizes one common factor of critical change events: they alter the normal structure and flow of life. To name something, a disaster implies that social norms have been disrupted (Carr, 1932). 'All that is necessary for a disaster to have occurred is the public perception that either a hazard threat exists or an impact has taken place' (Oliver-Smith, 2002: 37).

Students of disaster tend to focus on subsequent effects on the social system that generate a breakdown of normative and meaning-making structures (Comfort *et al.*, 2010; Masters and 't Hart, 2012; 't Hart, 1993). Another common thread in disaster literature is the evolution of perceptions about a disaster over time as those immediately involved (as well as those witnessing the disaster from afar) struggle to reconcile the event with what preceded and followed it and answer the question: *what the hell happened?*

Food plays an important role in the immediate response to disaster. Disaster managers evaluate the food supply, distribution of food aid and fabrication requirements (i.e. fuel for cooking). This includes evaluating supplies versus needs, structuring transport of food to the site of the disaster, setting up distribution points and ensuring sufficient energy and tools to cook and serve food (Alinovi *et al.*, 2008; Fisher, 2007). In this phase of disaster response, the primary concern is the delivery of sufficient nutritional impact for those affected by the disaster.

Once the immediate disaster has passed, food and the spaces in which it is prepared and consumed take on a new role different from the initial emergency provisions of nutrition. Food assumes its cultural role, as a realm of shared social meaning and a frame through which people make sense of their experience. The role of food in long-term recovery from disaster (and meaning-making in general) has received less attention than other factors of disaster recovery. Yet, the meaning it provides was central to addressing one of the most disorienting aspects of the New Orleans disaster – anomie.

Disasters are anominal because they alter existing schematic cognitive structures, and require those structures to be modified or replaced with new ones. In their study of trauma patients affected by displacement after Hurricane Katrina, Williams and Spuil (2005) found that even after the immediate impact of the disaster had passed and people began returning to the city, the sense of a 'new normal' never manifested: 'The usual channels for expression and for finding meaning remained absent and/or unavailable' (2005: 65). Disasters destroy mental schemas and maps that individuals use to understand their worlds:

A crisis can be defined as a *breakdown of familiar symbolic frameworks, legitimizing the pre-existing socio-political order.* Crises come to the fore when the everyday drama of public life are disrupted either by an exogenous event, by cumulative and hitherto insufficiently recognized unintended consequences of a process of organizational governance, or by the deliberate activities of particular groups bent on achieving such a perceptual breakdown. ('t Hart, 1993: 39)

The stories we tell about our experiences, like the preparation and consumption of food, bring meaning to them (cf. Bevir, 2011). Lance Hill, director of the Southern Institute for Education and Research, provides an example when he tells a story about going to get a po'boy sandwich. It matters where you get it in New Orleans: in a predominantly black neighbourhood corner store or a popular, predominantly white, Uptown eatery:

> The po'boy is an example. If you go down to the People's Grocery Store on Louisiana for a po'boy (and there quantity is quality) - they make a pork chop po'boy, and my wife used to get a liver cheese po'boy that had enough liver cheese to last an army for years - but they ask if you want cheese on a shrimp po'boy, and it's Velveeta cheese. And everyone is getting cheese. That is a very different po'boy than you get at Domalisa's [in Uptown].

> What outside food folklorists and cultural writers discover is a *part* of New Orleans cuisine and define it *as* New Orleans cuisine. I'm making the argument that there's a lot of variation in the food that we define as New Orleans food. And so, what we are sharing is a lot less than the cultural marketers would suggest. (Hill in Menck, 2012)

Food forms help us express who we are within our group; it is an indicator of that belonging to those we meet outside of that system. Food 'becomes a sign system that is socially qualified (as "distinguished", "vulgar", etc.)' (Bourdieu, 1984: 172). In short, food means something to those who eat it, binding them to their social system and the space it takes up. The po'boy (and how you 'dress it' with condiments) signifies the person who eats it, the city of New Orleans, and the groups within it.

Regardless of its variations and evolution, or perhaps precisely because of them, po'boys are a metaphor for New Orleans. In his 2010 speech commemorating the 5-year anniversary of Hurricane Katrina, James Carville told the audience how he explained to his wife why he wanted to return to live in New Orleans after Katrina. New Orleans was 'like a po'boy, sloppy and wet, and different from one restaurant to the next. If you want the same sandwich every time you go out to eat, go live in Iowa and eat at Subway' (Menck, 2012). Carville's sandwich is a metaphor for life and people in New Orleans, juxtaposing the perceived uniqueness of the New Orleans po'boy (and people) with the homogeneity of the rest of the country's Subway sandwiches (and people). Carville was implying that if you want the 'same-old, same-old' go anywhere else; if you want love, lust, art, taste and diversity – come to New Orleans.

Part of Carville's message implies that the uniqueness of New Orleans food, like the lace itself, is worth fighting for. The metaphor also expresses a larger narrative about how food is valued, and what it means in the context of the place. Food is a kind of *secret geography* (Duruz, 2002) of New Orleans – the things and activities of a place that bind communities to where they live. If you know where to buy a good po'boy you 'belong' – while those who do not partake 'are outsiders whose rejection of such culinary symbols implies disdain for the community' (Bienvenu *et al.*, 2005 : 109). We navigate our world when we know the stories we share with others, and we can reasonably expect that others know them as well, at least to a certain extent (Goffman, 1971). The breaking of bread and the conversations about the quality of ingredients in food, their combination in cooking, past occasions of food consumption and outstanding cooks help bridge the old normal and new conditions and help construct norms in the 'new normal' of disaster recovery.

MEANING AND NARRATIVES OF LEADERSHIP

Spaces of the food system (like restaurants, cafes and the farmers markets of Market Umbrella) are *re-place-ments*: new spaces in which individuals can connect and develop relationships that form a basis for increased social capital. These new spaces reinstitutionalize old rituals. Rituals, such as buying fresh food in a shared community space like a farmers market, are 'highly structured, more or less standardized sequences and are often enacted at certain places and times that are themselves endowed with special symbolic meaning' ('t Hart, 1993: 43). These may entail solidarity, reassurance and purification and animosity. Rituals build a sense of group cohesion through the embodiment of memory in performed acts (Stoller, 2004).

These spaces do more than permitting the re-enactment of old rituals in the new normal of disaster recovery. They provide 'social spaces - locations in which the unspoken riposte, stifled anger, and bitten tongues created by relations of domination find a vehement, full-throated expression' (Scott, 1990: 120). They provide venues to question existing identities and begin to understand new frameworks that alter those identities. They facilitate a certain type of leadership:

> [M]eeting and dealing with that voice of fear is the very essence of leadership: to facilitate the letting go of the old 'self' and letting come the new 'Self.' Then we can step into another world that only begins to take shape once we overcome the fear of stepping into the unknown. (Scharmer, Kindle Locations, 2007: 616–17)

Scharmer frames leadership in the context of adaptive change as moving from a present point to a future desired position in which organizations move from a position of seeing and sensing the present environment, through a process of presenting – or visioning – a desired future. Howard Gardner and Laskin suggest that:

> The formidable challenge confronting the visionary leader is to offer a story, and an embodiment, that builds on the most credible of past synthesis, revisits them in the light of present concerns, leaves open a place for future events, and allows individual contribution by the persons in the group. (1995: 56)

This closely aligns with Scharmer's idea of leadership, using narratives that weave together a group's story and suggest potential outcomes. Following disaster, the stories about what has happened and what it means becomes part of the process of recovery.

For example, when the Vietnamese community returned to New Orleans east in the weeks following Katrina they were confronted with near total destruction. The Mary Queen Viet Nam church served as a central organizing location for the community as it began the process of rebuilding. The initial mobilization of the community happened largely under the leadership of Father Vien, who led visioning sessions about the development of a new community garden as part of the recovery efforts in New Orleans east. Specifically, this community sought out more self-reliance as a way to build resiliency. If they could grow their own food, they would not depend on the grocery stores that were many miles away to supply them their sustenance. The lengthy process of finding a space, designing the garden and moving it through the required city, state and national regulatory process was part of a larger narrative of recovery. Food became a symbol of self-reliance as well as a cultural imperative. Father Vien did not construct this narrative; he facilitated the space for those in the community to gather, envision and develop their own desired outcomes.

'MAKING GROCERIES': MARKETS AS HOLDING ENVIRONMENTS FOR ADAPTIVE CHANGE

The experience of the Vietnamese points out that Katrina and its flooding brought disequilibrium to New Orleans, and with it a challenge to adapt to the changes. It created demands for new practices and arrangements that would allow the city to rebuild, and ideally, thrive. Ronald Heifetz (1994) suggests that these conditions of disequilibrium demand adaptive work of leadership, with and without authority (or in our terms: formal and informal leadership).

Adaptive leadership takes place in a space that Heifetz calls a holding environment. Venues for food production, provision, preparation and consumption may serve as holding environments. In his ethnography about restaurants, bars and cafes, Ray Oldenburg (1999) refers to them as third spaces, locations in which public issues meet private life:

> The eternal sameness of the third place overshadows the variations in its outward appearance and seems unaffected by the wide differences in cultural attitudes toward the typical gathering places of informal public life. The beer joint in which the middle-class American takes no pride can be as much a third place as the proud Vietnamese coffeehouse. It is a fortunate aspect of the third place that its capacity to serve the human need for communication does not much depend upon the capacity of a nation to comprehend its virtues. (Oldenburg, 1999: 20)

The case study of *cocina publicas* (public kitchens) in Mexico further illustrates the role of food in creating a third place. Public kitchens, primarily small-scale, women-led food stands, offer a variety of regional dishes to patrons. These stands are semi-permanent, in malls or open-air markets, and they represent the production of home recipes for sale to a wider public – and intersection of the public and private space. In her discussion of one of the vendors, Meredith Abarca finds:

> She shares part of her story as an entrepreneur with customers, and in the process she makes Gordita Cecy a site to discuss local politics and history, and to give advice to potential new market food vendors. (2007: 204)

We turn now to a specific instance of informal leadership within the food community of New Orleans to further recovery by literally providing residents of New Orleans the ingredients to make meaning from the preparation and consumption of familiar and distinctive food.

MARKET UMBRELLA

The city of New Orleans has a long market history. But as the food system has increasingly moved to a global distribution network, the system of local markets has largely been replaced with corner stores and larger big-box grocery stores. In 1995 Loyola professor Richard McCarthy saw an opportunity to refocus his work in political activism by reintroducing a farmers market into the Central Business District (CBD) in New Orleans. Working with fellow civic leaders John Abajian and Sharon Litwin, the group of three reintroduced a farm-to-market concept into New Orleans at the Crescent City Farmers Market. The market operated on Saturday mornings in the William B. Reiley Parking lot, festooned on two sides with an elaborate mural of rural life in Louisiana.

Originally organized in affiliation with Loyola University, through the Twomney Center for Peace, the initial mission was to develop rural–urban relationships by developing a strong regional food network. Working closely with regional farmers and fishermen, the organization developed into three markets serving not only the CBD, but also Uptown and Mid-City. By 2004, the farmers markets were organized under a central 'umbrella' mission defined by the Four M's: markets, mobilization, mentoring and models. This structure allowed the growing organization to engage in other food-related social justice issues such as the White Bucket Brigade, which works as an incubator with local fishermen to develop sea-to-market distribution channels beyond local markets into national and global systems. This marked a shift in focus from an organization dedicated primarily to farmers markets towards one that had a larger social goal:

> By learning, sharing and growing, we cultivate the field of public markets for public good. We develop tools that help other markets build capacity and evaluate impact, stage peer learning opportunities, and launch a number of innovative programs to grow agricultural enterprises. (Market Umbrella, 2010b

The Crescent City Farmers Markets transformed into an independent entity: Market Umbrella. Market Umbrella operates these 'public markets' as 'recurring assemblies of vendors marketing directly to consumers in a public setting,' with the goal of 'cultivating the field of public markets for the public good' (Market Umbrella, 2010a). The goal of this kind of direct marketing is to balance financial, social and human capital.

This paradigm operates on the following three assumptions:

i   That markets build social, as well as human and financial capital.
ii   That social capital improves community health.
iii That community health in turn builds human and financial health in a positively reinforcing spiral.

Market Umbrella works to build networks of food producers with consumers, developing forms of human and social capital within a community. The goals of Market Umbrella and others like it, reflect a desire to:

> [u]nderscore the influence of social and cultural capital such as customers becoming like extended family, instead of capital gain and fame... [moving] culinary practices from the sphere of domestic reproduction to commercial production without losing the familial ethical and moral values of caring, collaboration, and mutual benefit. This interconnection of spaces offers a paradigm that opposes the capitalist conception of professional kitchens. (Perez and Abarca, 2007: 139)

The localized market system is not only the antithesis of the industrial food system, it is not a 'system' at all; rather, it is a *relationship network* between producers and consumers. The market is about generating direct relationships where consumers can interact directly with producers who can tell their own stories about how the food is produced and brought to market. These relationships increase connections based on locale, developing denser networks of producers and consumers based on place.

The Crescent City Farmers Market is the type of localized food chain that connects local consumers with small-scale food producers like Pete Gerica, a fisherman who provides the shrimp for po'boys, and the fish and crabs for gumbo. Gerica's work represents both self and culture as it is experienced in a place. He tells the story about what happened to his family after Katrina, and what made him ultimately break down and cry:

> We were in my house when it blew out after Katrina. It was my mother, my daughter, my wife, and myself, and the dog - we got blown out and ended up in a tree, and I never shed a tear until two things happened. The first trip I made with DHH [Louisiana Department of Health and Hospitals] was to the Biloxi marsh. I saw the devastation to the marsh, and I broke down... I couldn't handle it.

> And the next time I went down to Delacroix Island with another biologist. When I hit the point of Reggio... which is a road I've been going down since I was a kid. We'd go pick up oysters down there

with dad in the truck, and I've been going down there all my life fishing. When I saw Lafitte skiffs hanging out of trees, and I saw the bayou filled up with mud, and grass, and stuff that wasn't supposed to be in there... I knew that the outside [of the bayou] had broke apart. So I just pulled over to the side of the road, and I just let it out.

That's the things that just break me down, because it's been a part of my life for so long, and you see it, and you feel it, and you live it and it's part of you. And that's what people don't understand about why people on the bayous who fish... why we keep coming back. It's in our blood, it's imprinted. (Gerica in Menck, 2012)

For Gerica, food is a visceral representation of belonging, a *solistalgic* experience (Albrecht, 2005) in which: 'each sense may be involved in lodging memories of home in the experiencing of the body, [and] work to construct "whole" experiences of home. The experience of wholeness here allows for experiences across distinct spaces and times to come together in specific moment of everyday habitual activity' (Warin and Dennis, 2005: 167). Gerica speaks of the emotional feeling the impact of Katrina had on him when he saw its impact on the land – the place that houses not only his livelihood, but also his memories.

Pete Gerica's experience after Katrina is an expression of loss at the damage to the physical place that threatens a disconnection between the individual and the land, but also the individual and their community. The interplay of the physical body within a place is both emotional and spiritual. It is that expression of physicality that makes the connection between the culture of the social group and its place (Berry, 1977; Loichot, 2004).

Relationships like those between Market Umbrella and Pete Gerica facilitate a social network between consumers and producers that add value and bring meaning to the places in which they occur. The group facilitates the transactions between farmers and consumers by creating the space for those things to occur – they mediated the relationships by providing the space and the structure for those to develop and evolve.

Katrina came at a critical time in the strategic planning process for the markets and their new structure under Market Umbrella. The mission of the organization was now in question: did anyone even want these markets, wondered the board and volunteers In the months initially following Katrina this question was answered through a series of surveys, and yes, indeed, people wanted their markets back. Vendors, customers and neighbours all indicated that they saw markets as a sign of normalcy in a city where the 'new normal' was still in negotiation. In November 2005, the market opened once again and became the self-proclaimed 'Department of Homeland Serenity'. Once farmers and fishers had been located, many affected by Hurricane Rita in September of that year, the customers and vendors used the market as a place to reconnect in the 'happiest place in New Orleans' (McCarthy in Menck, 2012).

By 2010, Market Umbrella continued to operate three markets in the city of New Orleans in its Crescent City Farmers Market initiative. The umbrella also includes bevy of other initiatives aimed at 'initiating and growing local economies' (Mark

Umbrella, 2010b). Market Umbrella was the first to bring Electronic Benefits Transfer (EBT) food stamps into farmers markets, working through a national grant to match dollar for dollar the amount used on the card. Most recently, Market Umbrella worked to provide $40 in free food dollars for any mariner in the region affected by the 2010 British Petroleum oil spill.

The initial idea of 'a public space that helps to alter the relationships and build bridges between people, bringing soft edges to the city' (McCarthy in Menck, 2012) has transformed into an organization that not only works to develop strong regional food systems, but also helps to foster economic growth through small business incubation and education for individuals and neighbourhoods interested in developing their own markets.

Individuals who returned to rebuild their neighbourhoods and communities found a new space familiar in some ways but different in both physical and emotional ways. Those things that had once been regular guideposts for life, including the production, provision, preparation and consumption of found had been altered. Re-establishing the spaces of daily living, like gardens, farmers markets, restaurants, cafes and grocery stores became a part of the process of emotional recovery, as well as a way for people to physically revision and reinvest in their physical space. This aspect of long term recovery and meaning-making, including the cultural narrative of food, fell to the informal leadership of the community.

It was with no small sense of irony that market Umbrella was deemed 'the Happiest Place in New Orleans' in 2005, and why wouldn't it be? With its mock 'Office of Homeland Serenity' tent, tables piled high with fresh local foods brought in by local producers (themselves affected by the disaster), and lots of smiling faces, this *place* was a vision of what normal might look like as soon as the 'new normal' arrived. Restaurants and other spaces of the food system, such as Market Umbrella, have the potential to serve as holding spaces for these visioning conversations and the activities of adaptive change between citizens and leaders.

CONCLUSION: MANAGING RECOVERY

The immediate response to disaster requires public managers to address the delivery and distribution of appropriate foods that will supply sufficient nutritional needs to those impacted by the disaster. Following this initial phase of disaster response, once some level of security and normalcy has been established, public managers and those leading response efforts can help to facilitate recovery from the event by establishing third spaces' for the communities they serve. These informal places allow individuals to collectively grieve their losses as a community, and begin the arduous task of visioning a new place. Food spaces, like farmers markets, restaurants, cafes and bars re effective locations for this kind of emotional work because they reinforce local cultural food traditions, feeding both the body and the soul.

This study finds that the anomie brought about by loss can begin to be at least partially addressed through community rituals such as food production and sharing. Because these activities are so seemingly trivial and mundane, they hold a potential path into the memory of what life was like before the disaster event, and they offer a glimpse into things that might be brought forward in the new landscape of the post-disaster community. The wordless communication that taste offers can be a conduit for connecting the future to the past. Public administrators and other community leaders can help to facilitate this process by opening up state and local resources to food production and sharing facilities like farmer's markets. Removing regulatory obstacles in times of crisis can help these community led groups re-ignite the connections between local food producers and consumers, thus establishing important social networks and increasing social capital.

Social capital is often identified as a key ingredient of societal resilience (Comfort et al., 2010). It is, however, rarely specified how social capital can be generated (especially in the short run) (Andrews et al., 2011). This study identifies a feasible way to both exploit and nurture social capital and canalize the subsequent social mobilization towards the re-erection of local institutions and rebuilding of the city. While the type of binding institutions will likely differ city to city, this article shows how simple it can be.

By generating community gathering spots in New Orleans, a venue for bottom-up change was created – a space where 'change is the identifying mark of those endeavours which seek a transformation in power relations, not simply a return to past conditions or the replacement of one elite with another' (Evans and Boyte, 1986: 158). The power of the space is its ability to hold the environment for self-reflection, shared experience and formation of identity. Farmers markets, cafes and other spaces of the food system are examples of places that allow for the telling of stories, the airing of grief and the formation of narratives about what happened in the disaster, and the negotiation of how it will become a part of the history of that place. The diverse spaces of the food system, public and private, provide a view into the construction of social space as a place to do the adaptive work of leadership, including recovery from disaster.

REFERENCES

Albrecht, G. (2005) Solastalgia, a New Concept in Human Health and Identity. *Philosophy Activism Nature*, 3 pp41–4.

Alinovi, L., Hemrich, G. and Russo, L. eds. (2008) *Beyond Relief: Food Security in Protracted Crisis*, Rome: Practical Action Publishing.

Andrews, R., Cowell, R. and Downe, J. (2011) Promoting Civic Culture by Supporting Citizenship: What Difference Can Local Government Make? *Public Administration*, 89:2 pp595–610.

Berry, W. (1977) *The Unsettling of America: Culture & Agriculture*, San Francisco, CA: Sierra Club Books.

Bevir, M. (2011) Public Administration as Story Telling. *Public Administration*, 89:1 pp183–95.

Bienvenu, M., Brasseaux, C. A. and Brasseaux, R. A. (2005) *Stir the Pot: The History of Cajun Cuisine*, New York: Hippocrene Books.

Boin, A., 't Hart, P., McConnell, A. and Preston, T. (2010) Leadership Style, Crisis Response, and Blame Management: The Case of Katrina. *Public Administration*, 88:3 pp706–23.

Bourdieu, P. (1984) *Distinction: A Social Critique of the Judgment of Taste* [Distinction], Cambridge, MA: Harvard University Press.

Brookings Institute. (2010) *The New Orleans index at five*. Available at http://www.brookings.edu/reports/2007/08neworleansindex.aspx (accessed 1 May 2010).

Carr, L. J. (1932) Disaster and the Sequence-Pattern Concept of Social Change. *American Journal of Sociology*, 38:2 pp207–18.

Comfort, L. K., Boin, A. and Demchak, C. eds. (2010) *Designing Resilience: Preparing for Extreme Events*, Pittsburgh, PA: University of Pittsburgh Press.

Durkheim, É. and Simpson, G. (1997) *Suicide: A Study in Sociology*, New York: Free Press.

Duruz, J. (2002) Rewriting the Village: Geographies of Food and Belonging in Clovelly, Australia. *Cultural Geographies*, 9:4 pp373–88.

Evans, S. M. and Boyte, H. C. (1986) *Free Spaces: The Sources of Democratic Change in America* (1st edn), New York: Harper & Row.

Fisher, D. (2007) Fast Food: Regulating Emergency Food Aid in Sudden-Impact Disasters. *Vanderbilt Journal of Transnational Law*, 40:4 pp1127–53.

Gardner, H. and Laskin, E. (1995) *Leading Minds: An Anatomy of Leadership*, New York: Basic Books.

Goffman, E. (1971) *The Presentation of Self in Everyday Life*, Harmondsworth: Penguin.

Heifetz, R. A. (1994) *Leadership Without Easy Answers*, Cambridge, MA: Belknap Press of Harvard University Press.

Loichot, V. (2004) Edwidge Danticat's Kitchen History. *Meridians: Feminism, Race, Transnationalism*, 5:1 pp92–116.

Market Umbrella (2010a) *Crescent City Farmers Market*. Available at http://www.crescentcityfarmersmarket.org/ (accessed 12 May 2012).

Market Umbrella (2010b) *Market Umbrella Website*. Available at http://www.marketumbrella.org/ (accessed 2009).

Masters, A. and 't Hart, P. (2012) Prime Ministerial Rhetoric and Recession Politics: Meaning Making in Economic Crisis Management. *Public Administration*, 90:3 pp759–80.

Menck, J. C. (2012) 'Recipes of Resolve: Food & Meaning In Post-Diluvian New Orleans'. Doctoral Dissertation. Available at Ohiolink Database http://etd.ohiolink.edu/view.cgi?acc_num=antioch1331074997 (accessed May 2012).

Oldenburg, R. (1999; 1997) *The Great Good Place: Cafés, Coffee Shops, Bookstores, Bars, Hair Salons, and Other Hangouts at the Heart of a Community*, New York: Marlowe; Distributed by Publishers Group West.

Oliver-Smith, A. (2002) 'Theorizing Disasters: Nature, Power, and Culture' in S. Hoffman and A. Oliver-Smith (eds) *Catastrophe & Culture: The Anthropology of Disaster* 23–48. Santa Fe, NM: School of American Research Press.

Pérez, R. L. and Abarca, M. E. (2007) Cocinas Públicas: Food and Border Consciousness in Greater Mexico. *Food & Foodways: History & Culture of Human Nourishment*, 15:3 pp137–51.

Scharmer, C. O. (2007) *Theory U Leading From the Future as It Emerges: The Social Technology of Presencing* 817–35. Leipzig: Meine.

Scott, J. C. (1990) *Domination and the Arts of Resistance: Hidden Transcripts*, New Haven, CT: Yale University Press.

Stoller, P. (2004) Sensuous Ethnography, African Persuasions, and Social Knowledge. *Qualitative Inquiry*, 10:6 pp817–35.

't Hart, P. (1993) Symbols, Rituals and Power: The Lost Dimensions of Crisis Management. *Journal of Contingencies & Crisis Management*, 1:1 pp36–50.

Tucker, R. C. (1995) *Politics as Leadership*, Columbia: University of Missouri Press.

Warin, M. and Dennis, S. (2005) Threads of Memory: Reproducing the Cypress Tree Through Sensual Consumption. *Journal of Intercultural Studies*, 26:1 pp159–70.

Williams, J. M. and Spruill, D. A. (2005) Surviving and Thriving After Trauma and Loss. *Journal of Creativity in Mental Health*, 1:3 pp57–70.

Abstract

Both academics and practitioners have recently discovered resilience as a core topic of interest. Resilience is widely viewed as a potential solution to the challenges posed by crises and disasters. The promise of resilience is an organization or society that absorbs shocks and 'bounces back' after a disturbance. While the idea of resilience is increasingly popular, empirical research on resilient organizations is actually quite rare. This article explores whether a relation exists between organizational characteristics, processes and resilience. Building on the insights of high reliability theory and crisis research, it probes this relation in two organizations that experienced deep crises: the California Independent System Operator (CAISO) and National Aeronautics and Space Agency (NASA).

THE RESILIENT ORGANIZATION

A critical appraisal

Arjen Boin and Michel J. G. van Eeten

Arjen Boin
School of Governance
Utrecht University
Utrecht
The Netherlands

Michel J. G. van Eeten
Faculteit Techniek, Bestuur en Management
Delft University
Delft
The Netherlands

THE RISE OF RESILIENCE

In recent years, the management of crises and disasters has become a key topic of concern for both practitioners and academics. Public and private organizations routinely prepare for a wide variety of adverse events. Academics, in turn, study the causes and dynamics of these threats, map patterns of organizational response and offer prescriptions (Weick and Sutcliffe, 2001; Boin *et al.*, 2005; Drennan and McConnell, 2007).

One of the dominant normative ideal-types that has recently emerged in this field of study is the resilient organization (Weick and Sutcliffe, 2001; Sutcliffe and Vogus, 2003; Sheffi, 2005; Hollnagel *et al.*, 2006; Flynn, 2008; Cascio, 2009; Christianson *et al.*, 2009; Comfort *et al.*, 2010; Välikangas, 2010). Long a dominant concept in the field of ecology, the idea of resilience is catching on in the fields of crisis management and organization studies.

The idea of resilience offers the promise of an intuitively plausible, attractive and seemingly attainable strategy to prepare for and deal with various types of adversity. The literature suggests that a resilient organization will maintain a high level of performance even when environmental pressures mount, threats arise and uncertainties deepen. In the face of unexpected adversity, the resilient organization is said to 'bounce back' quickly, without much effort (cf. Wildavsky, 1988). If disruptions are both inevitable and surprising, as the literature tells us, investing in resilience promises to be a more effective strategy than allocating scarce resources aimed at controlling the environment and defending against specific risks (Wildavsky, 1988).

The resilient organization is also quite remarkable from a theoretical perspective. The organizational literature typically identifies external shocks as potentially existential threats to an organization's health. The same literature predicts that organizations will find it hard to cope with such shocks. So here comes the resilient organization, which absorbs unexpected shocks and somehow emerges from crises without lasting damage. The resilient organization thus presents researchers with an enigma, as it 'works in practice but not in theory' (cf. LaPorte and Consolini, 1991).

While the idea of resilience is increasingly popular, empirical research on resilient organizations is actually quite rare. Much of the literature on resilience is prescriptive and normative; it spurs people to recognize impending dangers, learn on the spot, work in joint teams and high spirits, improvise their way around excruciating setbacks and emerge from crises stronger and better (e.g. Weick and Sutcliffe, 2001; Hamel and Valikangas 2003). But it is not quite clear how these skills can be built into an organization and its employees. In fact, we do not really know what causes resilience or how it is achieved. Is it the result of designed processes or perhaps the outcome of improvisation and luck?

In examining the relation between organizational *processes* and the *outcome* of resilience we encounter two problems. First, it is not clear what resilience is, exactly. Second, it is hard to recognize resilience in action. We do not know resilience when we see it – rather we assume it must have been there if an organization survives a crisis or disaster. If it end badly, the organization obviously was not resilient. If we want to study organizational resilience without conflating process and outcome, we must address these problems.

In this article, we explore whether a relation exists between organizational characteristics, processes and resilience. We make an explicit connection with the literatures on crisis management and so-called 'high reliability organizations' (HROs). We then use two well-known cases to probe the relation between organizational characteristics, the process of adversity management and the resilience: The California Independent System Operator (CAISO), which managed to keep the lights when the electricity market imploded in the summer of 2000, and the National Aeronautics and Space Agency (NASA), which suffered two Space Shuttle disasters.

RESILIENCE IN THEORY: TWO MODELS

There are many definitions of resilience to be found in a wide variety of academic fields including psychology, sociology, ecology, organization theory, public administration and political science.[1] These definitions pertain to different levels of analysis, ranging from the individual to the global level. In this article, we are primarily interested to understand resilience at the level of the organization.

Two elements typically return in definitions of resilience: (1) after a surprising danger manifests itself (2) the organization manages to restore order – i.e. bounces back to an acceptable state of normality (cf. Wildavsky, 1988: 77). The first element is conceptualized fairly consistently across the different definitions of resilience. It emphasizes that the disturbance 'fall[s] outside of the set of disturbances the system is designed to handle' (Woods and Hollnagel, 2006: 3). Standard operating procedures, in other words, will not suffice.

The second element leaves more room for diverging conceptualizations. Definitions vary along two dimensions. Some definitions simply focus on returning to a prior order, while other definitions refer to the capacity to emerge stronger from a crisis (Sullivan-Taylor and Wilson, 2009). The latter type infuses resilience with the idea of learning. Then there is the time dimension: does the 'bouncing back' occur early on in the crisis process (thus preventing further escalation) or does it occur after the crisis (building the city up after the earthquake)?

This leads to two very different models of resilience. The first type is *precursor resilience*, which we can define as the 'ability to accommodate change without catastrophic failure, or a capacity to absorb shocks gracefully' (Foster, 1993: 36). This is the type of resilience that prevents budding problems from escalating into a full-blown crisis or breakdown. A second type can be referred to as *recovery resilience*, which can be defined as 'the ability to respond to singular or unique events' (Kendra and Wachtendorf, 2003: 42), bouncing back to a state of normalcy. This is the type of resilience that we can witness: the organization or city that miraculously arises from the ashes of crisis or disaster (Vale and Campanella, 2005).

In the literature, many processes and structures are casually associated with resilience. Resilient organizations 'keep errors small and improvise workarounds that keep the system functioning' (Weick and Sutcliffe, 2001: 14). They possess 'an impressive capacity to grasp crisis dynamics... They resist tendencies to adopt and cling to an interpretation based on limited information and hasty analysis. They force themselves to continuously probe their situational assessments... [They] have created a culture of awareness... They expect crisis to happen. They look for them because employees know that they are expected to do that – even when it comes at the cost of task efficiency' (Boin *et al.*, 2005: 36–37; cf. Weick and Sutcliffe, 2001: 14). Hamel and Välikangas (2003: 54) write that in a resilient organization 'revolutionary change happens in lightning-quick evolutionary steps – with no calamitous surprises, no convulsive reorganizations, no colossal write-offs and no indiscriminate, across-the-board layoffs'. Kendra and Wachtendorf (2003: 42) speak of 'redundancy, the capacity for resourcefulness, effective communication and the capacity for self-organization in the face of extreme demands'.

The dearth of empirical data makes it hard if not impossible to relate with any type of certainty organizational characteristics and processes to resilient performance. We seek to address this lacuna. To facilitate empirical research, we need a theoretical framework that proposes precise relations between organizational attributes and processes, and specific types of resilience.

Studying resilience in practice

In this article, we are primarily interested to study what we defined above as precursor resilience: a resilient organization absorbs shocks and prevents emerging problems from escalating into full-blown crises. The research into so-called HROs provides us with a starting point for theorizing on conditions for precursor resilience (Weick and Sutcliffe, 2001; Sullivan-Taylor and Wilson, 2009: 253).

High reliability theory (HRT) began with a small group of researchers studying a distinct and special class of organizations – those charged with the management of hazardous but essential technical systems (LaPorte and Consolini, 1991; Roberts, 1993; Schulman, 1993; Rochlin, 1996, 2011). Failure in these organizations could mean the loss of critical societal functions and could cause severe damage, threatening thousands of lives. The term 'high reliability organization' was coined to denote those organizations that successfully avoid such failure while providing operational capabilities under a wide range of environmental conditions.

High reliability theorists set out to investigate the secret of HRO success (Bourrier, 2011; Rochlin, 2011). They engaged in individual case studies of nuclear aircraft carriers, nuclear power plants and air traffic control centres. Two important (if preliminary) findings surfaced.

First, they discovered that HROs share similar and rather distinctive features. The most important are:

- high technical competence throughout the organization;
- a clear awareness of core events that must be precluded from happening;
- an elaborate and evolving set of procedures and practices, which are directed towards avoiding disastrous events from happening;
- a formal structure of roles, responsibilities and reporting relationships that can be transformed under emergency conditions into a decentralized, team-based approach to problem-solving;
- a 'culture of reliability' that distributes and instills the values of care and caution, respect for procedures, attentiveness and individual responsibility for the promotion of safety throughout the organization.

A second finding relates to the *process* of reliability maintenance. The researchers found that once a threat to safety emerges, however faint or distant, an HRO immediately 'reorders' and reorganizes to deal with that threat (LaPorte, 1996). This reordering involves a combination of rapid decentralization and facilitated improvisation. However, very little is known how, exactly, this process unfolds and how it relates to constant performance under pressure and, by implication, precursor resilience.

The HRO framework thus offers a fairly precise (if only hypothetical) relation between organizational characteristics and precursor resilience. The crisis management literature offers additional insights with regard to the conditions for a rapid and effective response in the face of unexpected threats.

First, organizations need capacity to arrive at an authoritative definition of the situation. The coordination of an improvised response network requires that all participants are 'on the same page'. This, in turn, demands a form of dynamic sense-making: information must be collected, commissioned, analysed and shared in real time (Weick and Sutcliffe, 2001). It is no exaggeration to state that this is one of the biggest challenges that crisis managers encounter.

Second, crisis management scholars put a premium on the ability to improvise. Whereas HRT scholars view improvisation as 'the last 5%' only to be used when all else fails, crisis management scholars view it as an integral building block for an effective response. Plans and procedures cannot prescribe what an organization must do to address a major crisis (Clarke, 1999). In crisis, an organization must rally its resources and partners in creative ways to produce an urgent response to a unique problem.

Two empirical case studies revisited

To further explore if, and how, organizational characteristics and processes can be related to precursor resilience, we selected two organizations that have been extremely well studied and can be expected to have had at least the potential to be resilient.

The first organization demonstrated resilience in the face of unprecedented challenges. The CAISO is the focal organization for electricity transmission in California. The electricity crisis of 2000–2001 posed a major and unanticipated crisis for the CAISO. Much of the institutional design broke down – including the means with which to secure the reliable provision of electricity. Yet, the CAISO kept the lights on in California (Roe and Schulman, 2008).

The second organization is NASA, which suffered two major disasters in 17 years. This organization possessed many (but not all) of the 'right characteristics' for an HRO (cf. Boin and Schulman, 2008) and is known for its ability to manage crises ('Houston, we have a problem'). We will revisit NASA and consider why these organizational capacities were not enough to prevent two Shuttle disasters.

KEEPING THE LIGHTS ON IN CALIFORNIA: FROM CHAOS TO RESILIENCE

In 1996, California restructured its system of electricity generation, transmission and distribution. The state moved from a system of large integrated utilities that owned and operated the generation facilities, the transmission lines and the distribution and billing systems, and set retail prices under a cost-based regulatory system, to a market-based system consisting of independent generators who sell their power on wholesale markets to distributors, who then sell it to retail customers. The transmission lines were placed under the control of a new organization, CAISO, which assumed responsibility for managing a new state-wide high-voltage electrical grid.

The new system worked fairly well for the first few years. Then disturbances began to emerge and the system entered a period now known as the California electricity crisis of 2000–2001 (Roe et al., 2003; Roe and Schulman, 2008). The CAISO faced unanticipated volatility in the scheduling of electricity transmission. The scheduling is supposed to happen months, weeks, days or at least hours in advance, so that there is time to coordinate the complicated schedules and cope with congestion in the network. Real-time 'imbalance markets' were designed to take care of the last per cent or so of total load.[2] During this crisis, reality looked quite different:

> We had days where the load [was] forecasted to be 42,000 MW, but our scheduled resources in the morning were 32,000 MW, leaving us 10,000 MW short that day. How do we deal with this? 99% of the planning has to be done prior to real time. Real time is only to react to what you missed. Real time not 'I'm short 10,000 MW in the day ahead and I'm not doing anything.' Most of the time things come together, but at a very high price.

At one point, the markets stopped functioning altogether. 'I was here, working as new gen dispatcher, when I saw the market collapse. From one day to the other, there were no more bids coming [into the real-time imbalance market]', said a member of the California Energy Resources Scheduling purchasing team.[3] The CAISO did operate closer to the edge of failure than ever before – where failure means uncontrolled blackouts or, worse, grid collapse.[4]

Yet, CAISO somehow managed to keep the lights on. Notwithstanding the popular view of rolling blackouts sweeping across California during its electricity crisis, in aggregate terms – both in hours and megawatts (MW) – blackouts were minimal and comparable to previous years (Roe *et al.*, 2003).

CAISO: Characteristics of a resilient organization?

Drawing from extensive, long-term research on CAISO (Roe and Schulman, 2008), we can establish that this organization possessed the characteristics deduced from HRT:

High technical competence

The operational core of the organization consisted of approximately fifteen operators in the central control room in Folsom. Their key competence is to maintain peak load operations under time pressure. Rather than formal education, their background was dominated by operational experience, either in the electricity system or in similar environments, such as air traffic control. Extensive in-house training programmes prepared them for the job of real-time operations. Around this control room, the organization had wrapped, physically as well as organizationally, various staff units that focused on analytical competence, as witnessed by a high concentration of PhDs among its members. (The number of employees in these units was multiple times the number of control room staff.)

A clear awareness of core events that must be precluded from happening

It was both widely understood and formalized (in so-called Control Performance Standards) that the reliable delivery of electricity was a core value in CAISO. Failure to meet reliability standards, such as always maintaining a 7-per cent operating reserve, was sanctioned by the North American Electricity Council, an industry body that enforced the self-regulation of grid operators. Operators are under no illusion that they are in control; they understand how vulnerable the grid is, how limited the options are and how precarious the balance is; they keep communications lines open to monitor the state of the network and they are busily engaged in developing options and strategies to deal with disturbances.

An elaborate set of procedures and practices directed towards avoiding these events

CAISO was a highly formalized organization. The complexity of electricity provision through a market-based system requires extensive rules, regulations and procedures.

A formal structure that can be transformed under conditions of emergency into a decentralized, team-based approach to problem-solving

During the crisis, CAISO demonstrated that it could depart from its formal structure. As formal role descriptions no longer sufficed, operators had to reinvent new procedures and new lines of cooperation (for instance, with planners and analysts who also stepped outside their role descriptions). Interdisciplinary teamwork replaced hierarchical practices dominant in 'normal' times.

A 'culture of reliability'

Long-term research (Roe and Schulman, 2008) describes the strong organizational culture in CAISO. This culture emphasized the importance of the reliability value (described above) – it can also be seen as a source of stress for operators (who felt compelled to solve emerging crises through constant trial and error).

The process of resilience: Managing crisis in the control room

Scheduling transmission for a large, complex transmission grid is very difficult and highly risky, e.g. because congestion can overload paths and trigger cascading failures. In 2001, the markets that were designed to coordinate supply and demand stopped functioning, almost overnight. Strategic behaviour on the part of the generators caused them to withhold generation capacity in order to artificially raise prices. The most dramatic effect was that a large part of the load – approximately 10,000 MW out of a peak load of 40,000 MW – was not scheduled beforehand, but ended up in the real-time market. To schedule this amount under such intense time pressure is a recipe for blackouts.

The control room played an important role in CAISO's efforts to maintain reliability. The need to balance load and generation along with meeting other regulatory parameters is the key requirement of the CAISO control room operators. All kinds of telemetry measurements come back to the control room in real time. The Automatic Generation Control system connects the CAISO generation dispatcher directly to privately held generators; the Automatic Dispatch System connects the dispatcher directly to the bidder of electricity and the dynamic scheduling system in the CAISO connects to out-of-state generators.

CAISO survived this challenge through a number of adaptations that enabled them to rely heavily on real-time operations to ensure grid and service reliability. One such adaptation was to pull the wrap-around units into the control room and involve them in supporting real-time operations. Models, which were initially developed to do contingency planning for outages, were adapted to provide immediate feedback on real-time events, thereby helping the operators to quickly assess different options to deal with disturbances.

In addition, CAISO mobilized informal networks to coordinate supply and demand. Under dire conditions, operators contacted generators off the record – because it was illegal to have such contacts – and told them the truth about those conditions, motivating them to no longer withhold generation capacity, but to put it into the market – albeit at outrageous prices. They thus leveraged the interdependencies in the system, pointing out the threat of immediate massive cascading failure. They explained how other players, such as adjacent transmission grid operators, would also be greatly affected by such events, which made them offer generation capacity that they initially reserved for their own needs.

These adaptations enabled CAISO to pull the needed resources together at the last minute. Yet, CAISO also faced a series of problems during this crisis: reliability standard violations, computer failures, software disasters, data problems, late submissions by security coordinators, not enough bids in the beep stack, ignoring dispatch orders and shedding load.

In summary, improvisation in the control room proved crucially important in managing this emerging crisis. A combination of effective sense-making and decentralized decision-making enabled operators to make the right calls at the right moment.

What we describe in terms of real-time improvisation, operators described in terms of luck. They experienced real-time confusion and incomprehension and felt they somehow escaped from disaster. In recounting one bad day that turned out good, a shift manager in CAISO's control room described how 'just by sheer stroke of luck I had made a voltage change at that time and caught what happened'. But the holes were plugged and the lights stayed on.[5]

ONE ORGANIZATION, TWO TRAGEDIES: THE DEMISE OF SPACE SHUTTLES *CHALLENGER* AND *COLUMBIA*

On 28 January 1986, the Space Shuttle *Challenger* exploded within 2 minutes of its launch. On 1 February 2003, the *Columbia* Space Shuttle disintegrated during the final stages of its return flight to earth. High-level commissions investigated the causes of these disasters. Both Commissions – the Presidential Commission on the Space Shuttle Challenger Accident (1986) and Columbia Accident Investigation Board (CAIB) (2003) – criticized the safety organization and culture of the NASA. Both commissions discovered that NASA engineers had voiced concerns, which, if heeded, could have prevented the *Challenger* and *Columbia* disasters.

On the eve of the *Challenger* launch, Thiokol engineers had raised doubts with regard to the safety of the O-rings in cold weather (Vaughan, 1996).[6] The engineers suspected that the O-rings might not seal well in cold weather, which would pose a dangerous situation. After several phone conferences between the Thiokol team and the NASA managers, both groups finally agreed that there was no conclusive evidence to suggest that the Shuttle should not be launched. During the launch, the O-rings failed to seal.

The following explosion tore the *Challenger* apart. All astronauts on board of the Shuttle died.

The foam (and the associated tile) problem, which would ultimately cause the demise of *Columbia*, had a similar history. It was considered a dangerous problem in the early days of the shuttle programme. After well over a hundred flights, the NASA engineers thought that they understood the problem and deemed the risk acceptable. When NASA studied the tape of *Columbia's* launch (a standard procedure), it was noticed that a piece of ice knocked off some of the tiles (which protect the shuttle from re-entry heat). After extensive discussions between engineers and managers, it was decided that the risk of the observed tile damage was acceptably low. Upon re-entering Earth's atmosphere, the *Columbia* disintegrated over the skies of Texas.

NASA: A resilient organization?

NASA has been subjected to a tremendous amount of study.[7] Judging from these studies, there is a remarkable sense of agreement among observers with regard to NASA's organizational characteristics and core processes, which makes it possible for us to describe the organization in terms of HRO characteristics (Boin and Schulman, 2008).

High technical competence

NASA is home to the proverbial 'rocket scientist'. The core challenge for NASA has always been to match external demands (high expectations, insufficient budgets and tight schedules) with engineering brilliance. To save costs and to keep with the schedule ('before the decade is over'), NASA adopted a philosophy of calculated risk that was supported by the technique of systems engineering (Johnson, 2002). This philosophy demanded an unwavering commitment to 'sound engineering' principles and generated a powerful culture around expertise. Discussions are held on the basis of engineering logic; every flight risk and anomaly is assessed against the laws of physics and engineering (there is no room for 'gut feeling' or 'observations').[8]

A clear awareness of core events that must be precluded from happening

The people in NASA were intensely aware of the negative consequences that disasters in human spaceflight would cause to the programme. Many of the NASA engineers who worked on the Shuttles knew the astronauts (Vaughan, 1996); most would be aware of the negative consequences of media and political attention following a disaster.

An elaborate set of procedures and practices directed towards avoiding disastrous events from happening

Through what is called the acceptable risk process, NASA seeks to identify to establish whether engineers from the involved centres and contractors agree that 'the shuttle is ready to fly and to fly safely' (Vaughan, 1996: 82). If an identified hazard cannot be eliminated before launch time, NASA has to determine whether such a hazard qualifies as an 'acceptable risk'. Each mission is followed by a mission evaluation report, which identifies anomalies that occurred during flight (Vaughan, 1996). These anomalies have to be dealt with ('closed') before the next flight can take place. Each shuttle flight is preceded by a so-called flight readiness review (FRR). This formal review procedure is a bottom-up process designed to identify risks and bring them to the attention of the higher management levels. Because it is impossible and undesirable that top-level administrators review all possible risks and anomalies, the FRR aims to filter out the critical anomalies for senior management review.

A formal structure that can be transformed under crisis conditions into a decentralized, team-based approach to problem-solving

To invent the technology that would bring humans to the Moon and back, NASA created interdisciplinary teams and centres with high degrees of autonomy (Murray and Cox, 1989). The flexibility and resourcefulness of NASA was best demonstrated during the near-disaster that occurred when the *Apollo 13* experienced an explosion in space. The different engineering disciplines were represented in the Houston centre. The adherence of procedures enabled the engineers to figure out what had happened and what was possible. Yet, it was the capacity to be flexible and to *depart* from enshrined rules that gave rise to the level of improvisation that in the end saved the day (and the crew). It is not clear whether this characteristic was still present before and during the shuttle disasters.

'culture of reliability'

Time-proven safety mechanisms had become institutionalized in its organizational culture. If engineers provide an acceptable 'engineering rationale' that explains why a risk should be accepted (rather than redesigning the parts that posed the risk), the hazard is officially classified as an acceptable risk and the shuttle is launched. If that does not happen, the launch will be delayed (NASA has a history of launch delays).

The process of resilience: A failure of sense-making?

NASA abided by its safety system (the risk procedure and the FRR), but the processes in place did not stop the disasters from happening. In the absence of a disaster, these processes would have been quite remarkable for their thoroughness, commitment to safety and ability to deal with surprises. The failure to read the signals of impending disaster appears to be related to a crucial vulnerability in NASA's safety system, which remained unidentified and unaddressed in the wake of *Challenger*: the inability to deal with emerging uncertainties that could not be resolved through the normal 'sound engineering' discussion method. In other words, NASA had no proper procedures that would allow the organization to identify signals of doubts, coming from respected engineers, which were not substantiated by engineering data (see also Dunbar and Garud, 2005).

Revisiting *Challenger*

The infamous O-rings that caused the failure of the *Challenger* shuttle had been repeatedly subjected to the acceptable risk procedure (Vaughan, 1996). In the mid-1970s (well before the first shuttle flight), doubts arose with regard to the effectiveness of the O-rings. NASA would only fly the shuttle if Thiokol (the contractor that had designed the O-rings) could provide an acceptable rationale that convinced NASA that the O-rings were safe.[9] After years of extensive discussion, testing, more debate and more worst-case testing, engineers at Marshall and Thiokol finally and 'unanimously' agreed that, although the joint performance deviated from design expectations, it was an acceptable risk' (Vaughan, 1996: 104).

On 12 April 1981, the first Space shuttle flight took place. The inspection upon return showed no anomalies; the O-rings had performed according to the prediction. The rationale for accepting this acceptable risk was confirmed by experience – a most important argument in NASA's engineering culture, which held that 'a design is a hypothesis to be tested' (Vaughan, 1996: 109).

When Thiokol engineers discovered the first in-flight anomaly – motor gases had eroded 0.053" of a primary O-ring – they established the cause of the problem, designed a solution, which was then extensively tested. No erosion occurred on subsequent flights, which convinced the engineers that they had solved the problem. This would happen again and again: a problem would be found, analysed and fixed. The shuttle would fly and return safely. The institutionalized procedures seemed to prove their worth over and over again.

Before the fateful flight of *Challenger*, a few Thiokol engineers *suspected* that the predicted cold January weather (abnormally cold for Florida) could pose a problem for the O-rings. They were unable, however, to provide a compelling rationale for the intuition. In their rush to produce one on the eve of the launch, the Thiokol engineers committed the ultimate sin of presenting a *flawed* rationale to the NASA engineers. The NASA people – who had always been considered the more conservative group – were 'appalled' with the line of argumentation coming from Utah. The Thiokol engineers realized their mistakes and ended up voting for launching even though their worries remained. This is how a Thiokol engineer and a NASA engineer described what happened (Vaughan, 1996: 302, 307):

I don't believe they did a real convincing job of presenting their data [...] The Thiokol guys even had a chart in there that says temperature of the O-ring is not the only parameter controlling blow-by. In other words, they're not coming in with a real firm statement. They're saying there's other factors. They did have a lot of conflicting data in there. (Marshall's Ben Powers who agreed with the Thiokol recommendation)

I recognized that it was not a strong technical position [to recommend against launching], but yes, I basically supported that position. I had become very concerned during the presentation, however, when one of the [Thiokol] people seemed to indicate [...] that he had forgotten or didn't know about one of the recent warm temperature firings that also had a problem [...] And so it began, to my way of thinking, to really weaken our conclusions and recommendations. And I was already wishy-washy. And that one [chart] really hit me home when I began to think, gosh, you haven't really thought this out as thoroughly as you should have. (Thiokol's Bill Macbeth)

The analysis suggests that NASA's safety structure trumped sense-making capacities. NASA culture had no room for arguments that violate basic engineering logic. It could not handle 'feelings' or 'doubts' that were not supported by hard data. This was the entrenched norm that everybody in NASA knew and abided by – this was the way it had been done during the *Apollo* years.

In hindsight, it is easy to argue – as the Rogers commission did – that the doubts of respected engineers should suffice to snuff out the problem, to experiment and test, until safety can be proven. During the *Apollo* years, however, NASA had learned that this does not work with engineers: they will tinker, test and experiment forever (for they know that they can never prove the safety of an experimental space craft). The system in place had served NASA well: no astronauts had been lost in space until the *Challenger* explosion.

The *Columbia* disaster revisited

This tension between structure and sense-making played a crucial role in the demise of shuttle *Columbia*. The foam-caused damage to *Columbia* was not discovered until day 2 of the trip after the Intercenter Photo Working Group studied the film of the launch. The Photo Group formed a Debris Assessment Team (DAT), which was to consider whether the damage would pose a safety issue. Moreover, the photo material showing the foam hit was widely disseminated throughout NASA and its contractors by email. Both the media and the astronauts on board of *Columbia* knew of the problem.

Initial assessments did not provide any cause for alarm and 'may have contributed to mindset that [the foam hit] was not a concern' (CAIB, 2003: 141). Mission Control was under the impression that the foam strike fell within the experience base and waited for additional information to emerge from the DAT (CAIB, 2003: 146). This impression was confirmed by an email of Calvin Schomburg – whom Shuttle programme managers considered an expert on the matter – stating that the hit 'should not be a problem' (CAIB, 2003: 149). Boeing used a software tool ('Crater') to assess potential damage. The analysis did not give rise to concern.[10]

On Day 9 of the flight, the DAT presented its findings to a representative of Mission Control. The DAT engineers 'ultimately concluded that their analysis, limited as it was, did not show that a safety-of-flight issue existed' (CAIB, 2003: 160). As a senior engineer wrote to his colleagues 2 days later: 'I believe we left [the shuttle manager] with the impression that engineering assessments and cases were all finished and we could state with finality no safety-of-flight issues or questions remaining' (CAIB, 2003: 163). The CAIB pointed out that many uncertainties were noted in this presentation, but, as we have seen above, NASA culture did not allow for 'feelings' and 'observations'.

The many empirical accounts of NASA's culture all emphasize a deep commitment to the safety of astronauts. The process to detect emerging problems is transparent, smart and solidly based on engineering knowledge. In the months and weeks leading up to both shuttle disasters, this process played out in a neat and orderly fashion. Clearly, NASA had a safety structure in place that resembled the building blocks of an HRO.

A critical problem was NASA's inability to deviate from entrenched safety processes, which prevented an accurate assessment of the impending threats to the safety of the doomed shuttles. In addition, once the threat to *Columbia* was recognized, it proved hard to improvise or design a 'work around'. Intriguingly, it appears that NASA was hemmed in by the very processes and structures that had long been considered pillars of a vaunted safety culture.

DISCUSSION: RETHINKING RESILIENCE

This article explores the organizational antecedents of *precursor resilience*: the capacity to absorb an emerging crisis while maintaining a high level of performance. Other forms of resilience – notably *recovery resilience* – will likely require different strategies, structures and practices (and a different research agenda).[11]

We revisited two organizations that tried to be – indeed had to be – resilient. It is, of course, impossible to deduce any sort of generalized relation between organizational processes and resilience based on two case studies. Moreover, the cases differed with regard to the types of hazard they faced; the meaning and consequences of organizational failure; the character of political-administrative oversight and the organizational processes that are initiated in the face of impending crises. In revisiting CAISO and NASA, we were particularly interested in the differing organizational responses.

The case comparison brought us at least one intriguing insight: adherence to well structured safety processes is not sufficient for precursor resilience. The seemingly chaotic processes of decentralized improvisation and sense-making play an important role. This can produce internal tensions, as principles of crisis management (such as improvisation) do not always sit well with principles of HROs (as espoused in the 'high reliability' literature).

Both reliability and crisis management impose very different demands on an organization. Reliability must be exhibited continuously. Organizational structures and processes must be designed to facilitate it. Crisis management is typically used quite rarely (bringing the proverbial 'last 5%') and requires different types of training, preparation, facilitation and perhaps leadership. An organization that wants to be resilient must traverse simplistic distinctions between 'anticipation' and 'trial-and-error learning'. It must somehow create a highly structured environment in which various response modes can coexist (cf. Moynihan, 2012). We stand only at the beginning of the research that may tell us how that can be done.

The case studies bring to the fore several questions that may guide that research. For instance, we should study whether different forms of resilience require different skills, structures or processes. Another question, largely ignored in this article, pertains to the type of external relations that may facilitate or inhibit organizational resilience.

Future research should also consider the price of resilience. The literature on resilient organizations sketches an overwhelmingly positive image of resilience and rarely includes any discussion of the *costs* of resilience. This is awkward, to say the least, as resilience is often described in terms of redundancy and slack. But redundancy, as Schulman (1993: 353) reminds us, 'reeks of inefficiency' and usually comes at a cost.

Resilience will likely become increasingly important in the face of new threats. If we could design organizations to absorb small disturbances and shocks, surely the world would be a safer place. Recipes for resilience, however, are built on a rather weak empirical and theoretical basis. This article suggests that we should be careful to prescribe resilience before we develop a stronger grasp on the relation between organizational characteristics, processes and outcomes. Much more research is needed before prescriptions for resilience can be administered.

ACKNOWLEDGEMENT

We thank our reviewers who provided us with probing comments that helped us improve this article.

NOTES

1 For an extensive literature overview, see De Bruijne *et al.* (2010).
2 'Load' is the demand for electricity and 'generation' is the electricity to meet that load, both of which must be balanced within mandated periods of time, or otherwise service delivery is interrupted as the grid fails.
3 See Mensah-Bonsu and Oren (2001) for a detailed analysis of the causes of this crisis.
4 In thirty-eight instances, CAISO operated with 1.5 per cent or less operating reserves. The regulatory standard was to have at least 7 per cent.
5 Within the organization, the crisis exerted a price on the part of the operators in terms of burnouts and divorce, according to Jim McIntosh, then the CAISO's director of grid operations. CAISO later faced a court case because of the excessive overtime demands that its employees had been subjected to during that period.

6 An O-ring is a commonly used seal in machine design. In the shuttle, O-rings were used to prevent gases from escaping from the Solid Rocket Booster.

7 A few selected sources include Murray and Cox (1989), Vaughan (1996) and Logsdon (1999).

8 In the words of one famous NASA character ('Mad' Don Arabian): 'If anybody does anything technically that's not according to physics, that's bullshitting about something, I will forever be death upon them' (Murray and Cox, 1989: 361).

9 Ironically, Thiokol engineers complained about the overly conservative design mentality of the involved engineers. As one Thiokol engineer explained his objections against the continuous prodding of NASA: 'You take the worst, worst, worst, worst, worst case and that's what you have to design for. And that's not practical [...] All those worsts were put together, and [Marshall] said you've got to design so that you can withstand all of that [...] and you just can't do that or else you couldn't put the part together' (Vaughan, 1996: 99).

10 The CAIB discovered that the CRATER software was, in effect, not designed to perform this type of analysis nor were the Boeing engineers performing the analysis sufficiently qualified.

11 For instance, a focus on recovery resilience might well benefit from a study of emergency management structures in the US such as the Incident Command System (ICS) and the National Incident Management System (NIMS), which appear much less relevant for our study of precursor resilience (see also Boin, 2010).

REFERENCES

Boin, A. (2010) 'Designing Resilience: Leadership Challenges in Complex Administrative Systems' in L. K. Comfort, A. Boin and C. Demchak (eds) *Designing Resilience: Preparing for Extreme Events* 129–141, Pittsburgh, PA: Pittsburgh University Press.

Boin, A. and Schulman, P. (2008) Assessing NASA's Safety Culture: The Limits and Possibilities of High-Reliability Theory. *Public Administration Review*, 68:6 pp1050–62.

Boin, A., 't Hart, P., Stern, E. and Sundelius, B. (2005) *The Politics of Crisis Management: Public Leadership Under Pressure*, Cambridge: Cambridge University Press.

Bourrier, M. (2011) The Legacy of the High Reliability Organization Project. *Journal of Contingencies and Crisis Management*, 19:1 pp9–13.

Cascio, J. (2009) The Next Big Thing: Resilience. *Foreign Policy*, 8:3 May/June.

Christianson, M. K., Farkas, M. T., Sutcliffe, K. M. and Weick, K. E. (2009) Learning Through Rare Events: Significant Interruptions at the Baltimore & Ohio Railroad Museum. *Organization Science*, 20:5 pp846–60.

Clarke, L. (1999) *Mission Improbable: Using Fantasy Documents to Tame Disaster*, Chicago, IL: University of Chicago Press.

Columbia Accident Investigation Board (CAIB) (2003) *Columbia Accident Investigation Report*, Burlington, ON: Apogee Books.

Comfort, L. K., Boin, R. A. and Demchak, C. (eds) (2010) *Designing Resilience: Preparing for Extreme Events*, Pittsburgh, PA: Pittsburgh University Press.

De Bruijne, M., Boin, R. A. and van Eeten, M. (2010) 'Resilience: Exploring the Concept and Its Meanings' in L. K. Comfort, A. Boin and C. C. Demchak (eds) *Designing Resilience: Preparing for Extreme Events* 13–32, Pittsburgh, PA: University of Pittsburgh Press.

Drennan, L. and McConnell, A. (2007) *Risk and Crisis Management in the Public Sector*, Abingdon: Routledge.

Dunbar, R. and Garud, R. (2005) 'Data Indeterminacy: One NASA, Two Modes' in W. H. Starbuck and M. Farjoun (eds) *Organization at the Limit: Lessons From the Columbia Accident* 202–19, Malden, MA: Blackwell.

Flynn, S. E. (2008) America the Resilient: Defying Terrorism and Mitigating Natural Disasters. *Foreign Affairs*, 87:2 pp2–8.

Foster, H. (1993) 'Resilience Theory and System Evaluation' in J. A. Wise, V. D. Hopkin and P. Stager (eds) *Verification and Validation of Complex Systems: Human Factor Issues* 35–60, NATO Advanced Science Institutes, Series F: Computer and Systems Sciences, Vol. 110, New York: Springer.

Hamel, G. and Välikangas, L. (2003) The Quest for Resilience. *Harvard Business Review*, 81:9 pp52–63.

Hollnagel, E., Woods, D. D. and Leveson, N. (eds) (2006) *Resilience Engineering – Concepts and Precepts*, London: Ashgate Publishing.

Johnson, S. B. (2002) *The Secret of Apollo: Systems Management in American and European Space Programs*, Baltimore, MD: Johns Hopkins University Press.

Kendra, J. and Wachtendorf, T. (2003) Elements of Resilience After the World Trade Center Disaster: Reconstituting New York City's Emergency Operations Center. *Disasters*, 27:1 pp37–53.

LaPorte, T. R. (1996) Unlikely, Demanding and at Risk. *Journal of Contingencies and Crisis Management*, 4:2 pp60–71.

LaPorte, T. R. and Consolini, P. M. (1991) Working in Practice but Not in Theory: Theoretical Challenges of 'High-Reliability Organizations.' *Journal of Public Administration Research and Theory*, 1:1 pp19–48.

Logsdon, J. M. (ed.).1999. *Managing the Moon Program: Lessons Learned from Project Apollo*. Monographs in Aerospace History 14, Washington, DC: National Aeronautics and Space Administration.

Mensah-Bonsu, C. and Oren, S. (2001) *California Electricity Market Crisis: Causes, Remedies and Prevention*, Folsom, CA: CAISO.

Moynihan, D. P. (2012) A Theory of Culture-Switching: Leadership and Red Tape During Hurricane Katrina. *Public Administration*, 90:4 pp851–68.

Murray, C. and Cox, C. B. (1989) *Apollo: The Race to the Moon*, New York: Simon & Schuster.

Presidential Commission on the Space Shuttle Challenger Accident. (1986) *Report to the President by the Presidential Commission on the Space Shuttle Challenger Accident*. Washington, DC: Government Printing Office.

Roberts, K. H. (ed.) (1993) *New Challenges to Understanding Organizations*, New York: Macmillan.

Rochlin, G. I. (1996) Reliable Organizations: Present Research and Future Directions. *Journal of Contingencies and Crisis Management*, 4:2 pp55–9.

Rochlin, G. I. (2011) How to Hunt a Very Reliable Organization. *Journal of Contingencies and Crisis Management*, 19:1 pp14–20.

Roe, E. M. and Schulman, P. (2008) *High Reliability Management: Operating on the Edge*, Stanford, CA: Stanford Business Books.

Roe, E. M., Schulman, P., van Eeten, M. J. G. and de Bruijne, M. L. C. (2003) *Real-Time Reliability: Provision of Electricity Under Adverse Performance Conditions Arising from California's Electricity Restructuring and Crisis*, A Report Prepared for the California Energy Commission, Lawrence Berkeley National Laboratory, and the Electrical Power Research Institute, San Francisco, CA: Energy Commission.

Schulman, P. (1993) The Negotiated Order of Organizational Reliability. *Administration & Society*, 25:353 p372.

Sheffi, Y. (2005) *The Resilient Enterprise: Overcoming Vulnerability for Competitive Advantage*, Cambridge, MA: The MIT Press.

Sullivan-Taylor, B. and Wilson, D. C. (2009) Managing the Threat of Terrorism in British Travel and Leisure Organizations. *Organization Studies*, 30:2–3 pp251–76.

Sutcliffe, K. M. and Vogus, T. J. (2003) 'Organizing for Resilience' in K. S. Cameron, J. E. Dutton and R. E. Quinn (eds) *Positive Organizational Scholarship* 94–110, San Francisco, CA: Berrett-Koehler Publishers.

Vale, L. J. and Campanella, T. J. (2005) *The Resilient City: How Modern Cities Recover From Disaster*, Oxford: Oxford University Press.

Välikangas, L. (2010) *The Resilient Organization: How Adaptive Cultures Thrive Even When Strategy Fails*, New York: McGraw-Hill.

Vaughan, D. (1996) *The Challenger Launch Decision: Risky Technology, Culture and Deviance at NASA*, Chicago: University of Chicago Press.

Weick, K. E. and Sutcliffe, K. M. (2001) *Managing the Unexpected*, San Francisco, CA: Jossey Bass.

Wildavsky, A. (1988) *Searching for Safety*, New Brunswick, NJ: Transaction Books.

Woods, D. D. and Hollnagel, E. (2006) *Joint Cognitive Systems: Patterns in Cognitive Systems Engineering*, Boca Raton, FL: Taylor and Francis.

Abstract

An increasing number of disasters are generating consequences that extend beyond political boundaries. This article provides an economic framework for designing transboundary emergency management institutions and policies to address these transboundary crises. It emphasizes the importance of economic considerations in two ways. First, we disaggregate economic losses into direct and indirect components, which vary in terms of their transboundary potential. Second, we apply economic principles such as scale economies, externalities and public goods in analysing European cooperation in emergency management. The article concludes by identifying the type of consequences that might best be addressed by a wider geographic and political authority.

ECONOMIC CONSIDERATIONS IN DESIGNING EMERGENCY MANAGEMENT INSTITUTIONS AND POLICIES FOR TRANSBOUNDARY DISASTERS

Adam Rose and Tyler Kustra

Adam Rose
Center for Risk and Economic Analysis of Terrorism
Events
Price School of Public Policy
University of Southern California
Los Angeles, CA
USA

Tyler Kustra
Wilf Family Department of Politics
New York University
New York, NY
USA

140

INTRODUCTION

The number of disasters that have transboundary consequences appears to be on the rise. These disasters stem from increasingly powerful natural forces (Icelandic volcanic ash and the 2004 Asian tsunami), expanded use of imperfect technology (Chernobyl and the nuclear reactor failure following the recent Japanese Tsunami) and the increased interdependence of the world economy (mad cow disease and Severe Acute Respiratory Syndrome).

The economic consequences of transboundary disasters consist of several different but interconnected types of direct and indirect impacts. One example is the estimate that the largest single component of the business interruption (BI) losses associated with 9/11 attack was the nearly 2-year reduction in world airline travel and related tourism because of a 'fear factor' (Rose et al., 2009). Another one is the set of impacts stemming from the geographically far-reaching radiological contamination caused by the Chernobyl explosion.

The contribution of this article is to present an economic framework for designing emergency management institutions and policies to address transboundary disasters. Transboundary crises can be defined in terms of three dimensions: (1) cross-political, (2) cross-functional (with respect to systems) and (3) time scales (Ansell et al., 2010). In this article, we focus primarily on the political dimension. We begin by identifying the several categories of economic consequences from disasters and illustrate their relative size for a range of disasters. We subsequently specify which of the categories are most likely to transcend political boundaries, thereby providing a finer delineation of the potential benefits of the development of appropriate emergency management institutions and policies.

We present a set of economic principles that are especially well suited in providing a basis for cross-jurisdictional cooperation. This includes a discussion of how desirable policy and institutional design are affected by economies of scale, externalities and public goods, so as to better match policies with needs. The framework is illustrated by applying it to a terrorist attack using chlorine gas and to cooperative emergency management, with a special emphasis on the European Union.

ECONOMIC CONSEQUENCE ANALYSIS

The measurement of economic consequences of disasters is a critical input into policy decisions. The avoidance of various categories of direct and indirect economic impacts, multiplied by their probability of occurrence, represents the benefits of risk reduction. Moreover, the implementation of these policies also has direct and indirect economic costs that should be considered.

A broad conceptual framework for estimating economic consequences of terrorist attacks and natural disasters has recently been formulated to take all of these factors into consideration and is depicted in Figure 1 (Rose, 2009a). The methodology provides insight into how the various factors interact and indicate the breadth and some of the details of

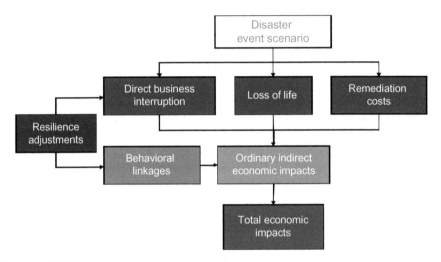

Figure 1: CREATE consequence analysis framework

economic consequence analysis. These distinctions also provide input for designing emergency response policies and creating institutions, including transboundary ones.

Until recently, economic consequence analysis focused almost entirely on standard target-specific effects in the form of ordinary economic impacts, such as direct BI and casualties. They also included ordinary indirect effects, referred to as multiplier, general equilibrium or macroeconomic impacts. The major expansions of the framework are the addition of resilience and extended linkages, which greatly affect economic consequences. Resilience adjustments refer to actions that mute the initial shock and that hasten recovery. Resilience can be quite effective in standard cases, potentially reducing losses by as much as 90 per cent (Rose *et al.*, 2007, 2009). They have the effect of lowering direct BI, a major category of target-specific economic impacts. Extended linkages refer to extreme behavioural reactions (such as fear of going to work or shopping in a high-risk area) or cascading system failures (mainly through interdependent infrastructure). They have the effect of significantly increasing the impacts.

Behavioural linkages can increase direct losses by more than an order of magnitude (Giesecke *et al.*, 2012). Direct remediation costs should be inserted into the analysis at an early stage, in part, because they, along with the two more standard features, are subject to indirect effects. The sum of all these positive and negative components yields a thorough bottom-line estimate of total economic consequences.

Actual estimation of the full slate of consequences is difficult. The problem is complicated by the fact that not only do a broad range of impacts need to be evaluated but, in a full risk analysis, the consequence estimation should be done for a probability distribution of magnitudes and likelihood of success of a given threat, meaning that an extensive array of consequence analyses may need to be performed.

Table 1: Summary of economic consequences of bioterrorism attacks (gross output losses, in billions of 2007 dollars)

Type of attack	Loss of life	Ordinary business interruption (BI)	Behavioural linkage	Resilience	Total gross output[a]
Stadium	−57.2	−0.5	−16.2	8.5	−65.4
Urban centre	−2.2	−8.2	Not measured	4.4	−6.0
Airport	−1.0	<$100 million	−220.0[b]	119.5[c]	−1,011.5
Lettuce	−0.054	−0.024[d]	Not measured	d	−0.078
Foot & mouth	<$100 million	−46.2	Not measured	4.2	−42.0
Water service	Not measured	−27.3	−2.6	26.7	−3.2

Source: Lee *et al.* (2008); Rose (2008).

Notes: [a]Total does not include stimulus from remediation.

[b]Adjusted for background economic conditions.

[c]Recent estimate added to the analysis.

[d]Resilience (via substitution of other vegetables for lettuce) is considered to offset domestic consumption loss, such that ordinary BI estimates represent only the decrease in export sales.

Table 1 presents the results of simulations for six different targets of potential bio-terrorist attacks (Lee *et al.*, 2008; Rose, 2008). The table illustrates the wide variability in the values of the various types of economic consequences within and across cases. Similar sizeable variations are likely to hold across attack modes (such as ordinary bomb blast and radiological or chemical attacks).

While the component estimates in Table 1 may at first appear random, some patterns do emerge. Several of the causes of variation are technical in nature, but several others are highly dependent on public policy and private sector decisions before and after an attack. The explanations can be summarized in the following categories:

- Lethalness of the biological agent
- Concentration of people and their ability to escape
- Vulnerability/security of the target
- Duration of the event
- Fear of replication on this or related targets
- Perceived ability to mitigate future attacks
- Extent of resilience.

CONSEQUENCES OF A TERRORIST ATTACK: AN ILLUSTRATION

An example of the diverse consequences of a terrorist attack can prove useful. Consider chlorine bomb attack at an industrial site (Giesecke *et al.*, 2010). The aggregate impact estimate is an indication of the potential severity of the event. However, it is the decomposition of the estimates in relation to the causal factors that will be useful in fine-tuning the appropriate planning and policy response.

Let us assume that such an incident takes place in a large city on the border between two countries. The gas plume from the event would extend into the neighbouring countries and kill or injure many people on the spot. The general lack of experience with such terrorist agents and the high levels of uncertainty surrounding the event's impact and control are likely to generate significant amounts of fear. Researchers have divided these into two major time-related categories. In the short run, media attention and rumours lead to a social amplification of risk that exacerbates fear (Kasperson et al., 1988). In the long run, the area is likely to suffer from a stigma effect (Slovic, 2004). Altered risk perceptions manifest themselves into behavioural changes, which can have severe economic consequences (Burns et al., 2010).

The translation of these effects into losses stems from reactions of individuals, such as requiring higher pay for workers and higher rates of returns for investors in the affected area, as well as requiring discounts for shoppers and tourists to frequent restaurants and purchase goods and other services in the area. This increased cost of doing business leads to direct price increases, which rob residents of their purchasing power, while also reducing demand for products in the area. Further problems arise from property owners walking away from their mortgages. This can lead to a real estate meltdown. A downward spiral can then ensue creating a situation of mass exodus. For the chlorine attack scenario, Giesecke et al. (2010) found that BI losses could exceed normal direct and indirect resource loss by almost three-fold (see Table 2).

ECONOMIC PRINCIPLES AND TRANSBOUNDARY SOLUTIONS

Several major economic principles are pertinent to the formulation of appropriate policies and institutions to address transboundary consequences of disasters. The effect

Table 2: Summary of economic consequences of the industrial site chlorine attack

Economic consequence category	Loss/ratio (in millions of 2008 dollars)
Total short-term (S-T) resource loss	67.5
Total S-T behavioural loss	62.8
Total S-T loss	130.3
Total medium-term (M-T) behavioural loss[a]	119.8
Total behavioural loss	182.6
S-T behavioural/S-T resource	0.93
M-T behavioural[a]/S-T resource	1.77
Total behavioural[a]/S-T resource	2.71

Note: [a]Discounted at 5 per cent.

of each of the principles discussed below depends, to a great extent, on how disaster costs are distributed across jurisdictions. The framework presented above can help to estimate these costs.

Economies of scale are an obvious consideration. Large facilities and operations can significantly reduce the costs of many activities, in part by reducing unnecessary duplication. At the same time, policy-makers must weigh the trade-off between cost savings from typically centralized operations as opposed to smaller decentralized ones. Centralized emergency management operations may become prime targets and therefore render systems more vulnerable. In addition, decentralized responses are likely to be the norm in resilient actions taken by industrial and household consumers (e.g. use of stockpiles, conservation, use of back-up electricity generators).

A related consideration is the reduction in transactions costs, which is often attained through mergers or consolidation in general. Governments often reduce disaster response costs by sharing rarely used equipment and resources. Mutual assistance agreements presume that disaster probabilities are uncorrelated. So, when one jurisdiction requires the material, its neighbours almost certainly would not. Transboundary disasters, however, affect multiple jurisdictions at once, and thus cause a surge in demand, meaning that governments that would have been willing to lend unused material to their neighbours may find that they need it themselves. As a result, mutual assistance agreements may not be entered into as readily and may lose some of their effectiveness.

In addition, many aspects of emergency management have public goods characteristics (i.e. they can be shared by many entities and without exclusion). This is an advantage in the dissemination of their services because this means that there is no additional marginal cost of service provision to additional users. At the same time, this poses a problem where some countries may not readily agree to cooperative efforts, hoping that other countries will provide the services. The reluctant countries will then be able to partake of these services as 'free-riders'. Examples include flood control projects and treating victims of an epidemic. The solution here is to improve cooperation among countries in equitably sharing the cost of disaster management.

Yet another consideration is that of externalities or spillover effects. This is, in fact, the essence of a transboundary problem, as some mitigation/interdiction/recovery costs, as well as consequences, cross country boundaries. On the pre-disaster side, many of the expenditures on disaster management can result in positive transboundary multiplier effects. Additionally, consequences can ripple extensively on a geographic basis (Galaz et al., 2011; Van Eeten et al., 2011). Prime examples include ordinary BI om flooding, earthquakes and many of the behavioural effects of terrorist attacks. An attack on an airport or airliner in one country is likely to instil especially heightened fear in others. Here, the solution involves 'internalizing' externalities by expanding the cooperation among countries likely to be affected.

EUROPEAN UNION COOPERATION IN THE FACE OF DISASTER

The European Union (EU) was designed to realize the benefits of European integration by reducing transaction costs and promoting gains from trade. Its powers now include areas that have direct and indirect impacts on the prevention of, and response to, natural disasters and terrorism. The EU claims a supporting competence in coordinating disaster relief, allowing member states to make use of these services if they choose so.

Disasters are rare events and pooling resources across multiple jurisdictions result in amortizing their costs over more deployments reducing their per-unit cost. But with twenty-seven member states in the EU, coordinating offers of and requests for assistance can place a great strain on governments already struggling to cope with devastation. Established in 2001, the EU's Monitoring and Information Centre acts as a clearing house for offers of assistance from thirty European nations to European and non-European countries facing disasters (European Commission on Humanitarian Aid and Civil Protection, 2011). The Centre quickly proved valuable. In the summer of 2002, heavy rains inundated the Czech Republic. A total of 220,000 people were forced to evacuate as 40 per cent of Czech land was affected by flooding. The Czech government contacted the Centre to request floating and submersible pumps as well as portable dryers. By coordinating the actions of dozens of EU members the Centre was able to reduce the cost of emergency response. In so far as efficient emergency response can lower ordinary direct impacts and causalities, the Centre helps to reduce these costs as well. Nonetheless, some governments chose to circumvent the Centre and deal with the Czech officials directly. The German government, concerned that the flood waters would soon flow downhill into its territory, stayed in direct contact with Czech authorities, demonstrating the difficulties national governments have in ceding power to supranational bodies when their own citizens are under threat (Ekengren et al., 2006).

While European integration has brought numerous economic and social benefits, it has also allowed criminals and terrorists to spillover from one country to another. The EU created Europol to facilitate inter-European cooperation on police matters, such as intelligence sharing. In theory, intelligence should be a public good because it is non-rivalrous in consumption. EU countries, therefore, should be willing to share it with their fellow members. The EU initially allowed its members to decide which information to share, on the understanding that the countries that generated the intelligence would be in the best position to decide whether other countries would find it valuable. While this rule was not designed to allow countries to hoard their most valuable intelligence, it quickly had this effect (Bures, 2006).

The Schengen Agreement was designed to make European travel easier by eliminating border controls between signatory states. While the agreement was successful allowing tourists and business travellers to journey throughout most of Europe without passports, it also allowed fugitives to flee across the continent. Once arrested, suspects had the right to fight extradition, resulting in costly and time-consuming judicial proceedings. To address this concern, the EU now has a European Arrest Warrant, which compels member states to extradite suspects within 90 days. Reaching an agreement on the warrant was time-consuming, however. The treaty creating the warrant was not finalized until 2001 and member states did not finish altering their legislation to permit the warrants until 2005 (Bures, 2006).

Even in areas where the EU's jurisdiction is clear and the danger is immediate, members have attempted to block and succeeded in stalling EU actions to protect the common good when these actions threatened national interests. After the British government announced that beef from cows infected with Bovine Spongiform Encephalitis (BSE, or colloquially 'mad cow' disease) could lead to Creutzfeldt–Jakob disease in humans, the EU instituted a ban on British beef exports. The UK government ceased cooperating with the EU in retaliation for the embargo. Understanding the importance of British cooperation in handling the crisis and the difficulties in forcing them to comply the EU agreed to relax restrictions on low-risk exports. In return, the British agreed to resume cooperating with the EU response, thereby showing that, while the EU may have the authority to undertake actions, the cost of enforcing this authority on a recalcitrant member is often prohibitive (Lezaun and Groenleer, 2006).

MODIFYING EUROPEAN COOPERATION TO ACHIEVE EFFICIENCY

There are two organizational forms within which individuals may interact to produce goods: firms and markets (Coase, 1937). Markets may be divided into ones where a Leviathan enforces contracts and ones that operates under anarchy (Dixit, 2004). Firms address spillover effects through centralized management that takes into account the effect of one unit's actions on the other parts of the organization. Markets address spillover effects through side-payments between the affected parties. The organizational structure that minimizes the production and transaction costs is considered efficient.

Making the EU directly responsible for disaster response would be analogous to using a firm structure (although with some key differences discussed shortly). International agreements enforced by the EU would be the equivalent of a market structure with government enforcement, while international agreements without EU or other third-party enforcement would be similar to market transactions under anarchy.

Placing the EU in control of disaster response could, in theory, be the most efficient way to respond to transboundary disasters within the Union. It could result in significant economies of scale and allow the Union to take a holistic view of its actions. Sandler and Siqueira (2006) note that a significant portion of anti-terrorism spending is for measures that do not decrease the number of attacks or the damage done, but merely cause terrorists to shift from one target to another. This spending is individually rational but socially wasteful. Unilateral reductions would be politically difficult to achieve, while a coordinated decrease would be not be possible because the benefits of defecting from the agreement would be too high. For instance, if anti-terrorism policy became the responsibility of the EU, it would have the incentive to take into account the externality created by deterrence measures.

A federation may not act in the best interests of all its members, crafting its policies to appeal to the politically powerful at the expense of efficiency. Researchers have found evidence of this problem with American disaster assistance spending. An American president is more likely to declare a flood a natural disaster, making the affected state eligible for federal aid, in years when he is running for re-election (Downton and Pielke, 2001). Battleground states receive twice as many disaster declarations as uncompetitive ones (Reeves, 2011).

Placing the EU in charge of disaster response would raise significant sovereignty concerns (Bossong, 2008). The EU is reticent to force its members to comply with its directives in the areas it is already the supreme authority, even when non-compliance may prove devastating. The Europol and mad-cow examples mentioned above are two examples. Another one is the European currency union. Under the Maastricht Treaty, countries that wish to use the Euro must have deficits lower than 3 per cent of GDP and a debt to GDP ratio of less than 60 per cent, so that they will not have an incentive to default on their debt. These requirements were widely disregarded for over a decade resulting in the European financial crisis of 2011–12.

If, on the other hand, the EU shared responsibility for disaster response with its members, this could lead to a moral hazard problem, where its members put themselves at undue risk because they will not bear the full consequences of their actions. This has been the case in other parts of the world, such as the United States, where local governments have used federal funds to promote post-disaster reconstruction on sites that are likely to fall victim to catastrophe again (Daniels et al., 2006).

According to the Coase theorem, externalities can be eliminated and efficiency achieved if individuals are able to bargain with one another using complete information and transaction costs (the costs of making and enforcing contracts) are negligible (Coase, 1960). For instance, a country could negotiate with its neighbours to provide assistance in its time of need, share information or abate a problematic spillover. These agreements could be enforced by a third party, an international organization like the EU, or their fulfilment could rest on the goodwill of the contractors.

Many disaster response policies rely on such agreements. Starting in 1949, the United States government began monitoring the Pacific Ocean for tsunamis. The Soviet Union and Japanese government soon followed suit. Recognizing that accuracy could be improved and costs reduced through cooperation, they, along with twenty other Pacific countries, formed the Pacific Tsunami Warning System in 1965 to share seismographic measurements and alert each other to possible tsunamis. The warning and evacuation orders generated by this arrangement have decreased tsunami deaths by 15.3 per cent since the system was put in place (Escaleras and Register, 2008).

Electric utilities in North America use mutual assistance agreements to provide one another with additional line crews during emergencies. These agreements have proved useful in many instances, including when the Red River, which follows north along the North Dakota/Minnesota state border, experienced a 100-year flood in April 1997. At the same time, an ice storm had knocked out electricity to 50,000 homes and businesses in the two states. These structures were protected with emergency dikes and relied on electric pumps to bail out any water that managed to seep in. However, without electricity, the pumps were useless, and Minnkota Power (the local electric utility) did not have enough line crews to restore power before the buildings were flooded. Manitoba Hydro loaned Minnkota Power over 100 employees to help to quickly restore power, thereby preventing billions of dollars of flood damage (Wachtendorf, 2000).

In these cases, however, all parties had incentives to keep to their agreements. With the Tsunami Warning System, cooperation was possible in large part because the information gathered was non-rivalous: its use by one nation did not diminish its value to others. Manitoba Hydro also had significant incentives to help Minnkota Power. The American utility purchases electricity from Manitoba Hydro and resells it to its customers, and under its mutual aid agreement with Manitoba Hydro it pays Hydro for the use of Manitoban line crews.

When the costs to their own interests are small, EU members are quite willing to cooperate. For instance, member states not directly affected by the Czech floods were willing to contribute and coordinate through the Monitoring and Information Centre. But when the costs are, or could be, substantial, such as with Germany during the Czech flood, members may put their self-interests first. EU members often make bold pledges of mutual cooperation only to retreat from them at the first sign they may entail costs as well as benefits (Boin and Rhinard, 2008). This behaviour extends to EU security and defence spending. As the costs of contributing to a mission decrease, smaller EU states are more likely to contribute to it and argue that, in return, they should not have to contribute to more costly activities (Dorussen et al., 2009).

Increasing sanctions for opportunistic behaviour could be effective (Dixit, 2004). However, the EU is loath to impose punishments. Dixit suggests that individuals shun those who have behaved opportunistically in the past, but his model focuses on medieval fairs, where dissatisfied customers could choose to do business with different merchants in the future. While European nations could attempt to extract additional concessions in future negotiations from countries that have behaved opportunistically in the past, it would be quite difficult and expensive for one EU member to shun another. The following sections of this article provide critical first steps in this direction. The analytical framework presented at the outset of this article for estimating the location and magnitude of disaster impacts can be used to understand which countries will bear what costs. The economic principles outlined in the previous two sections can then help to understand how countries will attempt to shift these costs onto others, either through strategically crafting international agreements or by refusing to honour agreements.

ALLOCATING EMERGENCY RESPONSIBILITES

We now turn to post-event emergency management and recovery operations. Losses that can be reduced by these actions include BI, economic productivity losses due to death and injury, costs of medical care and losses from behavioural overreactions. The examples below pertain primarily to the chlorine attack case discussed above but many of them are more generally applicable.

For many years, the focus of disaster management was mitigating against property damage and loss of life. There is growing awareness that BI losses can rival those of property damage (Rose and Blomberg, 2010). In contrast to property damage, which takes place during the event, BI just begins at that point and continues until some recovery target is achieved. The comparison of resource loss and behavioural loss effects offers yet another perspective. Our analysis divides the losses into the eight components listed in the first column of Table 3. In the third column, next to each loss type is a loss reduction action (either emergency response or recovery). The fourth column presents an assessment of the cooperation that might be warranted.

The second column provides a qualitative assessment of the potential for each consequence component to have transboundary effects. Terrorist attacks like the chlorine event are likely to be localized; a gas plume, however, broadens the potential of the direct BI, hence the 'low/medium' (L/M) designation of transboundary potential. Most natural disasters cause direct property damage within country borders; floods are a major exception, as many rivers serve as country boundaries. The 'direct impact on the surrounding area' is primarily related to a buffer or safety zone that might be designated in advance of an event for the purpose of evacuation. This zone will extend beyond the 'target' area, so it has also been designated to have low/medium potential. Indirect BI primarily refers to 'multiplier' or general equilibrium effects that readily transcend country boundaries through commodity trade, hence the 'high' designation. Deaths and injuries are designated as 'L/M' likelihood for transboundary effects for reasons similar to the direct BI at the site. Medical expenditures are given a 'medium' designation because cases involving chemical, biological or radiological attacks or accidents are also likely to involve a buffer/safety zone.

The behavioural effects relate to costs stemming from fear. Workers are likely to require a premium to return to an area that has been struck by disaster out of concern over repeat events or the safety of the site (e.g. lingering chemical contamination or structural instability of buildings). However, the workforce will typically come from

Table 3: Linking loss reduction actions to economic impact components

Economic consequence component	Transboundary potential	Example loss reduction action	Interjurisdictional cooperation
Resource loss effects			
Direct BI at site of attack	Low	Prompt and effective decontamination	Attacked country with mutual aid
Direct impact on surrounding area	L/M	Careful delineation of evacuation area	Attacked country with mutual aid
Indirect BI	High	Information clearinghouse for chlorine supplies	Many countries potentially affected
Deaths	L/M	Rapid emergency management response	Attacked country with mutual aid
Injuries	L/M	Effective critical care facilities	Attacked country with mutual aid
Medical expenditures	Medium	Effective use of medical resources	Many countries potentially affected
Behavioural effects			
Investor rate of return premium	M/H	Effective decontamination; risk communication	Attacked country; all affected
Wage rate premium	Medium	Effective medical screening; worker protection	All countries potentially affected
Customer price discounts	Medium	Effective decontamination; risk communication	Attacked country; all affected

roader geographic area than the disaster centre, hence a higher transboundary esignation. Moreover, the zone of fear is likely to include the buffer zone as well, rther moving the transboundary likelihood indicator up another half notch to 'medim'. Investors are likely to require a higher rate of return as well, but since investors e likely to come from an even much broader area, this component receives an even gher transboundary designation of 'medium/high' (M/H). Price discounts to attract oppers back to the affected area will also have negative economic consequences, but e considered to have the same geographic pool as the workforce. The exception ould be tourist destinations, which would command a higher score. Note also that the haviroural effects have multiplier effects of their own, which would have as wide-read effects as those associated with the direct BI listed in the first row of the table.

Key ways to reduce BI losses in this situation are to improve the effectiveness of contamination and to improve risk communication. Improved risk communication is ely to represent a rather small investment compared to the massive size of the losses.

In terms of transboundary considerations, risk communication has significant sensitivities to language and nuance. While a multi-lateral and cooperative approach among governments is to be considered, it must, at the same time, be fine-tuned to the needs of different populations including a diversity of ethnic, language and cultural groups within a city or region.

There are, of course, other complications that need to be addressed. One is the joint product benefits of several of the actions. For example, effective risk communication can reduce fear and thereby reduce the necessary wage and rate of return premia and customer discounts needed to attract people to the area. Synergies between the actions present another complication. For example, the reduction in injuries also reduces medical expenditures. More difficult to address is the issue of tradeoffs between actions. Death and injury can be prevented by evacuation, but, at the same time, evacuation increases BI. Moreover, unless the designated area is carefully selected it may lead to a stigma effect on a broader area than is necessary. Rapid decontamination will reduce BI in the short term, but scepticism of rapid clean-up may cause people to have doubts about its effectiveness, which leads to heightened fear and hence longer-term behavioural losses.

The various loss reduction actions take place in different time frames. This should make it easier than if they all had to be implemented simultaneously, and allows for learning and adaptation to the situation. Also, there is greater potential to make adjustments if the scenario unfolds slowly or if the emergency response period is lengthy. Of course, there is greater uncertainty regarding effectiveness with regard to those impacts that are further out in time. Also, the uncertainties related to stigma effects are much greater.

Many types of resilience are implicit in the analysis. Resilience refers to the ability to mute BI losses by using remaining resources more efficiently and recovering more rapidly (Rose et al., 2007; Rose, 2009b). Resilience extends beyond government actions to include the actions by businesses, households and other organizations. This can shift the burden of response and is potentially much more cost-effective. For example, as opposed to a major mitigation expense of a redundant system (e.g. parallel water line in case of emergency) or maintaining an expensive inventory (e.g. storing a spare electricity transformer), disruption of lifeline services can be more cost effectively addressed by customer conservation or substitution. Such actions can be empowering to the point where individual citizens can be major partners in reducing post-disaster losses (Flynn, 2008).

Finally, although we have not performed a formal cost-effective analysis, we can reasonably conjecture that one of the most cost-effective disaster response actions is risk communication (Casman and Fischhoff, 2008). Quelling fears does not necessarily require the massive costs of mitigation and reconstruction but has the potential reduce behavioural losses. Risk communication also has the potential to reduce fatalities and injuries through increased public understanding and compliance with emergency managers' orders for actions such as evacuation or sheltering-in-place (Sorensen *et al.*, 2004) or by educating the public on how to independently respond to chemical releases and other hazards without waiting for official orders after such incidents (Davis *et al.*, 2003). In the case of transboundary crises, it may behove emergency management officials in several countries to coordinate their communication efforts to put forth a consistent message, while at the same time accounting for cultural differences among the intended audiences.

Overall, all of the post-disaster loss reduction actions listed in the second column of Table 3 can be more effectively implemented by various types of cooperation among countries, while keeping in mind the desire of countries to shift costly responsibilities and outcomes onto their neighbours. More limited joint efforts are warranted in the case of direct effects, because these are concentrated in a smaller area than the other forms of losses. However, in the case of a transboundary crisis, all other seven types of losses warrant extensive cooperation for the various reasons pointed out earlier in this article. Indirect economic losses resulting from quantity multiplier effects or trade effects call for the largest geographic expanse of cooperation.

From an overall institutional perspective, extra effort must be made to deal with special characteristics of disaster mitigation and recovery. For example, individual governments are inclined only to take into account the benefits to their own country when regulating plant safety and deterring terrorism, leading to inefficient outcomes at the level of the broader community of nations. Similarly, improving risk communication in the wake of an attack is a public good and its non-rival nature means that it may be more efficient for a central transboundary agency to provide it. Government compensation and reconstruction efforts also have significant spillover effects onto neighbouring economies, meaning that they too may be under-provided.

CONCLUSION

This article represents an attempt at providing an economic framework for understanding the economic consequences of, and responses to, transboundary disasters. We explained some key economic principles that are operative in transboundary disaster management. We decomposed the consequences of disasters into various sub-categories for the express purpose of identifying those that are especially prone to transcend jurisdictional boundaries. This also provides a basis for estimating the relative magnitudes of various types of losses for the sake of prioritization of loss reduction actions. The article described major ways to reduce these consequences with an eye towards cooperative solutions among countries.

We conclude that transboundary problems are best addressed by transboundary solutions at different scales geared towards specific types of losses from disasters. Caveats are offered with respect to the need to account for cultural differences in such aspects as risk communication and warning. Also, cooperative efforts typically increase centralization, which may have some downsides in terms of increased vulnerabilities of emergency management centres and of the speed of response. In addition, ways need to be found to harness the decentralized nature of resilience of the general citizenry through individual motivation to contribute to recovery. This is a valuable, but often overlooked, complement to government efforts.

The article focuses on BI following a disaster in part because this is an oft-neglected area. We identify numerous opportunities to reduce the various types of BI losses through transboundary cooperation. By analysing economic interdependence and spatial connections, the article should be useful to businesses of any size and governments at all levels in seeking cooperative solutions to an ever-growing problem.

ACKNOWLEDGEMENT

The authors are grateful to the guest editors and two anonymous referees for their helpful comments. Any opinions and conclusion presented in this article are those of the authors and do not necessarily represent the views of the sponsor or the organization with which the authors are affiliated.

REFERENCES

Ansell, C., Boin, A. and Keller, A. (2010) Managing Transboundary Crises: Identifying the Building Blocks of an Effective Response System. *Journal of Contingencies and Crisis Management*, 18:4 pp195–207.

Boin, A. and Rhinard, M. (2008) Managing Transboundary Crises: What Role for the European Union? *International Studies Review*, 10:1 pp1–26.

Bossong, R. (2008) The Action Plan on Combating Terrorism: A Flawed Instrument of EU Security Governance. *Journal of Common Market Studies*, 46:1 pp27–48.

Bures, O. (2006) EU Counterterrorism Policy: A Paper Tiger? *Terrorism and Political Violence*, 18:1 pp57–78.

Burns, W., Peters, E. and Slovic, P. (2010) 'Public Response to 3 Crises: A Longitudinal Look'. Security and Human Behavior Workshop, University of Cambridge, Cambridge, 28 June 2010.

Casman, E. and Fischhoff, B. (2008) Risk Communication Planning for the Aftermath of a Plague Bioattack. *Risk Analysis*, 28:5 pp1327–42.

Coase, R. (1937) The Nature of the Firm. *Economica*, 4:16 pp386–405.

Coase, R. (1960) The Problem of Social Cost. *Journal of Law and Economics*, 3:1 pp1–44.

Daniels, R., Kettl, D. and Kunreuther, H. eds. (2006) *On Risk and Disaster: Lessons From Hurricane Katrina*. Philadelphia, PA: University of Pennsylvania Press.

Davis, L., LaTourrette, T., Mosher, D., Davis, L. and Howell, D. (2003) *Individual Preparedness and Response t Chemical, Radiological, Nuclear, and Biological Terrorist Attacks*, Santa Monica, CA: RAND.

Dixit, A. (2004) *Lawlessness and Economics: Alternative Models of Governance*, Princeton, NJ: Princeton Universit Press.

Dorussen, H., Kirchner, E. and Sperling, J. (2009) Sharing the Burden of Collective Security in the Europea Union. *International Organization*, 63:4 pp789–810.

Downton, M. and Pielke, R. (2001) Discretion Without Accountability: Politics, Flood Damage and Climat *Natural Hazards Review*, 2:4 pp157–66.

Ekengren, M., Matzén, N. and Rhinard, M. (2006) Solidarity or Sovereignty? EU Cooperation in Civil Protection. *Journal of European Integration*, 28:5 pp457–76.

Escaleras, M. and Register, C. (2008) Mitigating Natural Disasters Through Collective Action: The Effectiveness of Tsunami Early Warnings. *Southern Economic Journal*, 74:4 pp1017–34.

European Commission on Humanitarian Aid and Civil Protection. (2011) The Monitoring and Information Centre [online]. Available at: http://ec.europa.eu/echo/policies/disaster_response/mic_en.htm (accessed 30 August 2011).

Flynn, S. (2008) America the Resilient: Defying Terrorism and Mitigating Natural Disasters. *Foreign Affairs*, 87:2 pp2–8.

Galaz, V., Moberg, F., Olsson, E., Paglia, E. and Parker, C. (2011) Institutional and Political Leadership Dimensions of Cascading Ecological Crises. *Public Administration*, 89:2 pp361–80.

Giesecke, J., Burns, W., Barrett, A., Bayrak, E., Rose, A. and Suher, M. (2012) Assessment of the Regional Economic Impacts of Catastrophic Events: CGE Analysis of Resource Loss and Behavioral Effects of an RDD Attack Scenario. *Risk Analysis*, 32:4 pp583–600.

Giesecke, J., Rose, A., Muehlenbeck, T., Burns, W. and Barrett, A. (2010) *Economic Consequences of an Industrial Chlorine Site Terrorist Attack in Los Angeles: Implications for Emergency Management and Recovery Decision Making, Final Report to the Federal Emergency Management Agency*. Los Angeles, CA: Center for Risk and Economic Analysis of Terrorism Events (CREATE), University of Southern California.

Kasperson, R., Renn, O., Slovic, P., Brown, H., Emel, J., Goble, R., Kasperson, J. and Ratick, S. (1988) The Social Amplification of Risk: A Conceptual Framework. *Risk Analysis*, 8:2 pp177–87.

Lee, B., Gordon, P. and Moore II, J. (2008) 'Appendix C, Simulating the Economic Impacts Various Hypothetical Bio-Terrorist Attacks' in D. Von Winterfeldt, P. Gordon, and A. Rose (eds) *Support for Risk and Economic Analysis for the National Biodefense Analysis of Countermeasures Center*. Los Angeles, CA: Center for Risk and Economic Analysis of Terrorism Events (CREATE), University of Southern California, pp31–70.

Lezaun, J. and Groenleer, M. (2006) Food Control Emergencies and the Territorialization of the European Union. *Journal of European Integration*, 28:5 pp437–55.

Reeves, A. (2011) Political Disaster: Unilateral Powers, Electoral Incentives, and Presidential Disaster Declarations. *Journal of Politics*, 73:4 pp1142–51.

Rose, A. (2008) 'Appendix B: A Framework of Analyzing and Estimating the Total Economic Consequences of Terrorist Attacks' in D. Von Winterfeldt, P. Gordon, and A. Rose (eds) *Support for Risk and Economic Analysis for the National Biodefense Analysis of Countermeasures Center*. Los Angeles, CA: Center for Risk and Economic Analysis of Terrorism Events (CREATE), University of Southern California, pp14–30.

Rose, A. (2009a) A Framework for Analyzing and Estimating the Total Economic Impacts of a Terrorist Attack and Natural Disaster. *Journal of Homeland Security and Emergency Management*, 6:1, Article 4.

Rose, A. (2009b) *Economic Resilience to Disasters*. Oak Ridge, TN: Community and Regional Resilience Institute Report No. 8.

Rose, A. and Blomberg, S. B. (2010) Total Economic Impacts of a Terrorist Attack: Insights From 9/11. *Peace Economics, Peace Science, and Public Policy*, 16:1, Article 2.

Rose, A., Oladosu, G., Lee, B. and Beeler Asay, G. (2009) The Economic Impacts of the 2001 Terrorist Attacks on the World Trade Center: A Computable General Equilibrium Analysis. *Peace Economics, Peace Science, and Public Policy*, 15:2, Article 6.

Rose, A., Oladosu, G. and Liao, S. (2007) Business Interruption Impacts of a Terrorist Attack on the Electric Power System of Los Angeles: Customer Resilience to a Total Blackout. *Risk Analysis*, 27:3 pp513–31.

Sandler, T. and Siqueira, K. (2006) Global Terrorism: Deterrence Versus Preemption. *Canadian Journal of Economics*, 39:4 pp1370–87.

Slovic, P. (2004) What's Fear Got to Do with It? It's Affect We Need to Worry About P Slovic. *Missouri Law Review*, 69:4 pp971–90.

Sorensen, J., Shumpert, B. and Vogt, B. (2004) Planning for Protective Action Decision Making: Evacuate or Shelter-in-Place. *Journal of Hazardous Materials, A*, 109:1–3 pp1–11.

Van Eeten, M., Nieuwenhuijs, A., Luijf, E., Klaver, M. and Cruz, E. (2011) The State and Threat of Cascading Failure Across Critical Infrastructures: The Implications of Empirical Evidence From Media Incident Reports. *Public Administration*, 89:2 pp381–400.

Wachtendorf, T. (2000) *Interaction Between Canadian and American Governmental and Non-Governmental Organizations During the Red River Flood of 1997*, Newark, DE: Disaster Research Center, University of Delaware.

Index